AMERICA'S INADVERTENT EMPIRE

America's Inadvertent Empire

William E. Odom and Robert Dujarric

Yale University Press   New Haven & London

Designed by James J. Johnson and set in Melior Roman type by Binghamton Valley
Composition. Printed in the United States of America by Vail-Ballou Press.

Library of Congress Cataloging-in-Publication Data

Odom, William E.
  America's inadvertent empire / William E. Odom and Robert Dujarric.
      p.   cm.
Includes bibliographical references and index.
  ISBN 0-300-10069-8 (cloth : alk. paper)
  1. United States—Politics and government. 2. Power (Social
sciences)—United States. 3. United States—Economic conditions. 4.
United States—Social conditions. 5. United States—Foreign relations.
6. United States—Strategic aspects. 7. World politics—21st century.
I. Dujarric, Robert. II. Title.
  JK31.034 2004
  320.973—dc22
                                                                            2003015824

A catalogue record for this book is available from the British Library.

The paper in this book meets the guidelines for permanence and durability of the Committee on Production Guidelines for Book Longevity of the Council on Library Resources.

10 9 8 7 6 5 4 3 2 1

No one at the end of the twentieth century is less prepared [than the United States] for the competition that lies ahead in the twenty-first century.
—LESTER THUROW, 1992

The Cold War is over: Germany and Japan have won.
—SENATOR PAUL TSONGAS, 1992

Contents

Tables and Figures

Tables

Figures

Acknowledgments

We thank the Smith Richardson Foundation for the grant that made our research possible and Hudson Institute for supporting our writing over four years. The Smith Richardson Foundation also sponsored an editorial seminar, ably led by Nicholas X. Rizopoulos, that provided us with useful suggestions for the manuscript.

The Foundation for Teaching Economics helped our research by supporting interns who worked on this project for four summers in a row. Michishita Narushige, Nakabayashi Mieko, Devin Stewart, and Tanaka-Shichinohe Yoshiko organized seminars in Tokyo that helped Robert Dujarric develop ideas for this book. Daniel Aaron, Anka Begley, Louis Begley, Georges Berthoin, James H. Duffy, Harvey A. Garn, Nicholas X. Rizopoulos, Brian R. Sullivan, and Ron K. Unz read the manuscript and gave us very useful comments. The anonymous readers who refereed the manuscript for Yale University Press gave us a number of important suggestions for which we are grateful.

William Odom acknowledges the useful reactions to several key ideas in the book by students in his seminar on national security policy at Yale University.

The summer researchers who helped with the research for this volume were Luna Anico, Soraya Belghazi, Ludovic Butel, Rafi Cohen, Monica Downs, Laurence Fara, Fujiki Minako, Arjun Garg, Laura Habberstad, Jennie S. Han, Konishi Eiko, Elizabeth Lagresa, David C. Lam, Frank Lee, Lee Jung-Hwa, Terence Maguire, Matt Mooney, Nishino Masaki, Sarah K. Peterson, Kenneth Pick, Thomas Poirier, Shiga Sahoko, Takeuchi Takuro, and Yoshikawa Yukie.

At Hudson, Melody Campbell provided us with computer assistance and kept the network working while we relied on the helpful secretarial support of Carol Lynch and Diane Reed. Hudson Institute's librarians, Becky Cline, Gail Grouse, Charity Mitchell, and Susan Prostman, also provided considerable assistance. At Yale University Press, Jonathan Brent provided us with excellent advice, and Dan Heaton's remarkable editing skills have done much to improve our prose.

AMERICA'S INADVERTENT EMPIRE

Introduction

Abe Lincoln once said, "If we could first know *where* we are, and *whither* we are tending, we could better judge *what* to do, and *how* to do it."[1] Lifted from its domestic political context in 1858 into the global political context of the early twenty-first century, this proposition retains refreshing clarity. By the late 1980s, as the Cold War was ending, answers were being offered to Lincoln's timeless questions, and over the next decade several more followed. Some of them are now widely known by their slogans—"imperial overstretch," "the end of history," "the obsolescence of war," "the democratic peace," "the grand chessboard," "the clash of civilizations," and "globalization."[2] Others have captured less public attention, remaining relegated to academic circles.[3] None, however, has been widely accepted as explaining "*where* we are" or "*whither* we are tending," to say nothing of addressing the other two questions. Each proffered answer provides important insights—some more than others—and all taken together still do not suggest even a core of a consensus.

If that was not clear before the events of 11 September 2001, it certainly was afterward. Samuel Huntington's "clash of civilizations" seemed to say something about why those events occurred, and Zbigniew Brzezinski's view of Eurasia as a "grand chessboard" offered some insights into how to employ U.S. power in Asia, where the perpetrators of those attacks were located. The larger issues of the place and role of American power in the world, however, especially U.S. alliance relations, remain confusing.

The United States vacillates between accepting international leadership responsibilities and behaving like just one more sovereign state among all the others, looking after its own business and refusing to be more than marginally concerned about international rules and practices. Americans celebrate the breakup of the Soviet Union and its "socialist camp" of satellites, allies, and sympathizers but remain ambivalent about paying the price of maintaining the "capitalist camp"—the Western international system, which is the institutional matrix for the global economy and security. This attitude creates a lack of clear purpose that goes far in explaining why U.S. military actions since 1990 have yielded mixed results even when they have been operationally successful.

The attacks on the World Trade Center and the Pentagon have increased rather than reduced the ambivalence. When NATO voted to invoke Article 5 of the North Atlantic Treaty for the first time in its history in support of the United States after it was attacked on 11 September 2001, American leaders essentially ignored the resolution and initially rejected several NATO countries' offer of military support for U.S. military operations in Afghanistan. They simultaneously disdained "multilateralism" and appealed to it for creating a coalition to fight terrorism, apparently unaware that "terrorism" cannot be defeated, that it is not an enemy but a tactic—a tactic, moreover, that the United States has widely used.[4]

Whether Republicans or Democrats are in charge of American foreign policy seems to make a difference only in the nature of the confusion, not in the effectiveness with which American power is employed. Coming from opposite ends of the American political spectrum, both seem to misunderstand the scale and the nature of American power. They both misread, although in opposite ways, the importance of allies and many of the international organizations the United States established after World War II. The problem, it seems, is larger than Democrats and Republicans, leftish or rightish foreign policies and strategies.

Could it be that the world is really at a turning point in the nature of international politics? Does understanding it require a breakthrough in our thinking, somewhat like the change in scientific thought from Newtonian physics to Einstein's relativity theory and Heisenberg's quantum mechanics? At least two scholars apparently believe that it does. Both Francis Fukuyama ("the end of history") and Samuel Huntington ("the clash of civilizations"), in different and incompatible ways, describe the contemporary epoch as qualitatively different, not just more of that same old power politics among nations, punctuated by occasional efforts to govern by formulas for peace through disarmament, trade, and cooperation.

We reach a similar conclusion, but we interpret the nature of the change differently. As we see it, the United States is in a strategic position for which history offers no precedent. The root cause of the change is the sheer magnitude of American power combined with its manifold dimensions, a quantitative change that also brings qualitative changes. As a result, many of the commonly accepted maxims, propositions, and theories of international politics are as apt to mislead as to clarify our thinking about effective policy making. Not that they all are now invalid; rather, they apply in different or limited fashions.

The starting point for most of the book's chapters, therefore, is an appreciation of the magnitude of American power vis-à-vis the rest of the world. When the additional power of U.S. allies is included, the magnitude is truly staggering.

The next point is perhaps the most important: explaining the sources of American power. Several countries in the world have large areas and populations and are endowed with vast natural resources, but they have been unable to convert those assets into equally vast power. Some countries have amassed great empires, spanning large parts of the world, but none has come close to having either the quantity or the quality of American hegemony.

Yet another distinctive point concerns the many dimensions of American power, far beyond economic, technological, and military power. Others have described these dimensions as "soft power," a label that underestimates their importance and misleads about how they work for and against U.S. leadership in world politics. These various dimensions are not simply additive. That is, they cannot be summed up to yield an accurate measure of total American power. Most of them are derivative of economic and scientific power, but their effects multiply within certain institutional arrangements that the United States has built up in the world over many decades.

For example, the superiority of American business institutions and corporate governance may look like "soft" power, which Joseph Nye defines as the ability to attract others to take some desired action, as opposed to "hard power," which he defines as the ability to compel others to do something.[5] But when one compares the U.S. capacity to address its savings-and-loan scandal with Japan's creeping pace in forcing its banks to write off hundreds of billions of dollars in nonperforming loans, such power looks fairly hard because it confronts the delinquent institutions with a stronger U.S. economy that imposes stronger competition on them. Demographic

trends, favorable for the United States but unfavorable for Europe and
Japan, are not traditionally considered hard or soft indicators of
power although they were by monarchs in eighteenth-century Europe.[6] The effect of the brain drain from the rest of the world to American universities is difficult to quantify, but it contributes to hard U.S.
power. Although superiority in high culture and mass culture perhaps qualifies as purely soft power, it remains a hard fact that counterbalancing that superiority is difficult—if it can be done at all.

It is a mistake, however, to see soft power as working just for the
United States. America's allies, formal and informal, exercise considerable influence as well, constraining and nudging U.S. foreign,
economic, and military policies in many ways. In the chapters that
explain the large power gaps between the United States and the rest
of the world, it is also apparent that many countries profit greatly
under the American umbrella. This is true not only for defense and
trade but also for education, science, and culture. The benefits of
the dominance of American science and universities, for example,
are broadly shared, just as are those of U.S. military hegemony and
foreign access to American markets. That is why U.S. congressmen
sometimes make charges of "freeloading" against other countries.
This phenomenon might be described as interdependence, but that
term has a particular meaning acquired in the 1970s and 1980s connected only to first-world relations with the third world. The connections we describe are among first-world states and are more numerous and complex, suggesting that America's allies have no less
a stake in the mutual relations than the United States—and in most
cases a great deal more, because they could suffer more than the
United States without those relations.

Elaborating these three points tells us a great deal more about
American power than is generally appreciated, but it is difficult to
do without seeming to celebrate and boast. As much of the text will
reveal, that is not our aim. Instinctively most Americans know that
the arrogance of power is power's greatest enemy. Today, however,
more than a few American leaders from all points on the political
spectrum periodically forget it. Our accounting of American power,
therefore, is meant to induce reflective modesty in American political discourse so that responsibilities of that power can be properly
understood at a confusing time. Through most of the twentieth century, including much of the Cold War, it was assumed in the public
debate that the United States had a choice about those responsibilities. It could carry them as charity work for other countries or drop

them without great damage to its own peace and prosperity. That has been a false choice for some time. The wealthy countries in the world have become deeply entangled with the United States so that neither they nor the United States can easily disengage.

Understanding why, we suggest, requires recognizing that the United States has created, perhaps inadvertently, a new type of imperial regime. It is an empire, but not the traditional kind. Structurally and qualitatively it differs fundamentally from all past empires. Using the terms *imperial* and *empire* risks confusion because those words convey notions of a hierarchy of power, subordination, and dominance that are either missing from the American empire or only loosely institutionalized. Yet it is difficult to find apter terminology. How durable this new imperial system is remains an open question.

As the metropole, the United States may have great discretion in exercising power, but it built its empire by being willing to let its allies limit that discretion. On rare occasions it must exceed the limits to avoid the paralysis that has always beset large coalitions of states in which each has a veto over collective action. If the result in those cases is not productive for the empire, however, American leaders will have damaged the legitimacy of the imperial regime. In other words, this regime has an inchoate constitutional character deriving from America's constitutional philosophy.

At the same time, the empire is not simply based on principles of world federalism. Rather, it is a voluntary community of sovereign states, most of which have mature constitutional regimes. U.S. military power stands as the ultimate sanction against threats from outside the empire and enforcement of norms within it. To be politically effective, this sanction has to be exercised on the basis of military coalitions. Unilateral use of U.S. military power, while not precluded, is extremely risky for the health of the imperial order.

In principle, there is no reason why some other political center in the world could not lead this empire as long as it adhered to the general rules and was ultimately vindicated by results when it dared to violate those rules. A united Europe, for example, might prove able to lead it.

As we delve into the sources of American power and its spread in the world, we will elaborate several "subversive ideas"—that is, ideas that undercut much of the conventional wisdom now current in thinking about American strategy and foreign policy.[7] For example, we will show why a campaign to spread democracy to other countries is not necessarily a good idea. In too many cases that policy has prevented the development of civil society, human rights, and effective economic performance. For another example, violence and deadlocks in civil wars more often mark the road to constitutional order than do mediation, voting, and other peaceful efforts. For yet another, the number of countries outside the American empire that will become full-fledged members over the next couple of decades will be very small. New democracies may have come in waves in the past century, but truly constitutional regimes did not and have poor prospects of doing so in this century. Notwithstanding the immensity of American power, its evangelical capacities are limited except where they involve the use of decisive military force followed by several decades of occupation and tutelage institution building, or "nation building."

Finally, we call into doubt some of the contemporary views of what purposes U.S. military power serves. Many observers tend to ignore, even disdain, some of the major military tasks that a Liberal[8] empire must accomplish. Since the collapse of the Soviet Union the idea that only a visible threat can justify U.S. force structure and deployments is no longer adequate. The role of "military governance," or what has sometimes been called imperial garrisoning, has grown, although it remains an alien concept to contemporary Pentagon planners. Still other conventional views will be challenged here. Fixation on "exit strategies" for military interventions—so popular since the end of the Vietnam War—was never wise, and it is less so today. Deciding where to intervene now and over the long run is a key question for the United States today. The meaning of "victory" can no longer be what it was in World Wars I and II and during the Cold War. Unlike a football game, keeping the peace in key regions of the world has no time clock, no final whistle after which the victorious team can celebrate while the losers go quietly to the showers.

Less subversive of the conventional wisdom is our assessment of how and why economic power has grown primarily in limited regions of the globe. "Globalization" is not an explanation but a misleading description of sustained economic growth. Markets work badly without strong governmental institutions. As we will make apparent, strong government is so scarce that vast regions of the world cannot be rescued from poverty. Much of Eurasia and most of Africa and Latin America will not respond to the standard remedies recommended for their economic maladies. First world largesse to the third world simply cannot cure these maladies; it can and normally does make them worse.

These several points foreshadow much of our answer to the question of *where* we are. "*Whither* we are tending" is more difficult to know. We will have more to say about it in our conclusion, but our disposition toward a proper answer can be stated now. The future of U.S. global hegemony is uncertain. Anyone can make guesses about it, but no one can foretell it. It is true, however, that the objective bases of U.S. power are so great that one is encouraged to believe that American hegemony can endure indefinitely. Outside challengers are not a serious threat to it—neither rising powers like China nor Al Qaeda and similar nonstate organizations. They can cause the United States pain and damage, but they cannot destroy American hegemony. Americans, however, can do so.

The temptation to offer advice and suggest strategies for long-term maintenance of U.S. power is strong; in fact, friendly reviewers have encouraged us to do so. In several chapters, we make points about how to improve U.S. capabilities and to avoid serious problems with them, but these points are as much a part of the description of those capabilities as recipes for ensuring their long-term durability. A more realistic approach is to emphasize the uncertainties and to throw doubt on recipes, formulas, and programs. We simply cannot provide a big "game plan" for the United States to follow, assured of success in advance. There is no such game plan. Rational choice making in leadership can seldom be more than probabilistic guessing. And that grants fortune and luck a large role.

We can say with great confidence, however, that if Americans and their leaders recognize both the vastness of their power and its sources, including the United States' mutual dependencies with many other countries, they will understand that they have strong prospects for sustaining the American empire for a very long time. No leaders have ever had such capabilities at their disposal.

The most useful thing that observers can do is to provide study, analysis, and insights that reduce uncertainties and improve probabilities while avoiding doctrine or dogma. Leaders, of course, cannot avoid the challenge of working out programs and strategies, making day-to-day tactical decisions, and struggling to understand the results before proceeding too far on a course that is not succeeding. There are no ironclad rules for that kind of leadership, but critical study and analysis can help leaders gain occasional advantageous glimpses through the fog of politics and war. That is our purpose—to provide a critical exploration that may help not only leaders but also the attentive public to better appreciate where the United States is today.

We begin with a description of the special character of American institutions and how the United States has been led to create a new international system based on those institutions. Then we examine seven dimensions of American power—the military, demographics, economic performance, university education, science, media, and culture—showing the large gap in each between U.S. capacities and those of all other countries in the world and overwhelming gaps between the American empire and the rest of the world.

In the end, of course, we must face the question of what it all means, but much of the answer should already be clear from discussions of the gaps. Three troubling conclusions can be mentioned in advance.

First, the United States faces no rival, certainly not in the next several decades, but it could succumb to its own caprice and imprudence. No one else can take its power away, but it can throw that power away. The temptations for capricious American behavior are great, and the probable consequences are grave.

Second, the United States faces an internal contradiction. On the one hand, its concept of a limited state, constrained by checks and balances with political leaders accountable before the law and the electorate, has been projected as the supranational ideology of the American empire, embodied in its international organizations. On the other hand, it is impossible to construct checks and balances at the international level that the United States would, or safely could, accept. Moreover, many members of its empire would not accept them either, in light of the implications for their own sovereignty. Many of these nations would like to tie down the United States by such means but would reject such constraints for themselves. The most that can be achieved already exists: a kind of semiconstitutional network of international organizations that will hold together only so long as the United States provides adequate military power for last-resort enforcement that is done with sufficient prudence to avoid destroying the empire's basic norms of limited political power. Thus constitutional stability depends on a balance between multilateralism that will eventually undermine enforcement and unilateralism that risks eroding constitutional norms.

Third, the United States faces great uncertainties and dangers from regions outside its empire, not of the traditional military and

economic sort but rather of the kind that come from incredible poverty, social disorders, disease, and extremely weak governments.
The large majority of the world's population lives under such regimes. If our knowledge of how to deal with these problems has
improved, it is because five decades of experience have discredited
virtually all our theories about how to solve them through assistance
and guidance. Economic and social progress have been induced by
some assistance programs, but the unintended consequences have
too often brought more problems than were solved: oppressive dictatorships, radical political movements, disease and famine, and anger at the United States and its wealthy allies. Terrorism and proliferation of weapons of mass destruction are additional unintended
consequences. With the exception of nuclear weapons, these are not
new developments. Variants of them accompanied the modernization of Europe and North America in the eighteenth, nineteenth, and
early twentieth centuries. We will not deal with them in any comprehensive fashion because they are policy issues. We are concerned
primarily in understanding the structure of power and the institutional character of the American-led international order.

Many other books over the past dozen or so years have offered
interpretations of that order. They normally begin with devastating
critiques and sometimes outright dismissals of the previous ones.
Our approach is different. We relegate to an appendix the "state of
the debate" for those readers who want a brief summary of the literature on U.S. *economic* performance vis-à-vis the rest of the world.
From the growing body of broader literature on the nature of the
contemporary international order we take ideas and concepts selec-
tively, building on them where they offer insights, and identifying
some of their limitations. We also go back to a few old concepts of
political thought that have become distorted or forgotten, yet remain
powerful tools of analysis. We do not, however, provide a critique
of all the relevant literature.

1 The Sources of American Power

When one thinks of the sources of a state's power, land, natural resources, population, and favorable climate come to mind. These qualities are important indeed, but alone they do not explain why the United States is so powerful. Several other countries have large land areas, vast natural resources, large populations, and reasonably favorable climates but have failed to convert them into great power.

Why, then, has the United States been staggeringly more successful at converting these resources into unprecedented wealth and power? The answer is Liberal institutions.[1] Many Americans instinctively know this, but very few understand precisely why it is true.

By *institutions*, we do not mean organizations. Institutions are patterns, rules, and practices most often manifest in organizations—political, social, and economic—but not limited to them. They also include ideologies, which are made up of beliefs—religious, moral, and cultural—that individuals use to explain and rationalize the world around them.

Two propositions are critical to understanding the sources and distinctive nature of American power. Both are at odds with authoritative wisdom today. Together, they support a third proposition about the durability of American hegemony.

First, countries without Liberal political systems are unlikely to generate them quickly, and most will fail in the effort. While transitions to democracy have come in impressive waves, transitions to regimes with Liberal institutions have been remarkably few. There is little reason, therefore, to expect that the number will increase very much over the next several decades.

Second, for a country to become economically powerful and remain so more than temporarily, it must have Liberal political and economic institutions. The few apparent exceptions—authoritarian oil-wealthy countries, for example—depend on steady interaction with wealthy Liberal states to provide important innovations and new technology necessary to sustain their modernization. Or they have been short-lived, like such totalitarian countries as Nazi Germany and the Soviet Union. Cut off from the West, their modernity will become obsolete.

Third, in light of the first two propositions, the distribution of power in the world will not change markedly in the next several decades. The countries that are succeeding economically will continue to do so, while those countries with poor economic performance will continue to remain poor.

These assertions mean that China, Russia, India, or any other potentially large power simply cannot thrive without adopting Liberal institutions. That is, they will have to achieve constitutional breakthroughs and sustain them indefinitely. They may modernize, building considerable industrial power, but they cannot innovate effectively to sustain their modernization except by continuing to be closely linked with the United States and other Liberal countries. In other words, while Samuel Huntington's "clash of civilizations" thesis is highly compelling in some regards, it fails to convince us that non-Western civilizations can sustain their modernization and also clash with the West. They may indeed clash, but that will cost them lots of cash, while preventing them from remaining modern by borrowing.

Huntington is right that these states have little chance of Westernizing. They may have "democratic breakthroughs," but Westernizing requires "constitutional breakthroughs." Moreover, democracy without a durable constitutional order may well prevent achieving that order.

To make these claims compelling, we must first decouple two concepts that have been conflated in the American public mind—Liberalism and democracy. The two have always been in tension in the United States, and to good advantage, but the original idea of Liberalism has been transmuted, distorted, and pushed out of our public consciousness, leaving us unable to recognize the most important source of our power. Not only is a grasp of the original concept essential for understanding American power, but it also allows one to appreciate why a constitutional order is so difficult to establish and why democracy is as likely to obstruct a constitutional breakthrough as to facilitate it.

With that done, we must turn to the connection between political institutions and economic performance. Here again, category confusion makes it difficult for public discourse to avoid misleading conclusions. As we shall try to show, debating whether or not democracy promotes economic growth is asking the wrong question. Similarly, to argue that capitalist economies do not need powerful state institutions, as businessmen's political parties normally do, is to misunderstand what makes markets work effectively. The popular misconception that state direction of the economy can produce both sustained economic growth and great social equity has suffered setbacks with the collapse of the Soviet Union, but the equally popular misconception that market economies do not require state rule enforcement still enjoys a following.

To make this economic case, we will elaborate what seems to be an emerging understanding of how political institutions affect economic performance. We must also explore why countries find it so difficult to change their institutions, even when they recognize that those institutions are keeping them poor and weak.

The resulting picture should make clear why the United States in particular and countries with Liberal institutions in general are far more successful than other countries in converting land, labor, and capital into economic, political, military, scientific, and cultural power. It also provides the concepts and ideas for the arguments in the rest of the book.

Liberalism Versus Democracy

When Americans speak of democracy, they normally mean liberal democracy. Democracy is not the first idea, or even the most basic one, in American institutions. Liberalism is.[2] This is not the welfare transfer payments of the New Deal and the Great Society or Norman Thomas's version of socialism. It is the proposition that individuals have rights, which no state can justly abridge. Samuel Huntington has put it most succinctly: "The essence of Western culture is the Magna Carta."[3] By signing this document in 1215, King John agreed to a list of rights for his nobles which he swore not to violate, establishing a precedent that would become central to English and American political thought. (It is seldom remembered, however, that King John sought and received the pope's approval for breaking his oath within a couple of months after signing the document.[4] No English king thereafter agreed fully to such limits until the late seventeenth century.) In his history of European Liberalism, Guido de Ruggiero similarly traces its origins to the Middle Ages, "the period of the exclusive dominion of private rights. There are no such things as independent public rights" in a feudal regime. Liberalism also has religious roots. "Liberty is consciousness of oneself, of one's own infinite spiritual value; and the same recognition in the case of other people naturally follows from this immediate revelation." Such revelation requires the kind of "free examination" insisted on by Calvin and other leaders of the Protestant Reformation that made it "the source not only of religious liberty but of all modern liberalism," opening the door to rapid advances in science and technology.[5] Thus the political relation between the state and the individual in Liberal countries in modern Europe is the reestablishment, albeit in different specificities, of the contractual nature of that relation in the feudal state: limits and rights, obligations and liberties, for both.[6]

How does this European experience relate to the United States? The American pattern of highly diffused political power to state and local governments descends from feudal Europe, not modern Europe.[7] The U.S. federal system began with a very weak center characteristic of feudal monarchies. It never went through the centralizing absolutism that characterized the Europe of Louis XIV in France and Frederick the Great in Prussia. The makers of the American Revolution did not seek the abolition of the ancien régime, as did those who made the French Revolution. They defended the institutions of the ancien régime in reaction to King George III's abuse of traditional English institutions.[8]

Accordingly, the drafters of the Declaration of Independence and the U.S. Constitution did not set out to create a democracy. Most of them saw democracy as a danger to the very liberties they sought to ensure. Instead, they focused on how to limit the state, how to bind it so that it cannot abridge individual liberties. To do that, they had to take away the ruler's right to make a number of decisions, and that required them to find other ways to make these decisions. For example, who will be the ruler? And who will decide the laws by which he will rule? Establishing voting procedures for a limited set of citizens was the answer, as it was in England after the Glorious Revolution of 1689, and as it is everywhere that truly Liberal regimes have been established. When power passes from "the one" to "the few," voting becomes imperative as a decision-making procedure. It becomes a democratic procedure when voting is by "the many." Only about one-half of U.S. male adults could vote before the Civil War, and universal suffrage came only in 1920. Although federal law gave voting rights to African-Americans after the Civil War, in practice such rights were uncertain to nonexistent in the South until the 1960s.

The Declaration of Independence, in underscoring "life, liberty, and the pursuit of happiness," declared that citizens have political and economic freedoms—safety for one's life, the right to own property, and the right to pursue economic well-being through use of private property and one's labor. It says nothing about majority rule, and certainly nothing about democracy. Rather it asserts individual rights vis-à-vis the state.

The American founding fathers did not relegate democracy to a status below Liberalism only because they were concerned with limiting state power. Most of them were deeply distrustful of democracy, a disposition that the first decades of the new republic's political experience periodically vindicated. The founders established a restricted franchise to limit the potential mischief that illiberal majorities could make, but that is often forgotten today. Americans are keenly aware of their rights but associate them with democracy, not with Liberalism. Perhaps understandably, because "wherever one finds liberalism, . . . it is almost invariably coupled with democracy. . . . The converse proposition, however, has become less and less true."[9] This fact inspired one observer, Fareed Zakaria, to make the point more strongly, warning of the spread of "illiberal democracy" in today's world.[10]

Implicit here is an important proposition: while Liberal regimes inexorably become democratic, repeated and regular elections in illiberal democracies do not inexorably make them Liberal. In fact, it is difficult to find examples of their ever having done so. More than a decade of voting in Russia has not; nor have five decades of voting in India. A century and a half of voting in numerous regimes in South America has yet to produce a consistently Liberal polity there. The story is much the same outside of Europe and a few countries in northeast Asia. Belatedly this point is gaining some scholarly attention.[11]

Private property clearly must enjoy first place among the individual liberties.[12] This is true because private ownership of land and

capital diffuses power. A number of countries in the world today—
most former Soviet republics and many in Africa and South America, for example—guarantee the rights of free speech, free assembly,
and due process in law in written constitutions, but their citizens
cannot exercise them because they do not have the means to influence legislation and to curb state officials who obstruct their exercise of such rights. Citizens may freely vote for a parliament, but
without the power that private property conveys, they can neither
effectively influence the legislative process to ensure outcomes in
line with their rights nor compel the executive authorities to act
within the laws. Holding property, they may choose not to influence
policy making, but without property they cannot choose to influence
it. Where property rights are unstable or ownership is highly concentrated, other rights are in danger. As King John's barons knew in
1215, and as English parliaments remembered in the 1600s, if the
king owns most of the property, tyranny is inevitable. The right to
private property, therefore, is a precondition for other liberties.

Admittedly, private property begets great inequities in the distribution of wealth, but where property rights have been stable and
wealth sufficiently diffused to prevent outright monopoly, other
civil liberties have become a reality for increasing numbers of citizens. Where private ownership is not widespread and property
rights are not ensured by the state, civil liberties have been more an
aspiration than a reality, even in regimes with procedural democracy.[13]

Proponents of the contemporary welfare liberalism may not
agree. Socialists certainly will not, be they Marxist, national, uto-
pian, Fabian, or some other type. Nothing in the experience of the
Soviet Union or any other socialist regime offers evidence to support
the view that state ownership of most of the economy can coexist
with constitutionally governed politics. Likewise, nothing in the
performance of socialist economies suggests that they improve the
overall welfare of their societies, although they have achieved
greater equality of income, normally at impoverished levels compared with effective market economies.[14] Ironically, all of the socialist parties that have come to power in Europe have ruled over
market economies with private-property, not socialist, economies.
And where state ownership of large parts of the economy has been
tried—in Britain after World War II, for example—the result has
been declining performance.

This is not to dismiss the issues of social and economic inequities that characterize Liberal regimes. Charles Dickens provided an accurate picture of industrializing England, and many of the charges by American labor leaders against business practices have been well founded. The argument here is different. Liberties survived in England and the United States. Where the right of private property has not been ensured, liberty has never existed, as in Imperial Russia and China, or has perished, as in Nazi Germany and the communist states of Eastern Europe.

Democracy Versus Liberalism

It is instructive, even if somewhat repetitive, to turn the "Liberal democracy" coin around and look at the other side. Although democracy is the best-known and most popular American institution, it is not the source of American power. Democracy is an essential feature of the American political system, but it also has the potential to destroy American power by destroying Liberal institutions.

John Stuart Mill warned eloquently in his essay *On Liberty* of the danger of "the tyranny of the majority."[15] Rule of the majority is the banner of democracy. The primacy of rights is the banner of Liberalism. And the battle is ever joined in Liberal democracies. No statement of it has been clearer than the exchange between Colonel Thomas Rainsborough, speaking for the Levelers at the Putney debate against General Henry Ireton and Oliver Cromwell. The Levelers sought economic "leveling" at the expense of the rich. Rainsborough declared that "the poorest he in England hath a life to live as the greatest he."[16] Ireton and Cromwell asked in reply if he would violate God's "natural law" of private property in order to achieve such equality. They left the issue unresolved, but the practical implication of God's natural law as it concerned property was preserved in England.

There is no final resolution to this clash of political philosophies about "who gets what, when, how."[17] Because it embraces the clash, depending on repeated and continuing compromises, Liberal democracy entails an unending political struggle.

In academic circles, proponents of democracy increasingly gloss or entirely ignore the role of Liberalism.[18] The pages of the *Journal of Democracy* are filled with articles about "consolidating," "deepening," "rooting," and other processes of democratic development. Yet the flaws in the democracies that the authors of the articles want to rectify are almost always violations of liberties. These critics apparently do not see the illogic of their prescriptions because Liberalism in their vocabulary has been buried within democracy and wholly forgotten, leaving them talking a kind of nonsense about rights.[19] Others have not inadvertently buried Liberalism but believe it stands in the way of true democracy, presumably defined as much greater economic equality.[20]

Much ink has been spilt on defining democracy, obfuscating more often than illuminating the matter, but Joseph Schumpeter has usefully suggested that all definitions can be sorted into three types. The first defines democracy according to its source—for example, "the people." The second is based on democracy's purpose—that is, what democracy is supposed to achieve. The third type of definition treats democracy as a set of procedures for making decisions by voting. Implementing it requires establishing the procedures, which may vary widely.

As Schumpeter admits and as Samuel Huntington has more recently emphasized, only the third type of definition is operational, allowing it to be verified as indisputably extant or absent in a particular regime.[21] The lack of operational criteria for verifying the "source" or "purpose" of democracy leaves no practical way to judge whether or not a regime qualifies as truly democratic.

One might object that such academic subtleties of democratic theory are interesting but irrelevant, but if we want to remove the confusion in everyday political discourse, then theory is highly relevant. Democracy has been widely used as a brush by which to tar Liberalism with all the social ills that accompany industrial development, urbanization, and the breakdown of traditional social and cultural patterns. Marx, of course, and all of those "Social Democrats" who absorbed some version of his teachings, more effectively put the onus on Liberalism than anyone else until the early twentieth century. Then the Fascists in Italy and the National Socialists in Germany did the same, blaming it for all our misfortunes. Both ideologies required the destruction of Liberalism, first of all because of its strong defense of individual rights against the democratic majorities that Nazis and communists could produce to back their policies aims. It is fair to say, therefore, that democracy unleavened by Liberalism has served mankind very poorly.

Constitutions

Authoritative and enforced constitutions are the sine qua non for Liberal democratic regimes, but they tend to be taken for granted, left to the domain of lawyers, and believed to be valid and effective only when approved by a democratic referendum. This causes confusion in the implementation of the U.S. foreign policy goal of spreading democracy abroad. Letting democracy subsume Liberalism, and viewing democracy as primarily about voting, Americans can easily—although mistakenly—assume that spreading democracy is the way to spread American Liberal institutions. How is democracy to be spread? By introducing competitive elections. That, of course, is relatively easy to do, but as experience has repeatedly shown, it almost never produces stable constitutional regimes. If referenda and elections cannot do that, then how do such regimes come into being? How is the breakthrough achieved from a nonconstitutional regime to a constitutional one?

First, we must decide what criteria define a constitutional breakthrough.[22] How do we know that a regime has achieved a durable constitutional basis? The Russian case today, among others, makes clear what *does not* constitute a breakthrough: a written document approved by a popular referendum. Russia has such a constitution, but few observers contend that the Russian state is governed according to its official constitution, that autonomous Russian courts interpret the laws within the legal framework of the constitution, and that officials are obliged to abide by court rulings. Putting the issue the other way round, under what circumstances would the all these things to be true about Russia? Or for any other country striving to create a constitutional government?

Stripped to its bare essentials, establishing a constitutional order requires an agreement by the political elite on the following:

1. The rules to decide who rules.
2. The limits on state power—that is, individual "rights" that the state must defend and not abridge or violate.
3. The rules for making new rules.

A practical question immediately arises: who are the elite? They are people or groups who have sufficient power to violate rules with impunity if they chose. Those without such power are not critical for an initial constitutional agreement because they cannot disrupt the deal being struck. The Russian case is instructive on this point.

Although they do not publicly say so, several leaders and powerful groups do not accept the Russian Federation's constitution in practice. President Boris Yeltsin violated it with impunity on several occasions, and President Vladimir Putin has done the same. The secret police flout it. So do Russian military commanders in their treatment of their soldiers and junior officers. Several regional leaders reject it, insisting on the primacy of their local "national" constitutions, and Moscow has responded to separatism in Chechnya with brutal military oppression. The business "oligarchs," tycoons who became obscenely rich through privatization schemes during the early 1990s, show little regard for Russia's statutory law. Notwithstanding the public referendum that approved the constitutional draft in December 1993, the constitution has not become the effective law of the land. This is true not only for Russia but also for the majority of countries with written constitutions. To be effective, a constitution must bind a country's most powerful. That some people violate it is not a test of its effectiveness; whether violators are punished is. If the powerful—those who cannot be punished— violate the constitution, then they undermine the constitutionality of the state.

Second, to discover how constitutional breakthroughs are achieved, we must look at practical cases. In the United States, a constitutional tradition was inherited from England. Although most of the elite were socialized in the English Liberal tradition, they did not fully agree on a key issue: slavery. Thus their initial constitutional agreement eventually broke down. It took four years of civil war, 1861–65, to resolve an issue about rights that had been pushed aside in 1787. A constitutional breakthrough cannot be said to exist, therefore, until the deal has been internalized so deeply that no elite groups are willing to challenge it.

Looking at the historical record of emerging Liberal democracies in northern Europe, Dankwart Rustow emphasized the importance of a "great compromise" as the threshold point.[23] Reaching that critical point required a long period of conflict among the elites that ended in exhaustion and a willingness to strike a deal among competing parties. Another period, usually a generation in length, was required to "habituate" the terms and norms of the compromise. The "Glorious Revolution" in England and the "Great Compromise" in Sweden were Rustow's examples, but the Dutch Republic, several French Republics, and the German monarchy before World War I can be loosely fitted into his pattern. British colonies settled mainly by peoples from the British Isles—Canada, Australia, and New Zealand—took the English constitution as their own, allowing them to establish constitutional regimes without exhausting conflicts. Unlike the United States, they did not have slavery or some similar issue to divide them. In most other cases, however, the founding of a stable constitutional order has required violence and civil war, or invasion and occupation by the U.S. military, or strong influence by the United States on a country's domestic politics.

The reestablishment of a constitutional order in Germany and many other countries in Europe after World War II can also be explained by variations of Rustow's pattern of violence, exhaustion, stalemate, compromise, and a period of habituation. The U.S. invasion and long-term military presence in Europe imposed stalemates, encouraged compromises, and helped them to take permanent root. This proved easier in countries that have the legacies of Roman law and feudal institutions. Greece and Turkey do not, and both are still struggling to solidify constitutional orders.

Variants of the same pattern are also found in Asia. Beginning in 1850, Japan was under pressure from European and American traders and naval forces to open up to commerce. The struggle over how to cope with these foreign pressures catalyzed the Meiji Restoration in 1868. Copying of European legal systems and borrowing from other Western institutions progressed sufficiently by the end of the nineteenth century for Japan to claim that it had a constitutional system. During its subsequent occupation of Korea and Taiwan, Japan imposed its new legal institutions on those countries as well. Unfortunately, the collapse of the ruling oligarchy during the interwar period allowed the military, in collaboration with the emperor, to abrogate the constitution and destroy Japan's fragile Liberal order. Japan reintroduced a constitution after defeat in World War II at the direction of General MacArthur, but its speedy and successful internalization is attributable to the century of institutional change begun in Japan in the mid-1800s.

Since the end of World War II, Washington has successfully pressed Taiwan and South Korea to create constitutional orders. Each managed to avoid civil war on the way to a "great compromise." A fortuitous set of pressures and circumstances eased Taiwan's path: U.S.-imposed land reform, the Japanese legal legacy, and a threatening external environment that discouraged civil war. Chiang Kai-shek's Kuomintang Party held a monopoly of political power, but land reform and owners' compensation in the form of shares in industrial enterprises diffused economic power. Chiang's son and successor, Chiang Ching-kuo, struck the constitutional deal that broke the political monopoly, bringing it into line with the distribution of economic power. Thus far, the agreement has held. South Korea has come close to civil war on a couple of occasions, but the U.S. military presence and the threat of a North Korean invasion helped preserve the peace.[24] The legal institutions brought from Europe by the Japanese to Taiwan and South Korea have also made it easier for both countries to adopt a constitutional order, but it is too early to say whether the elite of either country have fully internalized it.

Singapore, some would contend, is actually a police state, but its government generally abides by constitutional arrangements, particularly in matters of property rights and contract law, which owe a great deal to institutional legacies from its colonial experience under British rule. India also has this British heritage, but only as a thin veneer over local non-Liberal institutions and cultural patterns; India remains in a domestic struggle to achieve a constitutional breakthrough. In the Philippines, four decades of U.S. tutelage "democracy" has left an electoral system but not a constitutional breakthrough. Numerous elites remain unhappy with the formal constitution and able to violate it without serious consequences for themselves.[25]

In sum, the experience of the thirty or so mature and stable constitutional regimes in the world suggests that constitutional breakthroughs result from long periods of war and violence, often followed by periods of dependence on U.S. military forces. War and violence, however, do not inexorably lead to constitutional breakthroughs. That seems to happen only when no single party or faction wins out, gaining monopoly political power. If a single leader or group wins the conflict—as happens in the majority of cases—then the country is no longer on a path leading toward a constitutional breakthrough.

This last point supports our proposition that not many countries will succeed in creating stable Liberal democratic regimes. It is too easy to be thrown off the path that leads to a stalemate. The Dutch provinces, England, Sweden, and a few others have been more fortunate than wise. The city-states of Northern Italy and the autonomous towns along the upper Rhine and in southern Germany at the time of the Protestant Reformation were pockets of the same kind of incipient Liberalism that won the day in the Lowlands and in

England. Kings and regional princes, however, eroded the autonomy of these urban polities, overtaxed them, and eventually absorbed them under absolute monarchies. The Spanish, English, and French monarchs tried and failed to do that to the Dutch provinces.

There have been, however, a few exceptions to the path of stalemate through war and violence. Where the U.S. military has intervened by invasion (as in World War II), or by peaceful garrisoning (as in South Korea), or by its military proximity and strong political presence (as in several NATO countries, such as Portugal and Spain), it has effectively caused stalemates under which successful breakthroughs emerged.

Most of the case for our proposition that Liberal regimes are few and cannot be created quickly should now be clear. The U.S. foreign policy of expanding democracy can actually impede constitutional breakthroughs. In the best circumstances, Liberal breakthroughs are highly problematic, and the number of new ones in the next few decades is likely to be small indeed.

We must now turn to our second and third propositions. To make them compelling, we must examine the connection between Liberal regimes and economic power.

Economic Performance and Political Institutions

Liberal political institutions account for the immensity of American economic power. That is, they make possible the United States' remarkable economic performance and, at the same time, an impressive standard of living for most citizens, not just a wealthy few. Today one can make this claim without incurring a lot of outrage or serious dispute.[26] That was not always so. The old debate about socialism versus capitalism fizzled toward the end of the Cold War, replaced by a search for "a third way," an endeavor likely to prove as quixotic as the search for socialism that can sustain growth. Claims in Europe that there is a unique Swedish socialism or a distinctive and compassionate model of German capitalism or a French *dirigisme* that constitutes an effective alternative are simply not credible. On close examination, they all turn out to have market economies on which they place very heavy welfare transfer payment burdens and other state-imposed costs.

The more important debates at the turn of the twenty-first century are about the limits of what can be explained by mainstream economic theory—that is, theory taught in economics departments at all major American universities, what is known as "neoclassical" economics, or "capitalism."

One such debate focuses on the role of the World Bank. Critics argue that it has had little success in contributing to economic development in poor countries. Its defenders disagree. This issue, of course, also concerns all of the money spent by the United States on foreign aid to economic development. The critics are awakening to the role of political institutions in economic development, something essentially ignored by the development economists in the World Bank, the U.S. government, and elsewhere over the past five decades.[27]

Political scientists have ignored economics to about the same degree that the economists have ignored political institutions. Economists who concern themselves with how to establish "democracy" in the Third World long ago noticed a significant correlation between economic development and democracy.[28] Whether the relation is causal has been widely but inconclusively debated. Explaining the "third wave" of new democracies decades later, Samuel Huntington still left the matter open when he concluded that economic factors have been "significant" but not "determinative."[29]

This indeterminacy may be a result of posing the wrong question. Instead of asking whether democracy causes economic development or whether economic development causes democracy, scholars should have been asking what makes possible more effective economic performance, particularly over the long term. Suppose that the answer is Liberal political institutions. If better economic performance requires Liberal institutions, which in turn expand democratic participation, then the democracy-economics connection would seem to be through Liberalism, leaving democracy with no causal role. Indeed, that seems to be the case.

This, of course, is to put the focus on institutional economics and economic history, which have been treated as poor cousins in the family of economics. Their reputation, however, received a considerable boost when Douglass C. North, an economic historian, received the Nobel Prize in economics in 1993 for his building on neoclassical theory to account for the role of institutions in economic performance.[30] His ideas provide a strong argument for our claim that Liberal political institutions account for the extraordinary economic power of the Liberal states of North America, Europe, and Northeast Asia.

In order to explain why there has been relatively little sustained

economic growth until the past couple of centuries, and then only
in limited parts of the world, North abandons the neoclassical assumption that "institutions are efficient." If they were, North observes, then economies everywhere should be advancing closer to
full performance potential. In his words, "The stock of knowledge
and the stock of technology set the upper bounds to human well
being," but they do not ensure that all economies will reach them.
"It is the structure of political and economic organization which
determines the performance of an economy as well as the incre-
mental rate of growth in knowledge and technology."[31] Ignoring
organizational factors, neoclassical economics suggests that all
countries, though at different levels of development, should be converging on a common efficiency level close to the "upper bounds to
human well being."

Why has this not happened? Because, according to North, both
political regimes and economic firms "are devised to maximize the
wealth of the principals by exploiting the gains of trade as a result
of specialization."[32] That requires that both kinds of organizations
(1) establish rules and regulations, (2) detect deviations and enforce
compliance, and (3) articulate an ideology that sets moral and eth-
ical norms for self-enforced compliance. As North explains, these
factors determine the terms of exchange between political leaders
and their constituents, most of whom are owners, managers, and
employees in economic firms. The political terms of exchange define the system of property rights and enforcement mechanisms
within which the economic terms of exchange must be devised.
Typically rulers, seeking their own revenue interests, devise inefficient property rights systems. The resulting political institutions
force economic leaders to shape their institutions to pay the resulting higher transaction costs. Consequently, economic performance
is inefficient, often far below what is possible.

Thus North explained why inefficient institutions exist, but he
also wanted to know why market competition has not weeded out
more of them and made sustained economic growth more general.
Why do not political leaders of "stagnant economies quickly emulate the policies of more successful ones? How can we explain the
radically different performance of economies over long periods of
time?"[33] If neoclassical economic theory cannot explain the failure
of most countries to follow converging paths toward a common level
of efficiency, what theory can?

Institutions emerged in some states that stabilized property

rights, ensured their more efficient allocation, and reduced transaction costs. Such change did not occur in other states. North observes that the Dutch provinces in the 1500s and England in the late
1600s, for example, moved onto a new path of institutional development which prompted unprecedented economic growth in both
countries for well over two centuries.[34]

Why did other European countries—for examples, Spain and
France—fail to follow? The rulers in England and the Dutch provinces were compelled to agree to changes in institutional arrangements that yielded much more efficient systems of property rights.
They also improved the flow of corrective feedback from markets to
help guide investments in order to better shape supply to meet demand and, especially, to encourage innovation. In Spain and France
the estates generals failed to impose controls on their rulers' power
to tax and allocate property rights, leaving them free to impose their
preferred—and inefficient—allocations of property rights in exchange for revenues. The resulting constraints disallowed corrective
feedback of the kind yielded by markets in England and the Lowlands.

Precisely what were the institutional changes that made such a
dramatic difference for economic growth? They were the conditions
that William of Orange accepted from the parliament in exchange
for his ascension to the English throne. Unlike the Stuarts and Tu-
dors before him, William could not claim that he was the absolute
ruler of England. He could not arbitrarily reallocate property rights;
they would be regulated by longstanding common law. Henceforth,
only parliament would have the right to levy taxes. Finally, he accepted limits to his power to appoint, remove, and influence judges.
These were the main outlines of the "constitutional monarchy"
granted to William, and they endured.[35]

Consider what these changes meant for economic activity. First,
the king could no longer trade property rights for revenues—deals
that distorted markets. Second, the reforms improved the ability of
judges to decide contract disputes according to law rather than by
political considerations. Third, an important change was effected in
the role of king's agents: the state bureaucracy became less predatory
and more of an honest rules enforcer. These changes greatly reduced
the costs of both governing and doing business—"transaction
costs"—as the English system evolved over the next several decades. The changes helped to vault England ahead of all other Eu-

ropean states by the late eighteenth century, as John Brewer and Niall Ferguson have explained in tracing the subsequent organizational and institutional developments.[36]

We need to underscore the consequences of the changing role of courts of law and the king's executive agents that resulted from this constitutional agreement. Neoclassical economic theory says nothing about why the agreed purchases and sales will be honored in actual practice—that is, why people will not cheat or violate promises. It simply assumes away the monitoring and enforcement tasks. To make this point absolutely clear, a metaphor may help.

Assume we are attending a game between two teams in the National Football League. The crowd is in the stadium. The bands are playing, and the teams are on the field, but there are no referees present, and there are no lines marking off the boundaries and yards on the playing field. Starting the game in these conditions will prove difficult, but suppose that one team owner rushes to the rescue, offering a set of referees, ones he pays. The other team owner, under the pressure of the impatient crowd, agrees to let these referees call the game. Because there are no boundaries and yard lines marked on the field, the referees are allowed to estimate where the lines should be in the course of play. The resulting game is unlikely to be the kind of performance that has made the NFL such a commercial success. Disputes leading to fights will be inevitable. The referees are sure to make calls that favor the team whose owner pays them. In retaliation, the other owner might send his agents to steal the box office receipts, refusing to share them with the other owner. If the NFL operated in this way, it would not endure for long.

The importance of monitoring violations and enforcing rules in a sports contest is obvious. It is no less so for market economies, but it is not always recognized. The popular image of laissez-faire capitalism is one of markets without referees—that is, without government regulators. Just as the players, coaches, and owners of football teams are the worst enemies of a well-refereed game, businessmen and political rulers are enemies of competitive markets. They will inexorably distort and destroy them unless there is some third party capable of enforcing the rules.[37] And as John Brewer would add, an efficient tax bureaucracy is essential to provide resources for this third-party enforcement instead of letting the referees cut their own expensive deals with the team owners.[38] According to Niall Ferguson, a national debt and central bank to administer it are also essential in order to spread the costs of the referees, stadium guards, and janitorial services over several generations through deficit spending in years of poor ticket sales.[39]

For North this matter is monumental. "The inevitable conclusion," he reasons, "is that complex contracting that would allow one to capture the gains from trade in a world of impersonal exchange must be accompanied by some kind of third-party enforcement."[40] The obvious candidate for the enforcement role is a state that has achieved a constitutional breakthrough, but the rarity of such breakthroughs makes effective third-party enforcement equally problematic.[41]

North's answer to "why" is different from but compatible with ours. He asks the question in a different way: why do leaders in poorly performing economies almost never adopt the policies of the more successful ones? We ask why they fail to adopt Liberal political institutions. His answer, "path dependence," is valid for both questions.

Path Dependence

Path dependence enjoys fairly wide use as a concept, though not always by that name. It is implicit in historical explanations based on cultural and structural continuities resistant to change. Observers of technological change also use it when they point out that once a large capital investment is made in a particular technology and the costs of training a workforce to use it have been paid, later and more efficient technologies are seldom adopted.[42] The large initial investment makes the change to the better technology look financially unattractive. An example might be the grip that the Microsoft Windows operating system has on the personal computer market. Apple's operating system is widely claimed to be more efficient in use of memory, more stable, and easier to learn, but most organizations and individuals who have already invested in Microsoft are not willing to pay the costs of changing to Apple's system. They are trapped in path dependence.

North adapts the concept to explain variations among countries in economic development. "The resultant path of institutional change is shaped by (1) the lock-in that comes from the symbiotic relationship between institutions and the organizations that have evolved as a consequence of the incentive structure provided by those institutions and (2) the feedback process by which human beings perceive and react to changes in the opportunity set."[43]

The feedback process in an institutional matrix may be "negative"—that is, corrective, providing for comparisons and evaluations of each choice against alternatives, allowing the less efficient ones to be discarded. Or it may be "positive"—that is, error-exacerbating, not error-correcting. As a series of choices is made without corrective feedback, inefficiencies accumulate, and each additional choice makes the cost of taking a different course more expensive, encouraging the lock-in to path dependence. Prices in competitive markets with low transaction costs more accurately reflect declining marginal returns and, in principle, prompt corrective activity. But this is not always the case, especially when the setup costs are high and networks of connections are difficult to change or abandon. In these cases, the less efficient activity produces so-called increasing returns, which are incentives to continue without a correction. As Paul Pierson describes it, "In an increasing returns process, the probability of further steps along the same path increases with each move down that path. This is because the relative benefits of the current activity compared with other possible options increase over time. . . . Increasing returns processes can also be described as self-reinforcing or positive feedback processes."[44]

Here we have North's answer to why leaders of stagnant countries do not adopt the policies of those with dynamic economies.[45] They become locked into institutional arrangements, which create strong disincentives to change. Not only the leaders but also many of their constituents have strong stakes in maintaining the status quo. In time, they internalize ideologies that justify those poorly performing institutions. Trapped in an "increasing returns process," they find the costs of breaking the institutional lock-in unacceptable, notwithstanding evidence that a different path would eventually make their countries richer.

All the foregoing analysis of political institutions and economic performance supports our key propositions: that a country must have Liberal political and economic institutions to become rich and remain so more than temporarily, that few Liberal regimes should be expected in the decades ahead, and that the distribution of power in the world will not change significantly in the decades ahead. Both poor and wealthy countries are more likely to continue on their present courses than to make radical changes.

Institutions as Computer Systems and Operating Software

A mechanistic analogy can corroborate the foregoing arguments, as well as more complex historical and technical ones.

Think of countries as computers and political institutions as the operating software for their economies. In their early stages of development, computers were big and slow. As long as the number of users was small and the number of operations the central processor had to perform was manageable, the overall performance of the system was impressive. As the number of users increased, however, they had to queue up for access to the central processor. As software applications became more complex, they required more time to complete a task. Even powerful supercomputers soon ran up against the limit imposed on sequential processing: the speed of light.

The institutional analogue is, of course, a centrally controlled economy in which central planners attempt to direct a large part of a country's economy, if not all of it. The Soviet command economic system went about as far in centralization of control as has ever been achieved. Buyers and sellers were not allowed to execute market exchanges unless those exchanges were already envisioned within the state plan.

As long as the size and complexity of the Soviet economy were limited, this institutional arrangement produced impressive macro results, although it was never effective at the micro level in centrally directing exchanges to meet the needs of buyers and sellers. Increasing size and complexity, however, soon overloaded the capacity of central planners to handle all of the decisions required for the trillions of exchanges. Predictably, economic firms and individual buyers and sellers were forced to queue up for their share of the increasingly scarce decision-making attention from overloaded central planners. The natural response by the state was to increase the planning bureaucracy at every level, a step that increased transaction costs and thus lowered labor productivity even further.

Attempts to retain a high level of central control over an economy are not peculiar to Soviet-type economies. In modern times it has been the practice in war mobilization economies. And it is the norm in military establishments and large business firms. Max Weber's rational-legal theory of a bureaucracy pertains to this kind of organization. Thus it is a general problem for complex organizations.

The East Asian economies that have experienced rapid growth since the 1970s—especially Japan, South Korea, Taiwan, and Singapore, but also others that prospered in the early 1990s until the crisis of 1997 in Thailand—have been described as providing a unique growth model, "Asian capitalism," implying that these countries have discovered a non-Liberal institutional matrix for better economic performance than the United States has. In all of these cases, the state has stepped in to make a number of investment and capital allocation decisions, overriding market forces. In particular, banks have lent money based on political direction rather than loan-performance criteria. This is a type of central direction that distorts the corrective feedback from markets and produces queues as business leaders seek the favor of key officials. This is not a problem peculiar only to East Asia—banks in a number of West European countries have also behaved this way—but it had become particularly acute in Japan and South Korea.

To return to the computer metaphor, the bottleneck created by a single central processor has been broken in two ways. First, as miniaturization of processors increased, it became possible to build "personal computers," small desktop machines. Instead of being tied by a terminal, along with many other users, to a single large processor in a large air-conditioned room, each user is now able to have an individual microprocessor on his desk. A huge number of such computers can operate simultaneously. This solution, "distributed processing," greatly reduces the queues, backups, and other delays.

If a large number of individual microprocessors (PCs) are to interact, exchanging processed information and working from common databases, they require compatible operating software and application software, as well as an electronic network to allow data to pass from one microprocessor to another. Such networking gives individual PCs far greater capabilities and efficiencies than they enjoy working alone.

The second way to break the bottleneck is through "massively parallel processing." In principle it does the same thing as distributed processing in that it allows many computer operations to be done simultaneously rather than in sequence. No longer, then, is the speed of a light a limit to the number of operations that can be performed in a given length of time.

The analogue to computers in this case is obviously a market economy in which private property and competitive pricing allow

large numbers of simultaneous market exchanges. Their networks
and "software" comprise Liberal institutions: a constitution, private
property rights, third-party enforcement, and so on. Many individual buyers and sellers can interact at the same time without first
getting the permission of the state's central planners. In contrast,
centralized and politically controlled economic decision making do
for economies what mainframe computers and sequential processing
do for information processing. As information sets become large and
complex, the command economy's institutions impede effectiveness.

Taking this analogy further, Liberal institutions not only make
"distributed processing" possible, but they also provide standardi-
zation among "operating systems" to permit the networking, aggre-
gation, and coordination of trillions of market exchanges. Just as
common interface standards are essential to allow computers of all
types to communicate over the Internet, and as compatible operating
systems and applications allow sharing and transfers of data, so too
Liberal institutions are essential for the stable allocation of private
property rights and effective third-party enforcement that allow
competitive markets to achieve impressive performance, both na-
tionally and internationally.

Consider what the computer industry has accomplished by over-
coming the rigidity of large central processors and designing smaller
and smaller microprocessors for all kinds of independent applications, then linking them broadly, via the Internet, and locally, via
networks. The most basic of all sciences, mathematics, would not
have advanced at the dramatic speed it has since World War II. Manufacturing design for staggeringly complex aircraft, management of
complex organizational systems, dramatic advances in medicine—
on and on goes the list of the fruits of microcomputational devices
and the distributed processing design.

Consider what Liberal institutions have done for economic performance and science since the 1600s. They have provided the operating context for the most effective market economies, and they
have justified and facilitated the culture of "individualism" essential
for innovations in science, organization, politics, and virtually every
other area of human endeavor. If non-Liberal institutions could
equal the performance of Liberal institutions, we would have examples of modernization independent of the West. To date we do
not.

Thus we can confirm our contention that Huntington obscures a

critical point in his "clash of civilizations" thesis by divorcing Westernization from modernization.[46] Non-Western countries may modernize without Westernizing, but only by borrowing the Western innovations that produce modernization. They can never equal, much
less exceed, the economic performance of Western countries except
by remaining closely tied to the West (including Japan, which
achieved a constitutional breakthrough after the Meiji Restoration).
To sustain that performance they must adopt Western institutions
in order to achieve the "distributed processing" of market equations.
Non-Western countries may retain their institutional equivalents to
big mainframe central processors, but they cannot make those institutions perform at levels equivalent to wide use of distributed microprocessors, working both independently and in networks.

This is not merely an academic point. Its implication is that no
non-Liberal state in the world can seriously challenge the economic
performance of the United States and its Liberal allies. An illiberal
Chinese superpower is not possible except temporarily through
comprehensive interaction with Western economies. This does not
mean that China cannot achieve considerable wealth and industri-
alization over several decades. It does mean that China cannot sustain that performance for the whole of this century without major
institutional change. The banking crisis in Japan, a product of illiberal policies, will inexorably bring Japan's economic decline unless
its political leaders can reverse those policies before the country is
locked into its present institutional path. And without a successful
constitutional breakthrough, Russia has no prospects of returning to
great power status. We will deal with this point in more detail in
the chapter on economic performance.

Liberal Regimes and Revenue

Liberal political institutions convey a capacity to mobilize
resources for all kinds of public concerns ranging from welfare in-
equality to waging modern war. They make states stronger precisely
because they can mobilize resources. In fact, capacity for direct taxation is the single best indicator of the strength of a state. Because
it is the most invasive form of taxation, it requires state penetration
and control of local government—roads, police, courts, and so on.[47]

By this measure, of course, the Soviet Union was a very strong
state, unrivaled in its capacity to extract resources and labor from

its population. Essentially a permanent war mobilization system, its command economy impressed the world for several decades only to fall into permanent decline after 1960.[48] Several earlier coercive regimes—for example, the Roman Empire—have demonstrated considerable capacity to extract resources from their populations, and to the degree they have, they have been politically stable, capable of repressing internal revolts, and able to finance foreign wars successfully. All nontotalitarian types of dictatorship, however, because they are especially poorly institutionalized, lack a large capacity to tax.[49] Accordingly, they are weak states, poor at keeping order and at providing public social services. During the Cold War, the United States supported several client states in the Third World against communist insurgencies. Most were dictatorships, and although they received large financial and material assistance from the United States, they did poorly against their insurgents because they could not tax effectively. The most notorious case, of course, is South Vietnam. Looked at closely, such "internal wars" turn out to be competitions in taxation.[50]

Charles Tilly also makes resource extraction central to understanding both the rise and the diversity in types of states in Europe. As rival rulers struggled for control over population and resources, they were continually at war. "War and preparation for war involved rulers in extracting the means of war from others who held the essential resources—men, arms supplies, or money to buy them."[51] Why, then, did the absolutist regimes of the sixteenth and seventeenth centuries do so well at taxation for a time and then lose out later on to Liberal states? And why did the totalitarian regimes lose to the Liberal regimes in the wars of the twentieth century? Liberal states proved better at managing wartime finance through national debts and taxation, raising revenues for much lower transaction costs, a consequence not only of formal Liberal institutions but also of informal ones: Liberal ideologies that disposed citizens to be more supportive of their governments. Britain's parliament after 1689 raised vastly greater sums for the monarchy's military than before, and its financial institutions facilitated the maintenance of a large national debt to cope with surging demands for money in times of war.[52] France became far more effective at taxation after its revolution, and Germany followed suit in the mid-nineteenth century, as did the United States and Japan.

What about the coercive methods of revenue extraction developed by modern totalitarian regimes, especially the Soviet Union?[53]

To conclude as a rule that Liberal states are better at taxation than all other types of regimes would not be justified unless we can deal with the apparent exceptions. Nazi Germany and wartime Japan can be explained by tax capacities they inherited from the Liberal regimes they displaced.[54] The Soviet Union proved capable of imposing a very high savings rate, even when it forced large numbers of its citizens to perish from incomes below subsistence level, and of extracting those savings for use by the state, as it did during collectivization of agriculture in the 1930s. Over a long period, however, its vastly higher transaction costs for coercive resource extraction and concomitant lack of economic growth left it unable to compete with Western Liberal regimes. The same is true of other communist regimes.[55]

The point for our larger argument, of course, is that Liberal institutions not only make it possible for market economies to outperform all others; they also give the state a huge tax extraction capability at relatively low transaction costs and the capacity to manage deficit financing through national debts, spreading public expenditure costs over generations. This explains why the U.S. government can implement a broad range of domestic programs—not only welfare transfer programs but also infrastructure investments, investments in education and science, and, equally important, unparalleled peacetime investments in military power—that need not threaten continued increases in the gross domestic product. Admittedly, government federal programs and expenditures can reach a point where they begin to weaken the U.S. economy's overall performance. This has long been the subject of political debates between the major political parties—the "tax and spend" party versus the party of "big business and millionaires."

This age-old American political debate touches on a weakness in all types of regimes that has been emphasized as the primary source of national decline.[56] In their early years, when institutions offer few constraints to competitive market behavior, a country's economy performs well. Groups pursuing business and social interests, however, begin to organize to pass laws and create rules that distort the market in their favor. Over time, the resulting accumulation of such rigidities makes the market less and less efficient, causing economic performance to decline. This and other dangers to American power must be considered, but let us defer them until later.

2 An Empire of a New Type

American institutions not only facilitated the generation of unparalleled domestic power, they made it possible for the United States to knit together and manage the network of global and regional organizations and military alliances known during the Cold War as the "Western camp." Its scope and diversity are unprecedented in history and not always recognized as a loosely integrated political, economic, and military system. In fact, it marks a qualitative change in the kind of hegemonic regimes that the world had seen as empires. It is a sui generis regime-type: unipolar, based on ideology rather than territorial control, voluntary in membership, and economically advantageous to all countries within it.[1]

The primary political, economic, and legal organizations of this unique regime-type include the United Nations, the World Bank, the International Monetary Fund, the General Agreement on Tariffs and Trade (now the World Trade Organization), and the International Court of Justice. Also global but with limited membership are the Organization for Economic Cooperation and Development, the Bank for International Settlements, and the G-7. The European Union, which traces its roots back to the European Coal and Steel Community in 1950 and the European Economic Community established by the Treaty of Rome in 1957, is the most successful regional organization. Others—the Organization of American States, the African Union, and the Association of South East Asian Nations—are loose groupings rather than effective organizations, imitative of those that the United States more directly sponsored.

The primary military alliances have been NATO and the U.S.-Japanese and the U.S.–South Korean security alliances. The U.S.-

Canadian combined air defense command, less well known, plays a key role. ANZUS (Australia–New Zealand–United States) is also important, though not as critically located. A number of other bilateral security ties, some formal (with Thailand and the Philippines, for example) and some informal (with Israel and Taiwan), are also part of the overall American military security architecture.

This network of alliances and countries closely associated with it comprises about 17 percent of the world's population but controls about 70 percent of the gross world product (see Table 2.1).[2] Because nearly all the developed economies are included, the network's share of science, technology, and corporate resources is closer to 90 percent of the world total. The military alliances compose the network's core, but other factors—political ideology and economics— also contribute to its coherence and durability. Most, but not all, countries within it share the key tenets of political Liberalism: limits on state power and basic human rights, especially private property. This political linkage facilitates vast flows of trade and investment. There were, for example, $7 trillion worth of U.S.-owned assets outside the United States and $9 trillion worth of assets owned by non-Americans in the United States in the year 2000.[3]

A Liberal Empire?

During the Cold War, Soviet propaganda described this U.S.-led system as "the imperialist camp," imputing to it all the world's evils, especially war and mass poverty. As the Vietnam War dragged on and as the antiwar movement in the United States gained strength, the charge of imperialism began to come from Americans as well. International leftist political circles increasingly charged the United States with "moral equivalence" with the Soviet Union. Some domestic groups agreed, notwithstanding the United States' record as the most successful proponent of decolonization by Britain, France, Belgium, Portugal, and Holland after World War II. In the aftermath of the Cold War, the imperialism charge continues to be made, in diverse contexts, and by diverse spokesmen, including numerous European officials, Russian generals and parliamentarians, and politicians in South Korea, Japan, and other East Asian countries. Americans may view as pejorative such labels as "only remaining superpower," "hegemon," "hyperpower," or "empire," but they are likely to stick. The sentiments behind them, however, are mixed. Many who use the labels are by no means eager to see

Table 2.1 Economic, Military, and Political Membership Status in the American Empire

Country	GDP in Billion U.S.$	Military Ally	Constitutional Breakthrough
North America			
1. U.S.A	$10,894	——	Yes[a]
2. Canada	760	NATO	Yes
3. Mexico	664	No	No
Europe			
4. Belgium	266	NATO	Yes
5. Czech Republic	85	NATO	Uncertain[a]
6. Denmark	190	NATO	Yes
7. France	1,531	NATO	Yes
8. Germany	2,145	NATO	Yes
9. Greece	146	NATO	Uncertain
10. Hungary	64	NATO	Uncertain
11. Iceland	9	NATO	Yes
12. Italy	1,278	NATO	Yes
13. Luxembourg	24	NATO	Yes
14. Netherlands	456	NATO	Yes
15. Norway	188	NATO	Yes
16. Poland	196	NATO	Uncertain
17. Portugal	130	NATO	Yes
18. Spain	710	NATO	Yes
19. Turkey	185	NATO	Uncertain
20. United Kingdom	1,646	NATO	Yes
21. Austria	218	Neutral	Yes
22. Finland	138	Neutral	Yes
23. Ireland	132	Neutral	Yes
24. Sweden	244	Neutral	Yes
25. Switzerland	285	Neutral	Yes
26. Bulgaria	17	NATO in 2004	No
27. Estonia	7	NATO in 2004	Uncertain
28. Latvia	9	NATO in 2004	No
29. Lithuania	13	NATO in 2004	Uncertain
30. Romania	47	NATO in 2004	No
31. Slovakia	25	NATO in 2004	No
32. Slovenia	23	NATO in 2004	Uncertain
Asia-Pacific			
33. Australia	436	ANZUS	Yes
34. Japan	4,229	Bilateral	Yes
35. New Zealand	62	ANZUS[b]	Yes
36. Philippines	83	Bilateral	Uncertain
37. Singapore[c]	95	Informal	Uncertain
38. South Korea	529	Bilateral	Uncertain
39. Taiwan[c]	302	Informal	Uncertain
40. Thailand	130	Bilateral	No

Country	GDP in Billion U.S.$	Military Ally	Constitutional Breakthrough
Mideast			
41. Israel[c]	108	Informal	Yes/Uncertain
Others[d]			

Source for GDP data: International Monetary Fund 2003 estimates.

[a] "Yes" means that constitutional orders are mature, at least twenty years old. "Uncertain" means that a country has a constitutional order less than twenty years old, or it appears to have achieved an initial constitutional breakthrough, but uncertainties about it persist.
[b] The United States has suspended military relations with New Zealand until it reverses its policy on U.S. nuclear-power ship visits.
[c] Taiwan, Singapore, and Israel have strong informal military ties to the United States.
[d] Micronesia, the Marshall Islands, and Palau are formally U.S. military defense responsibilities, but they have been omitted. They and many other small countries—e.g., Caribbean island states—have been left out because even in the aggregate they add very little to the power of the American empire although many of them technically could be included and some, but not all, would choose to be included.

American hegemony disappear. "Empire" need not necessarily connote negative sentiments.

Geir Lundestad calls the United States an empire, but one of a special kind, "an empire by invitation."[4] Including himself among the revisionist historians of the Cold War, he emphasizes American expansionism, but he differs from most others in documenting the record of the United States being "invited" into Europe, East Asia, and most other places. He reminds Europeans who accuse the United States of opposing European integration that Washington helped initiate and then sponsored and encouraged that integration. Overall, Lundestad offers a compelling case for why Americans should not blanch at the "empire" label.

Unlike previous empires, it is a money-making enterprise, not a money-losing one, the kind against which Paul Kennedy directs his "imperial overstretch" thesis.[5] Ben Wattenberg, reacting to Kennedy's warning, was among the first to make this point (and others) about the uniqueness of the American empire.[6] Countries struggle to become members; they do not have to fight to get out. None has left voluntarily, although a few have downgraded their military relations: France left NATO's military structure (but not the alliance itself) in the 1960s but made tentative steps toward rejoining in the 1990s, and the Philippines demanded the removal of all U.S. military bases from its territory (while keeping its defense treaty with the United States). In the mid-1980s, New Zealand denied U.S. naval ships the right to make port calls unless they were certified as having no nuclear weapons aboard. Washington responded by dropping all military relations with the country under the ANZUS Treaty. Although still a formal member, New Zealand has not yet reversed its policy, the condition for resuming those relations.

These cases are exceptions; more common is request for entry. The line of applicants now seeking membership in the American empire is long. All the former Warsaw Pact countries and at least three former Soviet republics have applied for NATO membership, but only Poland, the Czech Republic, and Hungary gained admittance in 1999. In November 2002 seven more countries seeking membership—Estonia, Latvia, Lithuania, Slovakia, Romania, Bulgaria, and Slovenia—were extended invitations to join the Atlantic Alliance in 2004. Mexico, long a bastion of anti-Americanism, reversed course entirely, joining the North American Free Trade Agreement. A number of other Latin American countries want to join as well.

Although Lundestad's "empire by invitation" captures a key feature of the American empire, it is an incomplete definition of this new regime-type, as the foregoing discussion shows. At least three features constitute a syndrome that more adequately defines it.

1. It is an ideological empire, not a territorial one.
2. It is a wealth-generating empire, not a wealth-squandering one.
3. Countries struggle to join it, not to counterbalance it.

Elaboration of each of these characteristics will demonstrate that they are not just slogans but simplifying labels for complex realities and relations.

The Ideology and Institutions of a Liberal Empire

On the face of it, "Liberal empire" is a contradiction in terms. Liberalism, which rejects colonial domination, values national sovereignty, and requires civil rights for all citizens, is the antithesis of imperialism. Indeed, it has been and still is incompatible with colonialism, slavery, and similar institutions of past imperialisms. Within the community of Liberal democratic states in the world today, however, Liberal values are broadly shared. These states constitute the primary members of the first Liberal empire.[7]

To be a full-fledged member of this empire requires a country to have achieved what we previously defined as a constitutional breakthrough. And it must have internalized its constitutional arrangements so that they are stable. In other words, it must be a mature Liberal democracy, meaning that it also has a market economy. Its level of social welfare transfer payments may be higher or lower than those of the United States, but its institutions are sufficiently compatible with U.S. institutions to permit peaceful and comprehensive economic, social, and political intercourse. Its military orientation toward the United States must at least be neutral; ideally, it will be a formal ally. Not all members meet these criteria, but the presumption is that they want to meet them and are making progress toward that goal.

Membership, of course, is voluntary. It is difficult to find a country with a stable constitutional breakthrough that does not want a reasonably close affiliation with the United States. Some countries, however, want to be members but do not yet meet the standards, political or military. Table 2.1 lists countries that probably would consider themselves as members. Only a glance is sufficient to identify countries that really do not meet the criteria. Mexico, for example, has not achieved a constitutional breakthrough as we defined it in Chapter 1; nor is it a military ally of the United States. Before the North American Free Trade Agreement (NAFTA) was signed and ratified, Mexico would not have been included in Table 2.1. By joining NAFTA, however, Mexico expressed a serious commitment to creating institutions that qualify it for membership. The European neutrals—Switzerland, Sweden, Finland, Ireland, and Austria—do not have military alliances with the United States, but they all have mature and stable Liberal political institutions that long ago allowed them to establish close economic relations.

It is one thing to have a community of like-minded countries. It is another thing to say that they constitute a political organization that provides supranational governance. Moreover, if that governance is to be Liberal, then it has to have a constitutional basis of the kind described in Chapter 1. That is, there must be agreement among the member states on (1) rules to decide who rules, (2) rules for making additional rules, and (3) limits on the empire's ruler.

John Ikenberry argues that something close to a constitutional break-through for an American-led international regime has been achieved in the course of the past half century. The Western international system has a "liberal manifesto" of "principles, which deal with organization and relations among the Western liberal democracies." He lists those principles as (1) economic openness, (2) joint man-agement of the political-economic order, (3) support for domestic economic stability and social security, and (4) constitutionalism in the sense of commitments embodied in institutional mechanisms.[8] He has further developed the idea of an "institutionalized" inter-national system based on the postwar settlements in 1815, 1919, and 1945, concluding that the institutional arrangements since World War II have become "path dependent" from an "increasing returns process."[9] Although generally compelling, Ikenberry glosses over a line in our analysis that we drew between post-1945 institutions and and those earlier ones. The later ones are marked by the ideological consensus imposed by the United States. In the earlier ones, the conservative and Liberal ideologies in the two halves of Europe cre-ated great tensions in the nineteenth century, and Wilson's demand for ideological consensus with his fourteen points at Versailles ut-terly failed to win the day after 1919. As Ikenberry notes, two sys-tems actually arose after 1945, one among the Western states and one between the Soviet and American camps; it is important to go further and emphasize that the American system is qualitatively dif-ferent from all previous ones in its ideological character, which is Liberal before it is democratic.

To describe the extant institutions of the American empire as "constitutional" is overly optimistic by the standards for constitu-tional breakthroughs described in Chapter 1. Still, it accurately de-scribes the principles that have long characterized American rhet-oric about the principles on which Western international organizations are based. They were instituted after the devastating violence of World War II, which occurred primarily in two of the major regions within the American empire today—Europe and Northeast Asia. Emerging as the wealthiest and strongest country after that war, the United States has had the power to make those principles stick most of the time since.

The United States might have successfully imposed its rule over much of Western Europe, Japan, Korea, and Taiwan, but it chose not to. Territorial expansion is not its aim. In principle it could expand if other countries wanted to come under the U.S. Constitution. The

Northwest Ordinance, passed by the Continental Congress in 1787, established rules governing the settlement of the West and admission of territories as states, which provided the framework for the expansion of the United States for the next century and longer.[10] In principle the framework could be used today to incorporate new territories into the United States federal system, but since early in the twentieth century the United States has forgone territorial expansion. That is one reason why it does not seek a formal constitution for its empire. Another reason is its sensitivities about limitations on its own sovereignty, which any new constitutional arrangements might limit. Moreover, all other members of the community are equally protective of their sovereignty. The most that can be achieved, or that any country wants to achieve, is what might be called a quasi-constitutionalism.

This could be dismissed as an unimportant "meta-issue" were it not for the effective governance the United States has provided to the international community of Liberal democracies for several decades. U.S. power relative to that of any member has been and remains so overwhelming that Washington can, and occasionally has, peacefully compelled members to refrain from violence in settling disputes.[11] Compliance has tended to be voluntary because Liberalism in its domestic affairs generally guides American behavior in leading this community. For the most part, American use of power internationally has been constrained by Liberal principles that Ikenberry describes as a "liberal manifesto."[12]

While our analysis generally builds on Ikenberry's, it differs in its definition of an American empire. Several of the institutions that bind the post-1945 international order, especially the United Nations, include many more countries than are listed in Table 2.1. Members of this smaller group, which have mature Liberal domestic regimes or are striving to achieve them, are linked more tightly, and therefore have more informal institutional coherence through the shared tenets of Liberalism. They also enjoy more formal institutional coherence in U.S.-led military alliances (excepting the "neutrals" and the "informals"). The idea that U.S.-initiated international institutions after 1945 have become path dependent is therefore more compelling for what we call the Liberal empire than for the United Nations membership as a whole. Moreover, we attribute considerable validity to Huntington's "clash of civilizations" concept in emphasizing that groups of states with non-Western culture—Islamic and Confucian, for example—can be and most often are very hostile to Liberal institutions. Their path dependency based on their informal cultural institutions confronts the much weaker path dependency that Ikenberry attributes to the post-1945 international order.

In any case, U.S. benevolence toward its Liberal allies, as well as other states, is not the only incentive countries have for tolerating American dominance. It pays economically.

The Economics of a Liberal Empire: Why Membership Pays

All of the arguments about the superior economic performance of the United States apply to some degree to the Liberal democracies within the American empire. Those that have accomplished constitutional breakthroughs and sustained them for a generation or more are locked into the "increasing returns" process of Liberal institutionalization. They have been able to make the state perform the role of "third-party enforcement," which allows their economies to capture greater gains from trade.

To be sure, not all of the countries listed in Table 2.1 have achieved constitutional breakthroughs; nor have they all established the most effective versions of Liberal institutions. That helps explain the considerably poorer performance records of several of them. Their institutions impose higher transaction costs in various ways, causing lower rates of return on investments. In some cases, the higher transaction costs come from greater corruption, misappropriation, and less effective monitoring and contract enforcement. In other cases welfare transfer payments are quite high, reducing savings for investment and raising production costs by making labor more expensive. A number of other explanations could also be devised to account for different performance levels. Notwithstanding these inefficiencies, the countries within the American empire account for about 70 percent of the gross world product. Table 2.2 shows the major countries outside the American empire. Only Saudi Arabia has a reasonably impressive per capita income (though not equitably distributed). It is an exceptional case with special explanations for its wealth, not a model that poor countries can follow. Saudi Arabia's wealth comes from its vast oil revenues, not from being a constitutional state with effective third-party enforcement. Therefore very few nations can hope to acquire wealth along the same lines.

Table 2.2 Major States Outside the American Empire in 2003

Countries	Population (Millions)	GDP (Billions $U.S.)	Income Per Capita, $U.S.[a]	Constitutional Breakthrough
Argentina	37	$112	$3,027	No
Brazil	163	488	2,996	No
Chile[b]	16	69	4,283	Uncertain
China	1,266	1,350	1,066	No
India	1,002	540	538	Uncertain
Indonesia	210	214	1,020	No
Iran	65	117	1,803	No
Iraq	25	26	1,060	No
Nigeria	114	45	394	No
Russia	146	387	2,650	No
Saudi Arabia	22	191	8,695	No
South Africa	44	106	2,402	Uncertain
Ukraine[b]	48	46	952	No
Uzbekistan[c]	25	9	346	No

Sources: For GDP data, International Monetary Fund, 2003 estimates, except as specified. For population data, *The Economist: The World in 2003*.

[a] U.S. per capita income, as a benchmark, is reported as $37,460 for 2003 by the IMF.
[b] GDP data come from *The Economist: The World in 2003*.
[c] Uzbekistan granted the United States military base access in the fall of 2001, but the permanency of the agreement remains to be seen.

In addition to better economic performance at the state level, the American empire provides a modicum of third-party enforcement at the supranational level. For example, U.S.-led international organizations have become more effective in managing disorders and disequilibria in international financial flows and currency markets. The G-7, the IMF, and the World Bank have been used to limit the spread of the effects of collapsing currencies and unpaid international debts. The meltdown of the Thai currency in 1997 affected most of the economies in East Asia, and its ripples were felt more broadly, but informal U.S. leadership among the finance ministers and the IMF, though initially dilatory, kept the consequences from being much worse. In recent decades, several debt crises and other threatening circumstances have been mitigated in similar ways.

The WTO offers another example. Founded by the United States after World War II as the General Agreement on Tariffs and Trade, it has achieved an overall downward trend in tariffs and protectionism and moderated occasional trade wars that have broken out among sets of its members. The United States, however, has not always been the best supporter of a rule-based WTO regime. Thus its regulatory processes at times appear feckless, but judged against earlier times, when no such supranational governance of trade disputes existed, or existed only on much smaller regional scales, its record is impressive.

Yet another example is the International Court of Justice in The Hague, which decides disputes among countries that might otherwise feel compelled to decide them by force, a more costly method. The ICJ, of course, is not entirely an American invention, although it is chartered by the United Nations. It is the successor to the Permanent Court of International Justice, created by treaty in 1921, and its statute is identical to the Permanent Court's.[13]

The American empire also contributes to better economic performance by lowering the costs for providing military security. The United States provides the lion's share of it, reducing the costs to other members of the empire. At the level of a single state, defense is a "public good," like clean air. If one person gets it, then all people get it. It cannot be distributed to some citizens and not to others (excepting, of course, that people in the military must risk their lives to provide the public good to the rest of the populace). At the supranational level, the "public good" characterization holds true only so long as military alliance commitments within the American empire are honored. Thus far they have been, allowing all members to enjoy the benefits of lower costs.

Naturally, countries outside the American empire enjoy some of the benefits of the supranational governance it provides through its network of international organizations and informal working relations among ministerial level officials in finance, business, law enforcement, and judicial matters. When those benefits are public goods, they cannot easily be denied to nonmembers. Still, much greater benefits accrue to members and partial members—countries that participate in the WTO and the IMF, for example, but not in military matters.

Why Opposing the American Empire
Does Not Pay

The security and economic benefits of cooperation with the American empire cannot fully explain why very few countries have left it and joined other groups of states to oppose it. Scores of voluntary leagues, alliances, and coalitions have been created on the basis of such benefits that did not last very long. Their temporary nature has been their most distinctive trait. The aphorism that a state has only enduring interests, not enduring friends, reflects the shifting membership and temporary nature of such groups. The idea of empire, however, does not call to mind a game of changing partners; it evokes a strong sense of permanence, precisely what has come to characterize the American-led Western international system over the past decade or so.

In Modern Europe—since the Renaissance—voluntary group behavior has been a pattern among sovereign states. Upon that historical record rests the "realist" school of international relations theory.[14] Although most international relations theories are arcane, realism is straightforward common sense. It assumes that the unchecked power of any state is a threat to other states and that the only way to check power is with power. When the balance of power among states is upset by the outcome of a war, or by disproportionate economic growth, or by the creation of a new alliance, that prompts a counterbalancing process of diplomacy or war or both that restores the equilibrium—that is, a new balance of power. The emergence of a hegemonic state, according to this theory, inexorably inspires alliances among weaker states to check, and if possible to reduce, its power.

Realism provides a reasonably satisfactory, although incomplete, explanation of European diplomatic and military history. But like neoclassical economics, which ignores the role of institutions and path dependence in economic behavior, realism cannot account for the role of institutions and the unique qualities of American power in world politics. Nor does it do well in explaining long periods of time during the Roman Empire or in clarifying the politics of Chinese empires. While it seems to account for the bipolar balance of power during the Cold War, it encourages one to ignore institutional developments within the U.S.-led Western international system.

More important for our argument here are the expectations that realist theory logically generated as the Cold War ended. Its proponents anticipated the breakup of U.S. military alliances and the decline of U.S. dominance in the international economy, and they also expected former members of the American empire to form counterbalancing alliances in order to check and reduce American hegemony.[15] Well over a decade after the disappearance of the bipolar balance of power, they are still waiting, but the American empire looks more stable than ever, notwithstanding some of the shocks President George W. Bush gave U.S. allies in 2001–3 and the resulting anti-American sentiment in Europe, South Korea, and elsewhere.

The U.S. Congress has repeatedly expressed concern about the limits of American power and the fickle character of U.S. allies. American opponents of enlarging NATO warned that such a step would drive Russia and China into a dangerous anti-American alliance. Moreover, Russia, China, and India have, in their various idioms, called for counterbalancing American power. The Russian slogan, "multipolarity," and the Chinese condemnations of "hegemony" are examples, but neither has been willing to form an anti-American axis that precludes their cooperative involvement with the American empire. Nor has India made it a three-way coalition to encourage multipolarity or discourage hegemony.

Why are both the students and the practitioners of world politics so apparently wrong? Kenneth Waltz, the dean of the realist school, defended the theory by saying that it "enables one to say that a new balance of power will form but not to say how long it will take."[16] That is not much help for policy makers. Nor is it very encouraging for theorists. The conventional wisdom is wrong because we live in a qualitatively new era of world politics where many long-standing axioms of international affairs, developed mainly on the basis of Europe's experience, have lost their validity in regions of the world where the United States remains fully engaged, namely in Europe and Northeast Asia.[17]

Two realities have defined this new era. First, Liberalism influences the way U.S. power is used, making it more benevolent and less threatening than all previous imperial power. In other words, guided by the ideology of Liberalism, leaders check their own use of power, something that "realists" assume can only be done by counterpower, not by the volition of leaders. Second, the quantity and dimensions of U.S. power are so overwhelming that no other state or potential coalition of states can reasonably hope to counterbalance it. The rhetoric of politicians in both Europe and Northeast Asia occasionally reveals that both regions could return to realist behavior without U.S. dominance. This unique combination of institutions and distribution of power makes the American empire sui generis.

A number of students of world politics have already begun to recognize one of these new realities, the quantity of U.S. power. William Wohlforth, for example, points out that after a decade of U.S.-centered unipolarity, there are no signs of its breaking down, even as it has drawn more states into the U.S. orbit.[18] Presenting comparisons between the distributions of power during the zenith of the Pax Britannica and during the Cold War, Wohlforth shows that the United States holds much greater advantages than Britain did at any time in its imperial heyday. He rightly observes, "Never in modern international history has the leading state been so dominant economically and militarily."[19] In addition to sheer power, he emphasizes the United States' "off-shore" geographical position as increasing the "likely longevity of unipolarity." Unipolarity, as he defines it, is a condition under which the concentration of power is so hegemonic that it does not pay other countries to balance against the hegemon.

In other words, Wohlforth is arguing that the ways in which realism theory has been most commonly applied are conceptually inappropriate to the present distribution of power. He does not reject the theory; rather, he adapts it to the present distribution: "A unipolar system is one in which a counterbalance is impossible."[20] By his measure, a summation of economic, military, scientific, and a few other capabilities, the United States not only controls more than 50 percent of the power in the world but it should be able to sustain unipolarity even if its share of the world's power dropped to the 30–40 percent range. For all his cogent analysis, however, Wohlforth ignores the ideological dimension of the U.S.-led unipolarity, treating it purely within the context of realist theory.

Although military alliances and diplomacy may not be able to counterbalance American power, some observers have worried that the diffusion of economic power in the world is undermining it. To date, though, there is little sign that this is happening. Ethan Kapstein concludes from an examination of global economic trends, "Any country or group of countries that would challenge this American-dominated order faces enormous systemic pressures, and there is little evidence that balancing against the United States is in fact emerging anywhere in the world."[21] Kapstein also disputes claims advanced at the very end of the Cold War that the new threat to the United States is Japanese economic power. That challenge, of course, has been undercut both by Japan's subsequent poor economic performance and by its unwillingness, even at the height of its economic power, to challenge the United States.[22] Japan neither could nor wanted to overthrow the U.S.-led international order. Robert Gilpin's argument that economic and military power shifts from core to periphery states will erode U.S. hegemony has not been borne out by the data since 1945, according to Kapstein. Nor is China an economic threat; if it succeeds in its transition to an effective market economy—not at all a certainty—it just becomes more dependent on the world economy.[23] Kapstein does warn, however, that one cannot assume that the United States will continue to lead in this international economy, not because it lacks the capability but because it may lack the domestic willpower to play by and enforce the rules of the international economic game.[24]

Qualitative change in interstate relations brought about by the Liberal character of the American empire has been noted by Joseph Joffe, a German scholar and journalist. Asking why U.S. alliances are surviving after victory in the Cold War, he answers that the United States "irks and domineers, but it does not conquer. . . . For the balance-of-power machinery to crank up, it makes a difference whether the rest of the world faces a huge but usually placid elephant or a carnivorous Tyrannosaurus Rex."[25] American ideas, fashions, goods, and culture enjoy remarkably wide and strong attraction in the world. "This type of power—a culture that radiates outward and a market that draws inward—rests on pull, not push. Worse, this kind of power cannot be aggregated, nor can it be balanced." If Europe, Japan, Russia, and China tried to gang up, "All their movie studios together could not break the hold of Hollywood."[26]

Thus Joffe effectively explains why we should doubt the universal validity of Waltz's axiom that "unbalanced power, whoever wields it, is a potential danger to others."[27] If American power, unbalanced in so many parts of the world, is really a danger to others, why would countries in Central Europe, for example, line up to make it more unbalanced by joining NATO? Mexicans, long hostile to the United States, seemed to have changed their mind about a decade ago, and today they are not seeking powerful allies to help them balance the unchecked American power hovering over their defenseless country. To be sure, American power has damaged some

peoples, but in the main, the record is quite the opposite. The failure
of U.S. leaders to assert "unbalanced" American power in several
places and times during the Cold War and after has been a greater
threat to others in the world than the use of that power. Yugoslavia
in the 1990s offers recent examples.[28]

A far more poignant case of the same argument was made more
recently by Régis Debray, the French leftist who was a Castro supporter a few decades ago, in a short work of fiction in which a
French civil servant retires early in Washington, D.C., and becomes
an American.[29] He writes to the narrator—in English, because he
now views French as a mere "dialect"—explaining his decision. He
advocates France's application for statehood. "Who's in this new
Western U.S.: Israel, but not the Arab states. Mexico excluding Chia-
pas. Maybe Russia, surely not China, maybe Turkey, surely not Central Asia or Africa."[30] He admonishes the narrator that "Bush,
whether you like it or not, is your president as well as mine."[31] The
European Union is not a political choice at all. It "lacks willpower,
is good for economics but is not ready to fight, to shed blood for
Europe." Thus "Europeans have the choice between two capital cities: Berlin or Washington. History shows that Washington has been
better for them than Berlin."[32] He warns that "military power is not
everything but when there is a real crisis, it's the sword, not companies' cash flows, that decide things."[33] Moreover, he points out
that if France had two senators, it would have more influence on
the United States than it now does as a sovereign country. The fictional character is killed in action while serving in a Defense Intelligence Agency unit in Turkmenistan in November 2001.

Obviously neither Joffe nor Debray's protagonist represents a
broad base of European sentiments, but that they express these
views so sharply reveals that they believe other Europeans privately
harbor or can be awakened to them, even as American unilateralism
has angered European political leaders.[34]

Clearly something has changed in the world. Both the distribution of power and the institutions for producing power in the present epoch are sufficiently different from those in the centuries before
World War II that conventional wisdom going back to Thucydides
and including contemporary "realism" can be grossly misleading for
understanding world politics. This is not to argue that conventional
wisdom is wholly wrong. Truisms, after all, are true, but misapplied
truisms can truly mislead. Rather it is to say that the proponents of
realism have missed a great deal of what is going on in the world.

Multipolarity and counterbalancing are useful ideas in analyzing the policies of states of a Europe where none was fully dominant over several centuries, but the world today is a replica of neither the Europe of the Peace of Westphalia nor the Europe of the Congress of Vienna.

In sum, it pays neither to leave the American empire nor to oppose it. Strong positive incentives promote voluntary membership, and strong negative incentives discourage balancing against it. Although it looks like any voluntary alliance, whose members normally treat it as temporary, it has acquired a permanency that approaches but does not reach constitutional government.

Apparent Alternatives to the American Empire

Among the several alternative ways to characterize post–Cold War international affairs, two merit attention because they capture aspects of the American empire; in fact, they are better understood within this empire than apart from it: globalization and the democratic peace thesis.

Globalization

The amorphous idea of globalization became very popular in the 1990s, spawning a voluminous literature.[35] Its meaning varies widely, depending on who is using it, but one definition includes the belief that international trade and finance have created, or soon will create, sufficient interdependencies among states to begin to have an autonomous constraining role on their actions as sovereign entities. Its forces operate globally, showing little respect for national borders. It transforms economies, produces unprecedented levels of wealth, as a kind of "invisible hand" in the marketplace writ large, transcending individual states and washing over the entire globe. Here we need only emphasize its lack of global enforcement mechanisms. To the extent there are any, they are parts of the American empire's institutions, which apply mainly to the advanced and postindustrial countries of the world, not to the so-called "emerging markets" that are mainly outside the empire. Thus they have higher transaction costs and greater risks for investments. Globalization looks like an alternative to the American empire only until one considers the problem of third-party enforcement. The American empire's governance has made the large advances in international trade and finance possible. Without the U.S. empire there would be wars and anarchy, and therefore, no globalization. The economic activity known as globalization is an effect, not a cause.

The Democratic Peace

The thesis that democracies do not go to war with each other has enjoyed popularity in academic circles, far less in policy circles.[36] It is based on research showing that there are no examples in modern times of democracies fighting among themselves. Overlooking the problem of definition—deciding, for example, whether Britain was a democracy during the War of 1812 against the United States and whether Germany was a democracy in 1914—the correlation is striking. Proponents of the thesis find a causal connection in the domestic politics in democratic states: leaders are constrained by legislatures, interest groups, and public opinion, all of which are reluctant to resort to war, especially against another democracy.[37] Dictators do not have these constraints, which accounts for their ability to make war when they choose and against whom they choose.

Indeed, public opinion and legislative controls do impose constraints on leaders if the democracies are Liberal—a point that some but not all proponents of this thesis acknowledge. Some countries they include in their set, however, have headed to war with each other only to be prevented not by their publics but by the United States.[38] Greece and Turkey have more than once been on the brink of war over small Aegean Sea islands. Without the U.S. military influence over both countries, their dispute could have led to war. Perhaps the clearest way to expose the problem with the theory of democratic peace is the anecdote about a young man who went out drinking three nights in a row. Imbibing Irish whisky and water the first night, he suffered a painful hangover the next morning. Turning to bourbon and water the second evening, again he had a hangover. After trying Scotch whisky and water of the third night without any relief, he concluded, "Boy, water really is strong stuff!" Democracy is not the whisky within Europe and Northeast Asia. U.S. military power is.

Some of the democratic peace proponents look to Immanuel Kant's proposal for a "perpetual peace" as support for their case.[39] Indeed, Kant's proposal is highly relevant because he puts more emphasis on the constitutional republic as the form of government, emphasizing the separation of legislative and executive powers as critical, mentioning democracy only in passing as one of the classical regime-types, along with tyranny and oligarchy. Most important, he insists that rulers of republics must establish this peace. It will not happen deterministically. Moreover, all member states to this peace must be constitutional republics in which leaders are accountable to and constrained by their publics. This established treaty, he insists, must be a "federation of nations," not a "nation consisting of nations," which, he argues, would contradict the republican principle of representative government.[40]

Thus Kant's concept comes very close to describing what the American empire has come to be in that its ideology is Liberalism and other countries join it voluntarily. Political leaders created it; it did not result from some immanent determinism. It shares Kant's emphasis on constitutions and representative government rather than democracy, but not his requirement for a formal treaty for a "federation." Nor does Kant deal with economic performance, as does our concept of a Liberal empire. Finally, the American empire provides military power to back up supranational governance—formal and informal. Kant, like the democratic peace theorists, leaves this enforcement role to the constraints that legislatures, public groups, and public opinion will place on leaders who are tempted to violate the treaty of the federation. His insistence that "perpetual peace" must be "established," however, implies some use of power to bring it about, presumably including military.

Military Power: Still the Final Arbiter

Neither the origins nor the maintenance of the American empire can be explained without including the central role of its military power. Armies created it and armies still maintain it. The end of the Soviet Union as an external military threat does not change this requirement for providing security to the three wealthiest regions of the world—North America, Europe, and Northeast Asia. Threats to Europe and East Asia during the twentieth century have included internal ones, not just the external threat of Soviet military power. World War I broke out because the major European powers could not manage peacefully the emergence of German power. Rising Japanese power in East Asia and Chinese nationalism led to the Sino-Japanese War in the 1930s and to World War II in the Pacific. While the settlements in 1945 in both regions brought peace, they did not entirely remove the antagonisms and divisions manifested in the wars. Mistrust of Germany, although it seems wholly unjustified, survives to this day within Europe and underpins continuing support for U.S. forces stationed there. A major reason that NATO expansion into Central Europe enjoys more support in Europe than in the United States is that the collapse of the Warsaw Pact opened the way for reemergence of several of the interwar struggles in this region. For example, large Hungarian minorities live in Slovakia, Romania, and northern Serbia, creating the potential for Hungarian irredentism against all three of these countries. Changes in Poland's postwar borders include gains on its western frontier at Germany's expense and losses on its eastern frontier to Ukraine, Lithuania, and Belarus. NATO expansion has thus far helped keep all of these issues quiescent, although rumblings have occurred in Slovakia, Romania, and Serbia.

Turning to East Asia, Japanese-Chinese and Japanese-Korean mutual suspicions have abated very little since World War II, far less than those in Europe. U.S. forces deployed in South Korea and Japan keep those suspicions from causing open hostilities and make it possible for all three countries to cooperate in certain respects, especially in trade and financial matters. The U.S. regional military umbrella also keeps peace between China and Taiwan. In both regions the peace has held mainly because of the military alliance arrangements that keep significant U.S. military forces deployed there.

Still, this enduring need for large U.S. military forces abroad after the Cold War is poorly understood, not only in the academic community but also by American political leaders in both parties, in the executive branch and in Congress, by experts in the think tank community, and by journalists.[41] Douglass North emphasizes, it will be recalled, that third-party enforcement is essential for capturing the gains from increasingly complex contracts and trade. The enforcement linkage between U.S. military hegemony and international contracting and trade is not formal, but informally it is a powerful factor. It exists in a subjective sense among most countries within the American empire, just as good law and order from an effective city or state police force exists for domestic trade and contracting. Preventing war and suspicions of warlike behavior among states lowers transaction costs for international trade, just as an effective police force lowers it for domestic trade. This is precisely why the long-term foreign deployments of U.S. military power in Europe and East Asia make a substantial contribution to all the economies within the operational domain of those forces. They are not a dead loss, a waste of "guns" that could be converted to "butter" without a negative impact on butter production. They are more properly understood as an "overhead cost" for the developed economies of the American empire.

A counterfactual scenario can help clarify this point. Imagine what would happen if all U.S. forces were withdrawn from Europe and Northeast Asia over a couple of years. Taiwan would either surrender to China or be invaded. War between the two Koreas would almost certainly break out, and if war produced a unified country, Korea would treat Japan as a hostile power and produce nuclear weapons. Both of these developments would leave Japan little choice but rearmament and acquisition of nuclear weapons. The businessmen of a rearmed Japan would not be welcome in most countries in the region. An economic meltdown in East Asia would inexorably follow, adversely affecting the U.S. and EU economies, as well as all East Asian economies.

Europe would suffer similarly, though more slowly. The first adverse development would probably be the European Union's inability to keep order in Bosnia and Kosovo. Civil wars would spread throughout the Balkans as European forces withdrew along with American forces. The European Union would soon lose its momentum, especially in dealing with new members in Central and Eastern Europe, leaving all these former communist states in the midst of unstable economic and political transitions. As their ability to act in unison declined, Britain, France, Germany, and Italy would resort to traditional balance-of-power diplomacy against one another. That, of course, would allow even a weak Russia to compete with them for influence in Central Europe, creating the kind of diplomatic competition seen there in the interwar period. At the same time, migration issues could radicalize domestic politics in Italy, Austria, Germany, and France.

This scenario could have any number of variations, all leading to poorer economic performance and less political stability in Europe. Americans may have a difficult time imagining such possibilities, and many ordinary Europeans deny that they can occur—but few political and military leaders are as sanguine. One scholar interviewed more than one hundred of them in the early 1990s to discover that the majority believed the removal of U.S. troops would return Europe to its traditional rivalries and conflicts.[42] A French author has recently written a fictional diary in which he reports the departure of American forces from Europe and then chronicles the efforts among European leaders to establish a Kantian treaty of peace.[43] The last diary entry is filled with forebodings, as the German "Chancellor Faust," who led the way to the European peace treaty, is assassinated.[44] The chancellor's name, of course, is an allusion to Goethe's Dr. Faust, who struck a deal with the devil. However one interprets this tale, it calls Europe's political stability and economic prosperity into doubt.

The United States could survive these adverse developments, but not without paying a large economic price. Both trans-Pacific and trans-Atlantic trade and investment would suffer dramatically. American consumers would no longer have the wide choices of consumer products that they now enjoy at low prices, and American businessmen would no longer have the international markets they now exploit.

Many Europeans, Japanese, and South Koreans do not find the American empire an appealing arrangement. Dependency on the United States is bound to offend their pride and dignity, but thus far the alternatives have been less attractive. The exception is the European Union, if it can become a full-fledged federation with a unified foreign and defense policy. Were Europe to achieve this goal, the American role would obviously no longer be necessary. To date, however, path dependence keeps Europe reliant on U.S. military support. Periodic European impulses to create a defense capability independent of NATO have faded because of the costs. Having gone far in constructing the military institutions within NATO, the European members are locked into that solution by increasing returns. That is, the costs of going back to the starting point of 1949 and taking another path for military security are vastly larger than those of remaining on the well-established NATO path.

Suppose, however, that Europe decides to pay the price and create a separate "defense identity." Would that necessarily destroy the American imperial system? Since a new European federation would have Liberal institutions, its compatibility with the United States should be assured in principle. A unified Europe, of course, would considerably change the distribution of power within the American empire. How both Europe and the United States would adapt to it and relate to each other is difficult to anticipate. In theory, if a unified and Liberal European entity became economically and militarily stronger than the United States, there would be no reason why the United States should not follow its lead and let it carry the burdens of this "empire by invitation." That would be a sensible way for Americans to maintain and enjoy their traditional values.

While Europeans often bridle at U.S. hegemony, Americans sometimes complain that the European countries in NATO are simply "free riders" on the U.S. defense budget. This old complaint about the lack of burden sharing is popular with U.S. taxpayers, but if it were really valid, then how has the United States become overwhelmingly richer during the five decades that it has been "ripped off" by its European allies? Mancur Olson's thesis about "the logic of collective action" probably best explains this puzzle.[45] He shows that if a group organizes to pursue a "public good," like "clean air" or in this case "common defense," then rational behavior for each member is to withhold its contribution to collective effort. At the point where the value of getting the public good is high enough to make it profitable for some single member to pay the whole price, it will do so. Because it is a public good, if one member gets it, all members get it. Thus all of those who did not contribute still gain the benefit by this free riding strategy. Indeed, the Europeans "free ride" in many cases, but still the United States profits. Americans may not like it, just as Europeans may not like overbearing U.S. hegemony, but carrying most of the burden of defense nonetheless profits Americans. Moreover, because no other country can supply this public good, an American refusal to provide it would mean its end.

This line of reasoning also applies to the U.S. military alliances with Japan and South Korea. Japan has never been as much of a free rider as popularly believed, but even if it were, the United States would have profited overall.

There is, actually, a strong case to be made against military burden sharing with Japan. Suppose Japan ceased "free riding" and spent 4 percent of its GDP on defense, or about four times what it now spends. To reduce the burden on the United States, of course, its forces would also have to take over some operational responsibilities, such as the defense of the Taiwan Straits and of South Korea. The negative political impact on East Asia would be enormous. The incipient arms race between China and Taiwan would widen to include China versus Japan. South Korea would react negatively as well. The resulting costs to the United States of providing additional forces to the region to contain these developments would be large. In other words, regional stability in considerable part depends on Japan remaining a free rider on U.S. military expenditures.

This argument also applies to Europe, though not in precisely the same way. Deep concerns have been expressed by the U.S. secretary of defense and other Americans over the "common security and defense policy" (CSDP) within the European Union and the European Security and Defense Initiative (ESDI) within NATO.[46] These critics fear that the common security and defense policy will draw military resources away from NATO, weakening the alliance. Precisely because members of the EU are notorious free riders on defense, the danger is more apparent than real and likely to remain so, unless the United States withdraws its forces from Europe. If a few countries began spending aggressively on defense and displacing the U.S. dominance, the intra-European balance and sense of mutual security would be upset.

Empire in its traditional sense does not describe what the United States has constructed, but it does convey an accurate sense of American hegemony and supranational governance. It misses, however, the qualitatively different institutional features. The American empire's ideology rules out colonialism as an imperial form of territorial control. It also dictates restraints on the exercise of U.S. power. While there may not be full international agreement on all of the "rules" that limit the American "ruler," the very concept of Liberalism requires that American hegemony be limited. It also requires that sovereign states voluntarily choose to participate as members of this empire.

If ideological commitment to Liberalism alone were the basis for this regime, then it would be very unstable. That has always been the weakness of international law and other schemes for removing war as an instrument of international politics, ranging from Kant's proposal for a perpetual peace to proposals for world government after World War II. None of those schemes accounts effectively for the realities of power. The new type of empire does.

By the end of World War II, the United States was the leading military power in the world. The Soviet Union came close to equaling the United States in military power by the late 1970s and early 1980s, but it could not produce the same levels of economic power, without which superpower status could not be sustained. The subsequent collapse of the Soviet Union has left the United States with unparalleled military primacy. This backdrop of power answers the need that "realists" rightly insist must be met for supranational rule. It means that, if absolutely necessary, the United States has the military power to punish any opponent or group of opponents with devastating violence; in less extreme circumstances the United States can persuade and prod it allies to take actions they would not if the decision were simply a matter of "one country, one vote" in an international organization or bilateral treaty.

Traditional empires built mainly on the power to compel faced high transaction costs in the maintenance of order and compliance with their rules. The American empire incurs much lower transaction costs because its Liberal institutions allow member states to prosper while affording them diplomatic and informal political influence on U.S. foreign, economic, and military policy. The incentives for voluntary compliance, therefore, greatly reduce the need for coercive measures. The most serious danger to the system is U.S. behavior. The United States alone has the capacity to violate the rules with impunity, as it unfortunately does on occasions. Such behavior will inevitably destroy the system if it is unchecked by the United States itself. No other state or set of states can effectively call it to account.

Those scholars who see the Western international system as "constitutional" are emphasizing an important aspect of the American empire, but they do not fully answer Waltz's charge that governance does not exist above the state level.[47] A constitutional breakthrough, as we explained in Chapter 1, is essential for a state to provide third-party enforcement. As North observed, when he underscored the criticality of such enforcement, no one today really knows how to turn a state into such an entity. Expressing skepticism that "the correct constitutional forms will restrain the tyrannical exercise of power," he approvingly quotes William Riker: "But every time I convince myself that I have found an instance in which constitutional forms do make a difference for liberty, my discovery comes apart in my hand. It is, of course, a matter of causality. . . . The question is this: Does constitutional structure cause a political condition and a state of public opinion or does the political condition and a state of public opinion cause the constitutional structure?"[48]

If this puzzlement arises over the explanation of constitutional systems at the state level, then it must be greater for explanations of constitutional arrangements at the supranational level, where it has never been fully achieved.

The American empire is unlikely ever to be entirely constitutional. At best it can achieve only a quasi-constitutionalism based on self-restraint. Its defense of liberties has become partially institutionalized in formal international organizations and treaties, but it is finally dependent on a combination of sustained economic growth and hegemonic military power. American leaders, therefore, can ignore any rule because no other country has the power to sanction them effectively. As a first or second party to an international dispute, they also remain the international "third-party enforcer" of last resort.

They are, of course, restrained by the U.S. Constitution, but are domestic constraints sufficient to prevent them from flouting the quasi-constitutionality of American leadership abroad? For the duration of the Cold War, U.S. leaders were sufficiently restrained, voluntarily or by U.S. domestic political forces and legal norms. Since the end of the Cold War, however, periodic fits of U.S. "unilateralism" in trade, diplomacy, and military affairs give grounds for concern about the future.

Unilateralism itself is not the problem. Without unilateral U.S. action within NATO at key points, this alliance could have gone the way of the League of Nations. This is a problem in Ikenberry's concept of an institutionalized international order becoming path dependent. If it were to achieve a lock-in, it would lose its capacity to adapt and take more efficient paths as they became apparent. American pressure on the United Nations to reform was to a considerable degree a reaction to bureaucratic decay and declining effectiveness of U.N. international agencies. That the permanent members of the Security Council no longer are the truly "great powers"—Germany and Japan are excluded, and the relatively weak states Britain, France, and Russia remain—is already the kind of lock-in that reduces U.N. effectiveness.

In organizations within the membership of the informal American empire, U.S. unilateralism has achieved more positive results. For example, on several occasions over the past five decades, when U.S. presidents adeptly imposed their policy preferences over strong resistance, they made NATO more effective in its pursuit of common goals. Admission of West Germany to membership in 1955, adoption of the military strategy of "forward defense" in 1967, the decision on deployment of intermediate-range nuclear forces in 1979, and the reunification of Germany in 1990 over British and French objections—all these developments depended to some degree on imposition of U.S. unilateralism.

The danger arises from the kind of unilateralism that undercuts the quasi-constitutionality of the American empire instead of reinforcing it. A few examples are the pursuit of the Vietnam War after 1965, failure to abide by WTO rulings, and evasion of responsibility to intervene in Yugoslavia in the early 1990s, and to do so more than half-heartedly in the mid- and late 1990s. The most recent example as of this writing is the U.S.-led invasion of Iraq. Conceivably that action could eventually bring a constructive result, but it seems more likely to produce a contrary result.

As we turn to assessments of the many dimensions of American power, it will become all the clearer that the major danger to the durability of this empire is American leadership. Can the member states of its empire devise enduring formal checks and balances to keep U.S. leaders from undermining it? And if they can, will that not risk creating an "increasing returns process" that results in decay? If a solution is to be found, it must lie in greater institutionalization of those truly Liberal regimes within the American empire, for it certainly will not be found within the United Nations or in some concept of "world federalism."

Still, keeping the boundary of the empire's membership reasonably open and ambiguous has been important to its success thus far. The unambiguous border of NATO, which declares formally who is "in" and who is "out" of the European part of the empire, has its disadvantages. The recent admission of seven new members gives formal status to highly illiberal countries while committing them to pursue Liberalism. Those denied admission may lose their incentive to become Liberal if their exclusion looks permanent or too long-term to count in their political calculations today. At the same time, the global Liberal institutions—for example, the WTO and the IMF—offer membership to countries that are unlikely ever to be genuinely Liberal.

One can argue that calling the roughly two dozen mature constitutional regimes an empire is counterproductive unless they are institutionalized more formally and governed as a separate unit inside the larger international order of the United Nations, WTO, and so on. We take a different view. Formalizing this core set of countries (and more than a dozen others that have formal or informal military ties to the United States) is ill-advised, but recognizing them explicitly and calling attention to what really connects them has two important advantages. First, it should heighten their awareness of the stake they have in keeping the United States strong and playing an effective leadership role. Second, it can diffuse the target for countries that want to undercut and counterbalance American power. For example, both Russian and Chinese leaders, instinctively and emotionally disposed to make the United States "enemy number one," are increasingly aware that to oppose the United States is also to oppose a large number of the states within the American empire.

As the evidence in the following chapters vividly demonstrates, U.S. power is overwhelming, but the aggregate power of the world's Liberal states is vastly greater. Although in the following chapters we emphasize the gaps between dimensions of American power and the rest of the world, that should not be taken to mean that the members of the empire do not count. Rather we shall reveal several reasons why the aggregate power of the empire is greater than the sum of its parts: American power as well as institutions draw them into international organizations, especially military and economic, that amplify the simple sum of their combined power.

3 The Military Power Gap

The gap in military power between the United States and all other countries is large, very large. The quantitative gaps in the various kinds of weapons and forces vary, some being quite large, others more modest. The qualitative gaps are impressively large across the board. The first purpose of this chapter is elucidating them, but the second purpose is more important—answering the question, "What is the point of keeping such large military capabilities?"

Never in its history has the United States enjoyed such a military edge vis-à-vis the rest of the world. Its defense budget for 2001 was more than the aggregate defense budgets of the fifteen next-highest-ranking countries. Before the 1950s, the United States had never maintained more than trivial peacetime military forces, but during the decades of the Cold War, large military budgets and big standing forces could be justified not only by growing Soviet military power but also by the military threats posed by several other states, including those of the Warsaw Pact, China until the late 1970s, North Korea, Cuba, and Vietnam. With the collapse of the Warsaw Pact and the Soviet Union, and the end of the Cold War, the United States has found itself with truly hegemonic military power. When the aggregate military capabilities of its allies in Europe and Northeast Asia are added, the military edge becomes even greater. Since the United States seldom goes to war alone and has a global network of military alliances, rough aggregate measures provide an idea of just how large the military resources at the disposal of this alliance system could be.

The North Atlantic Alliance has impressive levels of military spending and active-duty military personnel, as shown in Table 3.1.

Table 3.1 NATO Military Spending and Personnel in 2001

	Military Budgets	Active-Duty Personnel
NATO Europe	$165,416 million	2,317,500
U.S.	322,365	1,367,700
Canada	7,745	56,800
NATO totals	495,526	3,742,000

Source: IISS, *The Military Balance, 2002–2003* (London: Oxford University Press, 2002), 332–33. This does not include the data for the seven countries invited to join NATO in 2004.

The European members of the alliance maintain twice as many people in uniform as does the United States, but those forces are not as well equipped or trained. That is why U.S. military spending is greater than that of the combined European allies. While U.S. military spending declined precipitously after the first Persian Gulf War, dropping by more than 30 percent in the 1990s, it leveled out at the turn of the century. European NATO countries' spending on defense, in contrast, has continued to decline, as have levels of active-duty personnel. Still, the NATO totals are massive when the United States and Canada are included.

Table 3.2 offers a similar but less dramatic picture of U.S. alliances in the Asia-Pacific region. Japan is the biggest spender, and South Korea keeps the biggest standing force.

Table 3.3 reveals just how large a percentage of global military resources is at the disposal of the United States' alliance system. Although the system has slightly less than a quarter of global military manpower, it has an overwhelming two-thirds of the world's military budgets. Moreover, if the quality of military personnel were taken into account, the edge of the U.S. alliance system over the larger but less well-armed militaries would be equally impressive. The United States alone still holds the global lion's share of military resources, with 40 percent of the global budget, though its manpower share is only 6.6 percent.

These quantitative and static figures, of course, conceal far more about what constitutes effective military power than they reveal. What they reveal, however, is where the world's military resources are located, where they are heavily concentrated, and where they are sparsely present. Whatever they conceal, it cannot easily offset

Table 3.2 Asia-Pacific Military Spending and Personnel in 2001

	Military Budgets	Active-Duty Personnel
Japan	$39,513 million	239,800
South Korea	11,165	683,000
Australia	6,752	50,700
New Zealand[a]	664	9,200
Asia-Pacific Totals	58,094	982,700

Source: IISS, *The Military Balance, 2002–2003* (London: Oxford University Press, 2002), 332–37.

[a] New Zealand's membership in the Australia–New Zealand–U.S. (ANZUS) alliance has been ambiguous since New Zealand denied port access to U.S. nuclear-powered ships in the mid-1980s.

Table 3.3 United States and Allies, Global Military Budgets and Personnel, 2001

	Military Budgets		Active-Duty Personnel	
	(Millions of U.S.$)	% of Global Total		% of Global Total
NATO total	$495,526	59%	3,742,000	18%
U.S. Asia-Pacific Allies	58,094	7%	982,700	5%
U.S. & Allies Total	553,620	66%	4,724,700	23%
All Other Countries	$281,622	34%	15,691,000	77%
Global Total	835,242	100%	20,415,700	100%
U.S. Only	332,365	40%	1,367,700	7%

Source: IISS, *The Military Balance, 2002–2003* (London: Oxford University Press, 2002), 332–37.

the massive military resources in the hands of the United States and its allies.

These realities are widely acknowledged, but what do they mean? Do they assure U.S. military hegemony for the indefinite future? We must go into more detail than may seem necessary in assessing the U.S. military because unlike a market economy, militaries are large bureaucracies with very poor negative feedback, or corrective information, for military policy making. Like the political and economic institutions of countries, military institutions easily become path dependent and highly resistant to the restructuring necessary to be effective against changing threats and the uncertainties of future warfare. Wars themselves, of course, provide negative feedback information, but by then it is often too late, and costly in the best event. Moreover, even when political and military leaders recognize the need for military reform, they seldom can overcome the institutional "lock-in" that blocks it, though there are exceptions.[1]

A Road Map for Assessing U.S. Military Hegemony

Comparing the military power of countries has never been done with great precision.[2] The very nature of military power—a mix of technologies, organization, employment doctrines, morale, and domestic political support—is subject to so many variables that it never remains constant. Moreover, sustaining military power in periods of peace and rapid technological and social change is especially difficult. The best that can be achieved is a rough picture of the static balance of military forces combined with a look at key dynamic factors that have altered and will continue to alter that balance in the future.

To do this, we will use the first Persian Gulf War, although it transpired more than a decade ago. It still remains the best available comprehensive window into the U.S. military, not only (1) its performance on the battlefield but also (2) its strategic lift capabilities; (3) what is required to train such forces; (4) the quality of personnel required; (5) intelligence capabilities; and (6) the industrial base that produced such military forces. Three subsequent wars (in Serbia, Afghanistan, and Iraq) provide confirming insights, but they also mark an important learning process that has produced what one observer cogently defines as a distinctive "American style of war."[3]

Most important, we must clarify what U.S. military forces are for, and, more specifically, what missions they must perform. A related question, of course, concerns the economic burden: can the United States afford to play these roles indefinitely?

Finally, prudence demands that we ask whether we have overlooked any serious dangers to the United States' ability to maintain adequate military power and use it effectively. If no other countries can break U.S. military hegemony, are there other factors, subjective or psychological, that might erode it?

What the Gulf War Revealed

In the decade before the U.S.-led military coalition expelled Iraqi forces from Kuwait in early 1991, most experts judged the United States and the Soviet Union as roughly military equals. Not so after this war. With the collapse of the Soviet Union at the end of that year, no other military power, not even among U.S. allies, was remotely close to the United States. One superpower remained, and all others were third-level if operating on their own. Some of them, of course—namely Germany and Britain in Europe and South Korea and Japan in East Asia—could boast second-level status if they had modern military forces and were in active alliances with the United States, capable of interoperability for coalition warfare. The French military, not allowed to participate in the NATO military structure since 1967, experienced serious difficulties as a member of the Gulf War coalition.[4]

The media coverage of the war presented an image of awesome U.S. capabilities but ignored the most important dimensions of that might. Foreign professional military observers, however, especially Russians, did notice them, although not always clearly.[5] Let us consider what really makes the big differences in U.S. military capabilities.

On the Battlefield
AIR FORCES

U.S. air-power capabilities are overwhelming but not always effective. Consider the four major tasks they undertook during the first Gulf War and the significance of what was achieved in each.

The first was the destruction of Iraqi air power. Iraqi aircraft that dared to fly were shot down, and a large number were destroyed on the ground. Thus the U.N. coalition forces never faced Iraqi air attacks. The lesson was clear: no air force in the world, not even among American allies, is capable of standing up to the U.S. Air Force. None has modernized adequately or trained to the level of U.S. pilots. Nor does any have equivalent air management capabilities to control thousands of sorties over lengthy periods.[6]

The story of Iraqi air defenses is different. The U.S. Air Force proved able to degrade or evade them, but it never fully destroyed them. Soviet-made Iraqi air-defense weapons remained so effective that U.S. tactical aircraft were forced above 15,000 feet, where they were ineffective.[7] Iraqi air-defense radar actually picked up F-117 stealth fighters but could not support attacks against them.[8] The lesson is that air-defense technology today has the technological edge over most countermeasures, including stealth.

Second, "strategic bombing" of targets deep in an enemy's rear was intended to render a ground war unnecessary.[9] Not only did air power fail to "decapitate" the Iraqi regime; neither did it deny Saddam communications with his combat forces in Kuwait. The far more accurate bombing intended to break the Iraqi leader's control in 2003 also fell short of complete success.

Third, "interdiction" is intended to cut off enemy ground forces from reinforcement, and "close air support" is meant to destroy enemy units closely engaged with friendly ground forces. In the first Gulf War, this distinction was blurred as General Schwarzkopf gave the air force the mission of degrading Iraqi ground forces by certain percentages.[10] Accordingly, the largest part of the bombing effort—more than 23,000 of 35,000 strikes flown against targets in Iraq and Kuwait—was devoted to destroying Iraqi ground forces.[11] For all of this effort, the counts of destroyed weapons briefed to the president by the Department of Defense on 23 February 1991, the day before the ground war started, were 1,688 tanks (39 percent of those in the Kuwait theater of operations), 929 armored personnel carriers (32 percent), and 1,452 artillery pieces (47 percent). The director of central intelligence gave a much lower estimate, asserting that the CIA assessments confirmed only 470 of the armored vehicles and tanks destroyed.[12] If we use the CIA figures, it required 49.9 aircraft sorties to make each kill; even using the Pentagon figures, which yield a rate of one kill per 5.65 sorties, the effort was extraordinarily expensive. The CIA figures are probably closer to the truth, meaning that attacking ground forces accounted for well over 90 percent of the weapons destroyed.[13]

Proponents of such bombing have claimed it had the additional effects of lowering Iraqi forces' morale and keeping them from maneuvering against U.S. ground forces.[14] But later analysis based on actual Iraqi operational activity during the ground war suggests that, as Daryl Press puts it, "The ground attack would likely have gone very well for the coalition even if there had been no extended air war."[15]

During the war in Iraq in 2003, close air support and attrition attacks on Iraqi forces appear to have been far more effective. Given minimal Iraq air defense to protect the Republican Guard divisions around Baghdad and the speed of the ground maneuver forces closing toward these divisions, this was to be expected.

Among the most impressive aspects of the 1991 air war was the command and control of more than 2,400 coalition aircraft (about 1,800 of which were from the United States) in a relatively small air space. Approximately 118,000 sorties were flown from 16 January through 28 February 1991 without any "friendly kills" or other significant problems, an unprecedented feat of operational control. The management of these operations showed both the remarkable training competence of coalition pilots and the technological advantages of the Airborne Warning and Control System (AWACS) aircraft.

Fourth, "airlift" received far less public attention than it deserved. Yet it was, along with destruction of the Iraqi air force, one of the two most important achievements of air power in the war. At its peak period airlift reached 17 million ton-miles per day (MTM), making it "the greatest such airlift in history," almost quadrupling the next-highest MTM ever achieved, 4.4 MTM during the Arab-Israeli War in 1973.[16]

To sum up, the capabilities to gain air superiority quickly and to provide massive airlift were the most critical tasks of U.N. coalition air forces in the 1991 Gulf War. The results of strategic bombing were difficult to assess but were by no means decisive. Bombing to degrade combat forces had only marginal effects. Close air support was ineffective where there were ground-based air defenses.

The air war against Serbia reaffirms the foregoing assessment, but the more recent wars in Afghanistan and Iraq alter it. No detailed studies of the latter wars were available at the time of this writing, but they appear to mark a radical improvement in the effectiveness of close air support. U.S. ground forces in Afghanistan were initially composed of Special Forces teams assisting friendly Afghan fighting forces. After the Taliban government collapsed, more U.S. regular ground forces were deployed, but still relatively few, less than a division in total. The initial close air support against Taliban and Qaeda formations provided by carrier-based air seems to have been no more effective than during the first Gulf War. But then strategic bombers began dropping bombs guided to targets by

U.S. Special Forces teams using laser designators or providing map coordinates for bombs guided by a global positioning system (GPS). The accuracy of these strikes was so effective that weaker Afghan forces were initially able to defeat stronger Taliban units in several battles. As the Taliban adapted, however, they were not easy to defeat. As one analyst of this war concludes, "Precision firepower did not simply annihilate well prepared opponents at standoff range in Afghanistan. To overcome skilled, resolute opposition required both precision firepower and skilled ground maneuver; neither alone was sufficient."[17] Thus the Afghanistan experience shows that high-altitude bombers, which fly above tactical air defense systems, can, when supported by advanced targeting technology, deliver accurate and effective bombing in support of engaged ground forces. Making strategic bombers available when they were needed, however, proved difficult and sometimes impossible. For tactical bombers this problem was less severe.

As of this writing, it is too early to judge confidently what the war in Iraq demonstrated in 2003, but the initial impression is that Iraqi forces never resolutely stood and fought the way Taliban forces did. In any event, the unprecedented speed with which the 3d Mechanized Division moved on Baghdad and the close air support it received combined to overwhelm the Iraqi Republican Guard divisions. In this regard, joint air-ground operations were far more effective than were air operations in the first Gulf War.

Whatever its weaknesses, U.S. air power has no serious rival. In principle, a unified European air force and aviation industry could challenge U.S. superiority. Japan, too, could produce the requisite aircraft, but not without major investments and much learning in the techniques of systems integration required in modern aircraft production. Yet both Europe and Japan lack the worldwide set of air bases and facilities necessary to rival the reach of U.S. air power. Russia still has an advanced aviation industry that could compete, but its economy is too weak to support such an expansion. Although China is investing in its aviation industry, it cannot challenge U.S. air power for the next several decades.[18]

GROUND FORCES

Although U.S. ground forces in the first Gulf War were never seriously challenged by Iraqi defenses, four characteristics of their operational capacities were apparent to close observers.[19]

First, their weapons overmatched all Iraqi weaponry. The M-1A2 tank in some instances began identifying Iraqi tanks at 4,000 meters (about 2½ miles), killing them with first-round hits at 3,700 meters (2¼ miles). In these cases Iraqi tank units were destroyed before the Iraqis could even see U.S. armored formations approaching at 30–40 mph, shooting on the move.[20] Previously, tanks had to stop to fire accurately and moved at 5–15 mph when traveling cross-country. While the Iraqi army did not have the best Soviet tank, the T-80, it did have a large number of T-72s, the next-best one. The U.S. M-1A2 (a modified M-1 with a 120mm main gun) had no difficulty defeating the T-72. The Bradley infantry fighting vehicle (M-2), the MRLS (multiple rocket launcher system), and the Apache attack helicopter also performed very well. Except for the British and German armies, no other in the world has weapons in this class. A few Russian weapons may be close but not equal.

Second, the tank-killing efficiency of the M-1A2 tank deserves emphasis. When we compare the cost of a round of 120mm ammunition (about $1,000) and the cost of this tank (approximately $2.5 million) with the cost of a bomb or rocket (from $1,000 to several thousands) and the cost of the aircraft ($30–40 million) delivering it, it is clear that the tank was a cheaper means for destroying an Iraqi tank. Expensive U.S. aircraft ($30–40 million each) accounted for no more than 10–15 percent of Iraqi tanks destroyed, while U.S. tanks destroyed the other 85–90 percent. And this comparison is conservative because nearly all kills by M-1A2s were with first-round hits, while aircraft required several sorties and many bombs and rockets to make a single kill. In some cases, pilots repeatedly attacked the same tank hulls, unable to see that they had been destroyed earlier. To say that tanks were thousands of times more cost effective is to make a modest claim. Probably no other technological improvement in U.S. weapons provided so much gain in combat power as the M-1A2, a point again demonstrated in Iraq in 2003. Technology applications in the Apache helicopter, the MRLS, and in maneuver control also brought gains that received little notice during the first Persian Gulf War.

Third, GPS devices, added to tanks and other vehicles after they were already in Saudi Arabia, permitted armored formations to navigate the desert in order to make westward enveloping movements around Iraqi defenses without delay or confusion. Iraqi commanders, who knew the desert well, simply did not believe it was possible.

Fourth, modern weapons require highly educated and trained commanders, staffs, and troops. Two observations reveal something of the army's competence in this regard. First, at the brigade and lower levels, commanders were aggressive.[21] They proved able to exploit their weaponry and to manage an unprecedented speed of advance.[22] Second, at the division and corps levels, leaders were seldom as agile. They actually slowed the speed of advance in several cases, literally learning and feeling their way. The explanation for the greater competence at the lower levels is simple.

Most of the captains and colonels commanding tactical units had been through exercises in the army's National Training Center in California. This highly demanding facility had produced a generation of young officers practiced in handling newer, faster, and more lethal ground forces. No equivalent training exists for divisions and corps. Thus the generals commanding them in the first Gulf War had never led their units against live opponents in free-play exercises of two to three weeks' duration—the kind that take place in the National Training Center for brigade, battalion, and company commanders. Not surprisingly, then, division and corps commanders in the first Gulf War were forced to learn as they went. Since the war, they have been subjected to serious criticism, but most of it reflects a lack of understanding, even by the authors of the best single account of the war to date, of just what has happened in changing ground force weapons and equipment.[23] That the army division and corps commanders avoided major debacles is no small achievement. The combat power of a contemporary U.S. division and corps has so increased that most observers fail to understand what is required to control these units effectively.

In retrospect we can see that nine U.S. divisions were not actually needed for the 1991 ground war in Iraq to succeed, but that only makes more impressive the combat advantage demonstrated by U.S. ground forces in this war. Iraqi ground forces, except for front-line infantry along the Saudi-Kuwaiti border, reacted aggressively, and a few maneuvered skillfully to block or counterattack assaulting U.S. forces but were easily defeated.

The invasion of Iraq in 2003 confirms these conclusions: far smaller army ground forces, far less strategic bombing, and better close air support simply overwhelmed Iraqi ground forces. The 2003 war was also characterized by much better operational skill on the part of division and corps commanders than during the 1991 Gulf

War. In 2003 they matched the swiftness and aggressiveness of lower-unit commanders.

Are any armies a match for U.S. ground forces? German, British, and possibly French forces may be, but they are much smaller and do not have the same kind of training. Japan's ground self-defense force has modern weapons but is poorly trained. Chinese ground forces are both poorly armed and poorly trained. North Korean ground forces are no match. Russian forces have so deteriorated that they, too, would fare badly.

The war in Afghanistan demonstrated the value of U.S. special operations units, forces that played a limited role in the first Gulf War. Special Forces were designed for operations behind Soviet lines in event of a war in Europe. Yet these Cold War relics, including B-52 bombers, proved effective. By adapting new technologies in their operations, they have modernized almost unnoticed over the past two decades. Moreover, their umbrella command—the Special Operations Command (SOCOM)—has led this process. SOCOM has also integrated special units from the air force and the navy, making their operations truly "joint."

Still, they have not advanced as far as they could. Once C-17 transport aircraft became available, heavy army units—including M-1A2 tanks and Bradley fighting vehicles—could have been inserted into Afghanistan. In the 2003 invasion of Iraq, when no U.S. forces were allowed to launch an invasion from Turkey in the north, the 173d Airborne Brigade seized an airfield north of Kirkuk, and within a week, a small unit of M-1A2 tanks and some armed personnel carriers were inserted by C-17s. Thus the feasibility of this technique has now been established, but the limited number of C-17s constrains its scale. This little-noted event in which heavy ground forces were part of an airborne assault should presage a revolution in so-called forced-entry operations, rendering amphibious invasions largely obsolete.

In sum, U.S. ground forces have no peer in the world. Still, too much money is allocated to amphibious forces that have limited use ashore, too many technologies are poorly used or neglected by the army, and the army's capability to project its heavy forces great distances is underdeveloped.

NAVAL FORCES

In the first Gulf War, naval forces were present in large numbers but played a minor role. Three aircraft carriers sailed into the Per-

sian Gulf and three into the Red Sea, violating an age-old navy principle that in wartime carriers should never go into narrow waters
where they are vulnerable to land-based threats. About half of the
F/A-18s, the most modern navy attack aircraft, were actually based
on land in Bahrain.[24] Carrier-based aircraft had to fly long distances,
limiting the number of Iraqi targets they could strike. Naval vessels
in the Red Sea also participated by launching a few cruise missiles.
To complicate matters, naval air wing commanders were reluctant
to participate in joint operations under the control of the Central
Command (CENTCOM) air force component commander. Finally,
they accounted for only 10–12 percent of all the sorties flown. Thus
the navy, though its presence incurred a staggering financial cost,
provided nothing essential to coalition operations.

In the war in Afghanistan, carrier-based air was the earliest air
power available, but the number of sorties was limited by the need
for tanker aircraft for refueling to reach the fighting zone. Once
there, navy aircraft were not nearly as effective as were B-2 and
B-52 bombers in responding to U.S. Special Forces teams with the
anti-Taliban Afghan units. In the 2003 war in Iraq, naval air appeared to be much better integrated into overall air operations, a
sign of considerable learning in joint operations since the 1991 Gulf
War. Still, in all three of these wars, only a small part of the navy's
capabilities could be employed. Its surface fleet and its submarine
fleet—the larger part of the navy—offered nothing but protection to
the carriers, already very expensive airports.

The implication is key. In the twenty-first century, the U.S. Navy
has no potential "blue water" opponent now that the Russian navy
has decayed. A few budding navies are to be found—in China and India—but they could be quickly destroyed by land-based air and a few
U.S. attack submarines. Big naval battles fought entirely at sea, like
those of World War II, are highly improbable today. An exception
might be submarines versus submarines, as long as Russia maintains
a substantial submarine fleet or if China eventually acquires several
modern submarines. Two important conclusions follow.

First, the U.S. Navy simply has no peer. Even the Soviet navy
was never fully a "blue water" challenge during the Cold War. Moreover, a foreign country would require several decades to build such
a fleet. Since only friendly countries—Japan and West European
states—have the industrial and technological means to build such
a fleet, the prospects of facing a large, hostile, modern blue water
navy in the next fifty years are trivial.

Second, advances in land-based aviation, in ballistic missile accuracy, and in space surveillance have radically altered the nature of war at sea, forcing the U.S. Navy to devote more than 80 percent of its surface fleet to defense of its carriers. At the same time, carrier-based air wings have not significantly increased their offensive power over the past three decades.

By comparison, the range of modern bombers and air refueling capabilities allow land-based air to reach any part of the world from the United States itself, not to mention from many bases provided by U.S. allies in Europe and East Asia. Land-based air can sustain massive operations for months, as the wars in Serbia and Afghanistan demonstrated. Carriers can operate for only about seventy-two hours continuously at full capacity. This increase in the cost of defending a weapons system without a matching increase in the system's offensive power has been described as "senility."[25]

Another change confronts the navy. What naval power was to "strategic reach" in the nineteenth century and until the last third of the twentieth, air power and space-based reconnaissance have become to strategic reach today. This is true not only for projecting firepower and bombing to any place in the world but also for airlifting heavy combat ground forces between continents.

The submarine is an exception in this regard. Its ability to hide has yet to be neutralized, making it an important vessel for twenty-first-century navies. Smaller, faster, cheaper, and better-armed surface ships are probably best for twenty-first-century navies—better armed and too numerous to destroy easily.

In sum, the U.S. Navy can overwhelm all other navies in the world, and it can maintain this lead indefinitely. At the same time, it is becoming more vulnerable to cheaper land-based weapons systems.

JOINT OPERATIONS

Joint operations are imperative for the army because air and naval capabilities must facilitate the army's land campaigns, the decisive phase of a war. The navy and the air force have always considered joint operations anathema; each seeks to play the decisive role, and each insists that it can win wars alone. In the Pacific during World War II General Douglas MacArthur and Admiral Chester Nimitz waged a running struggle over who controlled joint operations. In the Korean War, the problem arose again, and during the Vietnam War, the navy and air force resisted the unified commander,

General William Westmoreland, in his attempts to integrate joint operations. The Holloway Commission, charged to review the "Desert One" hostage rescue operation of April 1980, found that improper use of the joint system for operations contributed to the mission's failure. As late as 1980 the Central Command, which General Schwarzkopf commanded during the first Gulf War, did not exist. President Carter forced the Defense Department to create such a command in everything but name, but until President Reagan ordered its formalization in the spring of 1981, the military services resisted. Even then, the navy quietly refused to commit forces to it. As late as 1987–89, the commander of CENTCOM was struggling to gain control of naval forces protecting Kuwaiti shipping from Iranian attacks in the Persian Gulf, the very center of his area of operational responsibility. The air force was only marginally more cooperative. Army commanders in Europe and Korea feared that CENTCOM would pull away their reinforcements located in the United States. Thus all of the services resisted critical preparations for the largest war since Vietnam.

Not surprisingly, in 1990, as the CENTCOM commander prepared for war throughout the fall, each of his service components developed its own war plan. The air force commander wanted to win through air power alone and made every effort to keep his strategic bombing plan from being integrated with ground operations. The navy commanders did not want their aircraft controlled by the air force component of CENTCOM, eventually submitting under strong pressure. The army and the marines developed independent ground campaigns. The CENTCOM joint staff tried, with mixed success, to help Schwarzkopf make it a truly joint operation.[26]

The twenty-first-century wars in Afghanistan and Iraq are still known mainly from news reports, but both appear to have been marked by much better joint operational planning and control. At the same time, giving every service a big share of the operations remains the practice, even when it is not an efficient use of force.

Strategic Lift

Before the first Gulf War, seven army divisions, two marine divisions, two armored cavalry regiments, and an armored brigade were moved into the Saudi Arabian desert. That necessitated construction of facilities for all the logistics, medical, and maintenance units, as well command and control elements. Food and potable water had to be provided for nearly half a million personnel. All in all, during the first thirty, sixty, and ninety days of the first Gulf War, more tonnage of weapons, equipment, and supplies was moved for the U.S. Army alone than in the same time periods in World War II, Korea, and, except for a few cases, Vietnam.[27]

Noticeable, too, was the sharp increase in airlift during the Gulf War, outstripping any other airlift operation in history, even that of Vietnam. Intratheater airlift was also unprecedented. It proved critical in the movement of the XVIII Airborne Corps to its western attack positions, and as the XVIII and other ground forces swept around the western flank of the Iraqi forces, C-130s dropped more than one thousand tons of food and drinking water to the leading elements of this attack.[28]

Equally impressive was the movement of air forces from the United States and Europe to the theater of operations. Well over one thousand fighter and bomber aircraft moved, with most of their ground support materiel and technical equipment, to air bases within range of Kuwait and Iraq, most to Saudi Arabia but many to Bahrain, Diego Garcia, Turkey, and Europe. Because the Saudi government had greatly expanded its airfields' basing capacity in the early 1980s, these air force units moved in more easily. Reconnaissance aircraft, electronic warfare aircraft, command and control aircraft, air refueling tankers, helicopters, intratheater airlift (C-130s), and several other kinds of support aircraft outnumbered the fighters and bombers.

The equivalent of about ten divisions moved from the United States and Europe to a theater virtually bare of support facilities and launched the largest tank battle in history, preceded by forty days of bombing equal to, if not greater than, any in history. The strategic significance of this movement is difficult to exaggerate. It marks a sharp change in the relationship between maneuver forces and long-range bomber and rocket forces.

Although strategic bombers and missiles can hit targets at intercontinental ranges, they cannot ensure control of the target country. That requires ground forces and destruction of the target country's military forces. So-called strategic offensive forces could have started a U.S.-Soviet war, but they could have not ended it. Just as the striking power of artillery and machine guns over enemy attacking forces produced a stalemate between Germany and the Allies in World War I, making a decisive outcome impossible, strategic offensive forces in a NATO–Warsaw Pact conflict probably would have done the same. The "defensive" form of warfare was dominant over the "offensive" form because ground maneuver forces could not reach the full depths of an enemy country to ensure its defeat and submission.

The first Persian Gulf War demonstrated that the United States and its allies indeed could project maneuver forces across great distances, that most countries in the world, if they went to war against the United States, could expect ground forces to arrive and occupy their territory, not merely strategic bombers and missiles to deliver bombardments that they might well survive. No other country in the world has the "offense" that can prevail over the "defense" at intercontinental distances.[29]

Strategic lift by air and sea made this change possible. As we have mentioned, the tempo of airlift during the first Gulf War was almost four times greater at its peak than in any previous case. What sealift had been to strategic reach in the past, airlift has become today. Wide-body aircraft construction and improved jet engine efficiency have greatly increased aircraft load and range capacities. C-5As and C-17s can carry M-1A2 tanks, the heaviest ground assault weapon. A fleet of 250 C-17s could pick up all the tanks in a heavy division and move them from the United States to the Persian Gulf in 36–48 hours. The full potential of strategic airlift has not been realized by the Pentagon, however, because the air force has never been willing to buy enough transport aircraft, even after it essentially wore out the already overaged fleet of C-141s and C-5As during the first Gulf War. Strains on airlift during the campaign in Afghanistan in 2001–2 once again made this need apparent.

Sealift, of course, retains a major role because of its lower cost and greater load capacity. Fast roll-on-roll-off ships, moving at 33 knots, can reach the Suez Canal from the east coast of the United States in eleven or twelve days, arriving in the Persian Gulf in thirteen to fifteen days. Thirty such ships could pick up an army corps and move it half way around the world in about two weeks.[30] Yet sealift has never enjoyed strong support in the Pentagon.

The 1991 Gulf War thus revealed a dramatic change in offensive power vis-à-vis defensive power, a shift that was reconfirmed in the later wars in Afghanistan and Iraq. The air war against Serbia in 1999 caused European leaders to recognize embarrassing gaps between their own and U.S. air-power capabilities. Although European aviation and shipbuilding industries could produce adequate strategic lift, political and other factors make it improbable that they will do so. Japan could build large strategic lift capabilities, but that could create regional instability. Russia can build them, but not without an unlikely and dramatic turnaround in its economy.

Strategic lift, while neither a widely discussed nor an eye-catching issue, is a major determinant of U.S. military hegemony, one that a few other countries have the potential to rival but are unlikely to do so soon.

Training Areas and Facilities

The space and cost requirements for training modern armies and air forces have greatly increased over the past several decades. This change constrains both small, wealthy countries and large, poor ones.

Some sense of the change can be grasped by comparing the size of the U.S. Army's National Training Center (NTC) in California's Mojave Desert with that of its major training area in Germany, Grafenwoehr. The NTC has 642,000 acres of space, of which 358,000 can be used for maneuver and another 89,000 are reserved as an impact area for live artillery and tank fire.[31] Grafenwoehr has only 56,000 acres, of which 48,000 are usable for maneuver. In other words, the NTC is eleven times as large as Grafenwoehr with more than seven times as much maneuver space.[32] The live-fire impact area at the NTC is half again as large as the entire Grafenwoehr area.

This means that a tank or mechanized infantry battalion can execute only limited maneuvers in Germany, and free live-fire exercises are impossible. Although training in Germany can produce moderate tactical competency, it simply cannot match the NTC's results.

The U.S. Air Force has an equivalent training facility at Ellis Air Force Base in Nevada. Fighter pilots fly against several types of foreign-produced fighters in aerial combat. Known as Red Flag, this facility accounts in large part for the extraordinary skill of U.S. pilots.

Many countries could find the land and air space for such training facilities, but they are not the countries with the wealth and industrial base to field modern forces. Western Europe is too densely populated and land is too scarce to permit construction of such facilities, although European militaries desperately need them. The same is true for Japan, Korea, and Taiwan. To escape such constraints, the German air force now operates Halloman Air Force Base in New Mexico. Both the available air space and the weather are vastly more favorable for flight training. Pilots can be trained in a fraction of the time required in Germany, where foul flying weather exists about three-fourths of the year. Some British and Danish pilots are trained at the Red Flag facility. Britain and Germany have tank gunnery ranges and training areas in Canada, and German air defense units train regularly at the U.S. facility in Fort Bliss, Texas. With the enlargement of NATO, of course, larger training areas can undoubtedly be found in some of the new member states in Central Europe, and large ones can probably be rented in Ukraine, but investments will have to be made to equip them with effective instrumentation and target arrays. Although Japan's air force has modern bases and can fly freely over the surrounding ocean, it has nothing like a Red Flag facility. Japanese ground forces have their largest training areas in Hokkaido, but the biggest one permits only limited tank fire and carefully controlled maneuver of small armored units. South Korea, with much larger ground forces, also is confined to small training facilities.

In other countries with large military forces—Russia, India, China, Ukraine, and Turkey—land and air space for training is available, but the governments cannot afford the investments required to build advanced facilities. Nor can they sustain the training tempo to maintain command competence in maneuvering modern forces. These realities mean that few countries can adequately train large modern ground and air forces within their own borders.

Finally, U.S. military training includes projecting forces across oceans and into regions where support facilities are extremely austere or nonexistent. It also involves liaison and coordination with other countries and their militaries. Beyond Britain and France, which project small military units into Africa and the Middle East, no other countries have significant experience in such operations. Training commanders and staffs to conduct such global operations remains a virtual U.S. monopoly. Neither Britain nor France can project significant combat power over long distances without assistance from the United States. Airlift, communications, and intelligence support has often been provided to them, as during the Falklands war between Argentina and Britain.

Military Personnel

The first Gulf War disabused the American public of the popular image that its soldiers, sailors, airmen, and marines are semiliterate,

rigid-minded automatons. On the contrary, they have to be well educated to master modern weapons and equipment. The educational
level of a state's population is yet another measure of its military
potential.

Without the infrastructure of a modern industrial society, any
country will find it difficult to raise its military personnel to a technical cultural level required for effective manning of modern military forces; even with that infrastructure, the achievement may remain difficult. The European manpower pool is as large as the U.S.
pool, and the technical cultural level of Europe is higher in some
cases. Objectively, then, Europe has an adequate personnel base, but
it lacks a common language. If it made English the European Union's
official language and pushed its universal use, this handicap might
be overcome in the next couple of decades.

Russia has a common language but lacks several other qualities
critical for first-order military power. In China, Mandarin is widely
spoken, but several other languages are used by about half of the
population. Still, China has a common written language. Spanish-
speaking Latin America also has a common language but lacks many
requisites. The same can be said of the Arab world, where political
cleavages are a serious impediment.

Military personnel requirements are one more dimension of
modern military power in which the American edge is considerable—not unchallengeable, but still significant. The smaller officer
corps of leading NATO militaries, however, can reach American
competency levels when they regularly engage in large multilateral
exercises and operations. Were these to include intercontinental
force projection, as to Afghanistan or the Persian Gulf region, or just
exercises back and forth across the Atlantic, the so-called capabilities gap between U.S. and European NATO forces would be overcome. The United States, having dropped virtually all such NATO
large-scale exercises in the 1990s, is partially responsible for the
growing gap, one that cannot be overcome by European countries
alone.

Intelligence and Surveillance Capabilities

The U.S. intelligence community may not be the world's best at
recruiting spies abroad and discovering enemy spies at home, but
its technical collection capabilities are unmatched. For modern military operations, these capabilities are especially important. That is

why General Norman Schwarzkopf in 1991 and General Thomas Franks in 2003 each had a remarkably comprehensive intelligence picture of Saddam Hussein's forces and their activities. Few commanders have ever held such an intelligence advantage.

This advantage was possible because the United States has the world's best science, technology, and industrial knowhow. In particular, the U.S. space architecture, consisting of a complex constellation of satellite and ground sites deployed around the world, would not be easy to duplicate. Europe could build an impressive space-based architecture over several decades, but no single European country could do so alone. Japan has the wealth and the technology base, but it would have trouble establishing a network of ground stations.

The U.S. intelligence community, however, is not wholly independent. Collaboration with several allies gives it vastly more reach and capacity than would otherwise be possible. It is not a one-way street, however; allied countries gain far more than they contribute, making it a bargain for them.

Global telecommunications networks are the backbone that holds a global technical surveillance regime together. Any country may lease such communications from private suppliers, but none has the U.S. military's proprietary satellite communications architecture. The Soviet Union built a system of military communications satellites, but that system has deteriorated. China also has considerable space communications capabilities, but it nonetheless faces technological constraints. In sum, then, Western European countries, if they could pool their resources in a single program, are the most capable potential competitors in worldwide communications capabilities.

For intelligence to support all policy making, not just military operations, the U.S. advantages remain large and include additional assets. For assessments of a foreign government's capabilities and behavior, U.S. media coverage and university research provide remarkable breadth and depth, often far better than what can be learned from intelligence-collection means. In economics and business intelligence, the private sector—banks, think tanks, business schools, and university economics departments—produces more and better analysis than the intelligence community. Here again, the United States has greater private-sector capabilities than any other country in the world. When U.S. policy makers need political and economic intelligence analysis, the majority of it comes from the

private sector and open sources. In military intelligence, the proportions are reversed. The media and research centers did nothing
to help CENTCOM learn the number and disposition of Iraqi forces
or the technical parameters of Iraqi air defense radars, but they did
provide political and social knowledge of Iraq.

U.S. intelligence superiority, however, has vulnerabilities.
Changing communications technology can erode it. Continued U.S.
superiority depends to a degree on cooperative allies. Moreover, alternative collection means may emerge surprisingly in certain areas,
temporarily giving a hostile power an edge. All this fluidity notwithstanding, the U.S. lead will not be easy to overcome.

The Military Industrial Base

The U.S. economy also provides a unique military industrial
base. More advanced than any other, it is also more flexible in adapting to increases and declines in weapons development and pro-
curement. Nearly autarchic, it depends on few foreign suppliers,
and they are almost entirely located in countries belonging to the
U.S. military alliance system—primarily Germany, South Korea, and
Japan.

The first Gulf War stunned several foreign military observers,
waking them to the U.S. leads in advanced weaponry, strategic mobility, and intelligence capabilities.[33] They realized that their countries' economies simply could not provide such capabilities, not
even in very small quantities. To modernize their forces, they will
have to purchase weapons and equipment from U.S. firms. Although
they can turn to Russia and Western Europe for advanced weapons,
most will not have leading-edge technology, and some will not be
available. The gap between U.S. production capabilities and those
in all other states is uneven but still large in the aggregate.

Although no country can easily close this gap anytime soon,
leading European defense firms are struggling to make the European
Union a serious competitor.[34] While there is much talk in Europe of
doing that, the larger EU members continue to cut their defense
budgets, ensuring that European military industrial firms will have
smaller and smaller markets.[35]

As Richard Bitzinger describes the hierarchy of international
arms industry, the United States, Britain, France, Germany, and Italy
are the "first-tier" arms-producing countries, accounting for about
75 percent of the world's armaments production.[36] "Third-tier" pro-

ducers—for example, Egypt and Mexico—have limited capabilities and low technology. "Second-tier" countries—for example, Argentina, Australia, Canada, Israel, Japan, Norway, South Korea, Sweden, Taiwan, and Turkey—stand between these two categories. They have small but sophisticated weapons production capabilities that cannot rival first-tier producers. Changing markets, technological hurdles, and the unequal dynamics of cooperation between first- and second-tier arms producers make it unlikely that second-tier states can reach the first tier. Thus they will have to restructure and possibly shrink their military industries.[37]

China, a second-tier arms producer, therefore will not soon possess the quality military power that has often been predicted. Russia's defense industries, once in the first tier, have survived in some sectors and struggle for international markets, but they are unlikely to return to their former robustness and comprehensiveness over the next few decades.

In sum, a static assessment puts the United States far ahead of any competitor, but a dynamic view of military industries around the world, especially in Europe, Japan, Russia, and China, raises prospects for considerable change and uncertainty. The prospects for the United States to keep the lead, however, are good because it has a larger and more stable market for materiel and weapons than any other country.

Missions for U.S. Military Forces

A key problem for U.S. defense policy is recognizing that the military missions for a Liberal empire are considerably different from those of a traditional great power, or even a superpower in the age of bipolarity. The strategic environment is both different and the same: different in that U.S. military forces confront no single power or group of states that have equivalent forces, the same in that some countries will still be inclined to initiate wars against U.S. interests.

Thus the first U.S. military mission remains maintaining the capability to win wars involving heavy combat with modern forces. Defeating Germany and Japan and preparing to defeat the Soviet Union posed great uncertainties: victory could not be assumed. Today the United States faces no such challenges, even from China. Winning wars, therefore, in the sense of defeating an opponent's armed forces, can be assured. (Winning the postconflict political settlement is another matter.) Yet the war challenge remains because countries still start wars although their defeat is certain. Iraq, Serbia, and Afghanistan's Taliban regime chose to fight the U.S. military and lose. No doubt, many other small states will do the same in the coming decades. A large heavy combat power projection capability therefore is and will indefinitely remain the cornerstone for the American empire, and to the degree possible, it should include allied forces.

The second mission is homeland security. Not new, this imperative was called continental defense during the Cold War, but today it must deal with changing threats. A Department of Homeland Security was authorized by law in 2002, the largest such cabinet reorganization since the National Security Act of 1947. It has long been overdue. The fragmentation of border control and security responsibilities, a product of haphazard organizational developments dating from the nineteenth century or earlier, goes a long way in explaining why the Qaeda organization was able to destroy the World Trade Center and damage the Pentagon.

Dealing with terrorists and saboteurs as well as other kinds of direct attacks on the continental United States is a mission that seems likely to retain high priority for a long time. How it is accomplished will be as important as its effectiveness. It might be done in ways that abridge individual rights and threaten the Liberal character of the political system. It might be made excessively expensive, raising transaction costs for transportation, crossing U.S. borders, and controlling immigration to the detriment of economic performance. Or it might be only talked about but never effectively accomplished.

In any event, it is important to understand that terrorism, like crime, can be reduced but not ended. Terrorists have never destroyed a Liberal regime, but acts of parliaments have ended a few. Keeping this perspective while improving homeland defense is essential for sustaining American power.

The third mission, harder to define accurately in a single term, might be called military governance. This task involves the deployment and use of military forces to serve as a stabilizing backdrop for regional stability, and in some places it includes providing military occupation governments dedicated to establishing Liberal political regimes. This military mission is not unlike the "imperial garrisoning" that traditional empires provided to maintain peace and stability within their domains. A visit to Hadrian's Wall in northern England will call to mind the demilitarized zone (DMZ) in

Korea. Three Roman legions garrisoning that wall controlled population movements and kept the local peace for three centuries. The
U.S. 2d Infantry Division and South Korean military forces on the
DMZ have done that for half a century. In the Balkans, U.S. and
other NATO forces essentially perform a garrisoning mission in Bosnia, Kosovo, and Macedonia. In Iraq an initial strong disposition in
the Pentagon against assuming a garrisoning mission there has begun to weaken. U.S. forces are likely to remain there for a very long
time.

The U.S. Army has spent more years in nation-building activities
than in war. That was the army's task in the westward expansion to
the Pacific Coast in the nineteenth century and during Reconstruction in the South after the Civil War. Forty years of nation building
in the Philippines yielded mixed results, but it can hardly be considered a complete failure. The Marine Corps' occupation of Nicaragua and Haiti kept order but never involved the creation of new
political and economic institutions. Germany, Japan, South Korea,
and a few other post–World War II examples were remarkable successes. Only Vietnam was a failure. Yet that example has given nation building a misleading reputation, largely because it was not a
direct occupation but a form of "colonialism by ventriloquy" in
which the U.S. paid a weak and corrupt regime to "talk" the nation-
building game without "playing" it.[38]

The Pentagon, long accustomed to justifying and sizing its forces
based on perceived threats from potential adversary militaries, has
never taken into account this governance mission. In fact, the military services brush it aside as a distraction, not their proper business. American political leaders have also failed to understand it.
The Bush administration came into office in 2001 belittling so-called
peacekeeping missions, obscuring the technical definition of *peacekeeping* as developed by the United Nations in the 1950s. U.N. "blue
helmets" are supposed to stand between warring parties that have
already reached a truce; they are not deployed to fight and "make
peace" between warring parties. The military governance mission
includes peacemaking as well as long-term peace sustaining and
"nation building."[39]

As we explained in Chapter 2, U.S. military forces stationed in
Japan and South Korea and in Western Europe have also performed
this governance role since the end of World War II and continue to
provide reassurances of stability in both regions. Europe's continuing dependence on U.S. military hegemony for good relations

among NATO members was visible in 1990 during the diplomatic process that led to German reunification. Britain and France opposed reunification outright. The first President Bush prodded them into line behind a change in NATO's nuclear weapons doctrine essential to secure Moscow's acceptance of reunification.[40] Without military hegemony in the whole of Europe, Bush would have failed in this diplomatic effort. Thus this governance mission has always included more than the occupation of Germany; it is a regional task as well, carried out through NATO. Moreover, the rationale for enlargement of NATO in 1999 and 2002 has been to extend this governance umbrella over countries that mistrust each other as well as to confront potential domestic instability from ethnic minorities.[41]

In Northeast Asia the same thing was true throughout the Cold War and remains so today. Many South Koreans and Japanese have long seen each other as enemies, and each views U.S. forces as protecting them from the other.[42]

Beyond these two regions within the American empire U.S. military forces are engaged in a governance mission in the Persian Gulf region. President George W. Bush's "war on terrorism" is generating additional governance challenges, namely in post-Taliban Afghanistan. If the war against terrorism spreads to other countries, the question of governance after military operations will arise as well. So too will the nation-building question. Will governance in Afghanistan and Iraq include installing Liberal institutions and transforming these countries in the way that South Korea, Japan, and Germany were transformed? Or the way Bosnia, Kosovo, and Macedonia will eventually have to be transformed? Or will some more limited governance goal be designed?

Thus the military mission least understood and most disliked by the Defense Department is already the largest one it faces and promises to grow. Since the end of the Cold War, failure to appreciate this mission has resulted in dubious judgments about what constitutes a proper military force structure. If U.S. military hegemony is to be sustained, these views will have to change in the Pentagon. That requires a recognition that the centerpiece for U.S. military capabilities must be forward deployed ground and air forces in Europe and Northeast Asia. Additional forces will long be needed to fight small wars and conduct special operations in other regions as well—for example, the Persian Gulf area. These "threat-based" missions can best be performed by ground forces with tactical air support, projected at unprecedented speeds to intercontinental ranges by airlift and fast sealift—in days and weeks, not months, as in the first Gulf War. Thereafter, governance forces will be needed indefinitely.

This mission will never be properly understood without a recognition that it cannot end with "victory" in the traditional sense of the word. Nor does it normally have an "exit strategy." Curiously, no one expects police departments to win a decisive victory against crime that allows them to "exit" the scene. In a sense, the U.S. military has become the world's policeman, like it or not. This undesired mission is an "overhead cost" that keeps all members of the American empire prosperous as well as safe.

Military Coalition Leadership

The United States' military power is not just a matter of the size and capabilities of its own forces. It is also a matter of allied military forces. Coalition military leadership is therefore a critical skill for maintaining the empire. Bilateral military ties exist with South Korea and Japan, but only in NATO does the United States have multilateral military relations. Several years of negotiations and exercises have produced a large degree of interoperability there. Since the end of the Cold War, however, the United States has reduced its commitment to large-scale multilateral exercises in Europe, the mechanism that builds and sustains interoperability. U.S. reluctance to take on the lead role in combined occupation of Bosnia and Kosovo, inclining instead to dump the responsibility on European NATO states, seriously damaged the U.S. moral and political capacity to handle military coalition leadership. "Unilateralism" in the early months of the war in Afghanistan, as the United States turned down offers of military forces from several European countries, was particularly hurtful. It carried on to the war in Iraq and helps explain the failure of U.S. diplomacy in obtaining support for that war from the U.N. Security Council.

The costs of unilateralism are not just political but also economic. The coalition that fought the first Gulf War also shared the costs, minimizing the U.S. share. The U.S. costs of the less extensive coalition for the 2003 war in Iraq appear to have been well over $100 billion when all the payoffs to reluctant members are included. Unless the damage is somehow repaired, the governance that

U.S. and allied military forces provide within the American empire will be undercut. As Churchill once remarked, the only thing worse than having allies is not having them.

The Financial Costs of U.S. Military Hegemony

Can the United States afford to maintain the military forces necessary to deal with these challenges? Can it sustain its large advantage in military capabilities, constantly modernizing them, without threatening its own economic well-being? Without question it can. Table 3.4 shows the trend in military spending by several countries, including the United States. Among them, Russia and China could prove troublesome in future conflicts. India, far less likely to clash militarily with the United States, is included in the table because of its size, its significant military forces, and its ties with Russia. In the unlikely event that an anti-American military bloc arises in the decade ahead, China, Russia, and India are prime candidates for membership. Japan, South Korea, and Taiwan are included in the table because they are the front-line states in the security system in Asia. The trends in that region reflect a slow but certain military buildup that is absent in Europe.

As the figures for military spending as a percentage of GDP show, the United States has been on a downward trend for more than a decade, leveling out above 3 percent. Russia and China are above 5 percent.[43] Japan and India have steadily increased defense outlays with only minor changes in percentage of GDP devoted to defense. Taiwan and South Korea have increased defense spending but with a drop in military percentage of the GDP. Clearly defense is not nearly the burden for the United States that it is for these countries—except for Japan, the only one among them that could potentially approach U.S. military spending levels.

Table 3.5 shows the record of U.S. military spending during the Cold War both as a percentage of GDP and as a percentage of the total federal budget. Two figures stand out. First, with periodic exceptions, military spending as a percentage of GDP generally declined throughout the Cold War. Second, domestic spending competed well with defense, pushing it down from nearly two-thirds of the federal budget to less than one-quarter toward the end of the Cold War. By the end of the century, ten years after the Cold War, military spending had fallen to about one-sixth of the federal budget

Table 3.4 Military Budgets as a Percentage of GDP (billions of dollars, 2000 prices)

	1985 (GDP%)	2000 (GDP%)	2001 (GDP%)
United States	$390.3 (6.5%)	$304.1(3.1%)	$322.4 (3.2%)
Russia[a]	364.7 (16%)	52.1 (4.3%)	63.7 (4.3%)
Japan	30 (1.0%)	40 (1.0%)	46 (1.0%)
China	29.4 (7.9%)	38.4 (3.9%)	39.9 (4.0%)
Taiwan	9.7 (7.0%)	17.6 (5.6%)	10.4 (3.7%)
India	9.4 (3%)	14.8 (3.1%)	14.2 (2.9%)
South Korea	9.5 (5.1%)	12.7 (2.8%)	11.2 (2.7%)
North Korea[a]	6.3 (23%)	2.1 (12.7%)	2.1 (11.6%)

Source: The Strategic Balance, 2000–2001 (London: IISS, 2000), 297–99.

[a] The 1985 figures are for the Soviet Union. To appreciate why 16% is absurdly low, see Clifford G. Gaddy, *The Price of the Past* (Washington, D.C.: Brookings Institution Press, 1996). The figures for 2000 and 2001 are probably too high because IISS uses "purchasing power parity" dollar figures for 2000 and 2001, which exaggerate the reality. For similar reasons, the data on North Korea are also absurdly low.

and to near the 1939 level as a percentage of GDP (slightly below 3 percent).

Sustaining the present level of military spending as a percentage of GDP should be a light load for the United States. Given that the U.S. economy grew steadily throughout the Cold War, it seems difficult to argue that 3–4 percent of GDP for defense for the indefinite future will seriously hurt economic performance. In fact, doubling the present defense budget should not adversely affect the economy.

Are Americans Up to Sustaining Military Hegemony?

Although the objective foundations for sustaining American military hegemony are surprisingly strong, there are several reasons for not taking for granted its long-term maintenance. Several reasons have already been cited in connection with path-dependent military force structure expenditures, but there are yet others.

The first and most serious bears repeating: the quality of American leaders. Some of them may not know how to maintain and use military power effectively in the management of the American empire. In the 1990s, officials in both the executive branch and in the

Table 3.5   U.S Military Spending During and After the Cold War

Year	FY 1996 Dollars Outlays (Billions)	% of GDP	% of All Govt. Outlays
	Cold War		
1955	$296.9	10.8	62.4
1960	280.3	9.3	52.2
1965	267.7	7.4	42.8
1970	336.6	8.1	41.8
1975	239.5	5.5	26.0
1980	244.7	5.1	22.7
1985	329.9	6.1	26.7
1990	354.3	5.2	23.9
Average	296.2	7.28	37.6
	Post–Cold War		
1995	259.5	3.7	17.1
2000	281.2	3.0	15.7
2001	293.9	3.1	15.8
2002 estimated	330.5	3.2	16.1
2003 estimated	360.9	3.2	17.0

Source: Historical Tables, Budget of the U.S. Government, Executive Office of the President, Office of Management and Budget. "Outlays" for the post–Cold War years are different from U.S. defense spending reported by the IISS, used in earlier tables, because those figures were "authorized," not actually spent in that fiscal year. Figures for the Cold War years are outlays. Authorized budgets are normally slightly higher than outlays.

Congress, as well as in both major political parties, seemed to believe that the governance of the global economy does not depend on the backdrop of U.S. military power. This was manifest in their occasional calls for reducing U.S. military forces in Korea, Japan, and Europe, sometimes masked in the illusion that withdrawing land forces while maintaining large forward-based maritime forces would have no adverse impact on those regions. Withdrawal to the sea, to the air, or to space is withdrawal pure and simple.

The 1990s were characterized by painful demonstrations of how an American president can squander military influence. Neither the periodic bombing attacks on Iraq nor the missile strikes on suspected terrorist sites in Afghanistan and Sudan achieved any noticeable result, except perhaps to reassure Osama bin Laden that the

United States was not really serious about stopping his activities. The air war against Serbia is another example. President Clinton's flat refusal to use ground forces to invade Serbia produced a long air war with mixed outcomes, placing severe strains on key European governments. As we have mentioned, the George W. Bush administration not only failed to regain Europe's confidence but damaged it further by a number of arbitrary actions that came close to creating an irreversible decline in NATO political solidarity during the summer of 2002 and through the invasion of Iraq in the spring of 2003.

Second, the "zero casualties" syndrome—a legacy of the first Gulf War—throws doubt on the competence of American political leaders to use military power. When U.S. troops are told, as they repeatedly were in Bosnia and Kosovo, that their mission there is not worth the life of one soldier, they wonder why they are there. Taking risks is part of their profession. The message, as they see it, is that they are doing nothing of value. The deleterious effect on their morale is obvious.[44]

Third, this reluctance to risk casualties reflects a larger problem, a gap between the public and political and military leaders. Table 3.6 presents findings from an interview and polling study conducted at Duke University. The public's judgments about acceptable casualty levels differ greatly with those of the leadership in all three cases. The study leaders cogently conclude that the public is less "casualty averse" than "defeat averse." In other words, if the president had decided not to withdraw from Somalia in 1993 when eighteen American soldiers were killed, and instead had launched a campaign to find and destroy the guilty Somali warlord and his entourage, the American public would have rallied to his support. The public quite sensibly dislikes taking casualties if its leaders accept defeat.

The shock of 9/11 seems to have dissipated the fear among U.S. leaders that the American public can no longer accept more than trivial casualties in foreign military conflicts. Public support was high for both wars since then, in Afghanistan and Iraq, but the numbers of casualties were low. It is too early to judge whether the change is temporary or permanent, but if it is only temporary, then the capacity of America's leadership to manage its empire will remain in doubt.

Fourth, the present system of recruiting U.S. military personnel, especially the officer corps, has an adverse impact on the quality of

Table 3.6   Casualty Aversion

QUESTION: *In your opinion, what would be the highest number of American deaths that would be acceptable to achieve this goal?*

	Average number given by 623 military officers	Average number given by 683 civilian leaders	Average number given by 1,001 members of general public
1. To stabilize a democratic government in the Congo	284	484	6,861
2. To prevent Iraq from obtaining weapons of mass destruction	6,016	19,045	29,853
3. To defend Taiwan from an invasion by China	17,425	17,554	20,172

Source: Peter Feaver and Christopher Gelpi, "How Many Deaths Are Acceptable?" *Washington Post,* 7 November 1999.

the American political elite. Until the 1990s the political elite included a significant sprinkling of military veterans. For a full generation now there has been no draft, and ROTC is no longer present at most elite colleges. The potential importance of this issue is highlighted by a recent study correlating the makeup of the executive and congressional branches of the government from 1812 to 1990 with the propensity of the United States to use military power. When veterans were more numerous in the political elite, leaders were more cautious, but they also used force more massively. When veterans were fewer in government, leaders acted with less caution but with more graduated force, and often less successfully.[45]

Can American leadership in the world, for which the use of military power is so fundamental, be effective if no American leaders have had military experience? Can the military continue to play a positive role in racial and social integration if the middle class does not populate a significant part of its ranks? Probably not.

A fifth danger is that the Defense Department will prove unable to take advantage of the many lessons of the first Gulf War, the air war in Serbia, and the wars in Afghanistan and Iraq about military inadequacies. Congress can also be an obstacle to needed change. The record of U.S. military modernization before the Cold War was not good, and insightful speculations and case studies on how militaries best modernize are rare and at odds.[46]

In short, the American public is up to the tasks of military hegemony, but American leaders may not be.

For all their many sound insights, none of the theories about the nature of the post–Cold War world—from the "end of history," "globalization," and "the clash of civilizations" to "realism" and "constructivism"—adequately addresses the role of military power. In this chapter we have at least begun a proper examination. Five points tie its arguments together to explain why military hegemony is essential for the American empire and to highlight trends and factors that can undercut it.

First, U.S. military power is huge, flexible, and unprecedented in its quality. It has no rival as long as alliances remain solid. Were they to dissolve, the American empire would be short-lived.

Second, hegemonic U.S. military power provides the ultimate enforcement for the quasi-constitutional system regulating interstate relations within the American empire. Thus it is essential not only for the security of the empire but also for its economic performance.

Third, the costs of U.S. military power are comparatively small for the size of the American economy. The defense budget could be doubled without causing more than a ripple in the economy, although such a large budget is not actually needed.

Fourth, path dependency resulting from an increasing returns process in force structure is the major obstacle to effective U.S. forces. The sustainability of U.S. military power depends on a continuing series of improvements in force structure, command and control, personnel policies, and other areas, especially coalition leadership. While there is much to celebrate in U.S. military capabilities, there are many problems that cannot be ignored indefinitely without compromising U.S. military power.

Fifth, a change of mind about military missions and their priority is critical, not just for political and military leaders but also for the public at large. The end of the Cold War produced expectations of a large "peace dividend." In the event, the defense budget was massively reduced, down from the average Cold War level by about a half, but the view that the United States needed little or no military power any longer proved an illusion. The disappearance of the So-

viet threat did bring large changes in the military security environment, but it did not end the threats. Rather, it changed the mix and
priorities. If American leaders cannot adapt to recognize the change
and use military power effectively to meet these new threats, then
the sustainability of the empire will be in doubt.

The governance role that U.S. forces and military alliances must
fulfill cannot be overemphasized. It is both a crucial instrument for
enhancing collaboration with U.S. allies and the ultimate barrier
against the collapse of the present international order.

4 The Demography Gap

Fertility has been declining across the planet, but at different rates. The higher fertility rates of American women, compared to Europeans and Japanese, combined with massive immigration to the United States, will lead to a greater increase in the U.S. labor force in the foreseeable future, leading to a widening gap between the size of the U.S. economy and that of its partners.

In this chapter we will touch on two other aspects of the "demography gap." We will survey the impact of immigration on the United States, explaining how immigration strengthens the American economy and its position in the world. We will also deal with the difficult challenges of immigration policy for Europe and Japan. Afterward, we will see how the West has benefited from improvements in the position of women in society. This progress allows the United States and other Western countries to make better use of the female half of their populations for their economy but leaves Japan lagging behind among developed nations.

America's Demographic Position

The institutional similarity between Liberal economies ensures that improvements in productivity in one country can be copied in others. Capital moves freely and rapidly from one market to another; no country lacks capital as long as it offers profitable opportunities. Land availability has little impact on national income now that agriculture is but a small component of national income. The single most important variable in explaining the difference in the size of GDPs of Liberal economies is the volume of the workforce. The most populous countries in the developed world are the

United States, Japan, and Germany. They are also, in the same order, the three biggest economies. The next-largest GDPs are those of Britain, France, and Italy, each with about 60 million inhabitants. Smaller countries follow, with their rankings in population and national income more or less aligned. In the rest of the world, the rankings are much less correlated to population size because there is great diversity among economic institutions and concomitant diversity in efficiency at using available manpower.

Whereas a nation can import capital, the mobility of the supply of labor is limited by immigration regulations, language, and inertia. Economies must, to a considerable extent, make do with the stock of domestic labor they have. And unless there are major wars or plagues, demographic science can generate relatively accurate predictions for one or two decades. Consequently, to quote Lord Keynes, demography gives us "a considerable power of seeing into the future."[1] From 2000 to 2025 the American workforce will increase by 14 percent, while the Japanese workforce declines by as much as 16 percent and Europe's by 9 percent (though increased immigration could mitigate that decline). Thus it is highly likely that the American GDP will outweigh those of Japan and Europe even more in 2025 than it does today. The European Commission recognized this fact in a 2002 report: "These persistent differences in potential [demographic] growth rates between the EU and the U.S. could result in large changes in their relative economic importance in the world."[2] Projections for periods beyond 2025 also point to a continuation of these trends, though the accuracy of demographic forecast diminishes as the time frame expands.

The World Demographic Situation

In many poor countries, the large number of citizens under twenty years of age generates enormous pressures. Although fertility rates have declined dramatically in most underdeveloped nations, demography has put most third world states on a high-speed treadmill—they must run fast just to keep up with their increasing population. These nations, many of which have populations in which the majority is under twenty, will find it hard if not impossible to provide jobs for all their young citizens once they reach adulthood.

In China the consequences of the one-child policy will be a swift rise in the ratio of retired individuals to workers. China will have to adjust to this unprecedented rapid aging of the society as a poor nation with fragile institutions, making the management of the costs of a growing senior population more arduous than in rich and stable polities. Another demographic challenge that China will face results from the infanticide of baby girls and the abortion of female fetuses. The coming shortage of women could leave many men with no prospects of finding a mate. This situation has potentially explosive consequences—an increase in disturbances caused by poor young men who do not benefit from the "pacifying effect" of marriage, for example, and the use of violence to acquire the resources necessary to find a spouse.[3]

Africa is being devastated by HIV. AIDS, unlike diseases that prey on the weak, kills large numbers of young adults in their most productive years. African nations will grow even poorer than they already are unless an effective, easy-to-administer, low-cost cure for the virus is discovered soon. Outside of Africa, other underdeveloped countries are at risk from a breakout of AIDS into large segments of the population. The virus has so far been successfully contained in developed nations.

Russia is facing a demographic catastrophe. By 1999 life expectancy had regressed to the levels of four decades earlier.[4] While fertility is well below replacement level, mortality due to cardiovascular diseases and accidents (injuries, suicides, murders) is so high that "Russian men in their 40s and 50s are dying at a pace that may never have been witnessed during peacetime in" an urban industrialized society.[5] Russia may also be on the verge of an AIDS epidemic. Unless there is a radical transformation, especially a drastic reduction in alcohol intake, Russia will remain, medically and metaphorically speaking, a sick nation.

The demographic situation in most countries outside of the American empire is generally negative despite some recent improvement. Within the countries of the American empire, the United States is in a more favorable position that its European and Japanese partners, a situation that will likely increase the relative weight of America within its empire.

Unlike exchange rates, the population ratios between Europe, Japan, and North America do not fluctuate dramatically. But over time the changes have been enormous. In 1900 the U.S. population was only about 50 percent greater than Japan's and less than a third of that of Western Europe. By the early twenty-first century, the U.S.-Japan gap had grown considerably and the U.S.-Europe one had narrowed dramatically (America's population was 72 percent that of

Western Europe). From 1967 to 2000 the aggregate East and West German population grew by less than 6 million (about 7 percent), whereas the U.S. population rose by 82 million (41 percent). In other words, the number of German residents has stagnated, but in less than thirty-five years the United States added an entire Germany to its population base. In the 2001–25 period, it is projected that while the U.S. population will increase by 61.5 million, the Japanese population will fall by 6 million and the Western European one will gain only 5 million.[6]

For a generation to be replaced women must on average give birth to about 2.1 children. The United States, alone among the major rich nations, has a fertility rate slightly above two children per woman (2.07), whereas its partners are well below replacement: 1.38 in Japan, 1.51 for Western Europe as a whole, including 1.37 in Germany, 1.26 in Italy, and 1.26 in Spain. Rates are closer to replacement level in France (1.85) and Britain (1.66).[7] As a result of its near-replacement fertility rate, boosted by immigration, the United States population will continue to grow significantly in the coming decades.

Current Japanese and European total fertility rates (TFR, the number of children a women has over her lifetime) may understate future birth rates. Some of the recent decline is a result of women delaying rather than avoiding childbearing. In the United States rates fell in the 1970s and 1980s but recovered later as Americans had children later in life. But the Japanese total fertility rate and those of several European countries have fallen well under the lowest U.S. numbers ever recorded, making it unlikely they will soon return to replacement levels.[8] The longer nations maintain their low fertility rates, the harder it is to reverse population decline, because fewer and fewer women are of child-bearing age. Thus even if in one decade Japanese and European women have on average 2.1 children, they will only be ensuring the renewal of their generation, which is smaller than previous generations. Moreover, there is a time lag of between fifteen and thirty years between birth and entry into the workforce. Increases in fertility in the mid-2000s would not affect the supply of labor until the 2020s and 2030s. Consequently, projections up to 2025 that show a shrinking labor force in some nations would not be significantly affected by a "baby boom" in the early twenty-first century. Beyond these years, projections are admittedly less reliable, and one should note that even short- and medium-term forecast can be affected by changes in migratory trends.

The change in the working-age population has also been, over several decades, quite dramatic. In 1950 both Germany and Japan had a working-age population that was about half that of the United States. By 2020, however, the German working-age population will be about 27 percent that of the United States, and the Japanese labor force, which rose relative to the United States until the 1970s, will be 36 percent of the American force.[9]

While the Japanese and possibly the European labor forces may shrink, the percentage of elderly within those populations will increase. Japan's evolution is particularly striking, since that country will go from being one of the developed nations with the fewest elderly to one with the most. In 1950, 4.7 percent of Japanese were sixty-five or older, compared with 9.8 percent for Germany and 8.1 percent for the United States. By 2020 the percentages will be 26.8 percent for Japan, 21.4 percent for Germany, and 16.5 percent for the United States.[10] Age-related public spending will thus rise. Aggregate educational costs diminish as fewer children need to be schooled, but the relative weight of health and pension outlays for retired citizens in the national budget increases as population ages. The overall economic consequences are negative. By some estimates it is 2.5 times as expensive to support someone sixty five or older than a child under twenty years of age.[11] Moreover, schooling is an investment in the future, while consumption by seniors is not.

A growing proportion of elderly voters in a country affects politics. Older individuals want increases in retirement and health benefits. We may thus witness what the French essayist Nicolas Baverez calls "a senior citizens' democracy: a government of the elderly, by the elderly, and for the elderly."[12] Societies will suffer from the conflicting demands of the economy (raising the retirement age, curbing medical expenses and pensions) and of the political market (increasing entitlements to satisfy senior citizens). Thanks to its younger population, the United States will be less at risk than Europe and especially Japan, though by no means immune from the consequences of an aging population.

Some Europeans see smaller age cohorts as a positive sign, arguing that as the labor force contracts, the number of unemployed will decline. This outcome is not guaranteed. Those who are unemployed may well lack the skills that are in demand. The unemployed are not jobless because there are too many Europeans looking for too few jobs. In numerous cases they are out of a job because the workings of the labor and product markets, combined with their lack of skills, have shut them out of the economy. The continuous demand for migrants demonstrates that there are jobs in Europe. Moreover, a collapsing demography is likely to slow down the economy and will lead to increased taxes to pay for the elderly, including possibly higher nonwage costs that will discourage employment. To see demographic collapse as salvation is a delusion. If a country's population declines indefinitely, it will cease to exist. It will have zero unemployment but no inhabitants.

Demographic trends also have military implications. Combat remains a physically arduous activity best performed by young men. Japan and Europe may find it more difficult to staff their military establishments, or at least more costly as the demand for scarce potential recruits brings up the wages they command. Moreover, an aging society's pension and medical costs will put defense budgets under growing pressure.

We can observe demographic trends but cannot easily pinpoint their origins. As life expectancy and economic well-being increase, fertility rates tend to decline. The smaller number of children is compensated by longer lifespans and much lower infant mortality, thus allowing the population to expand at the same rate over the long term. Most societies will thus go through population aging as fertility rates decline and lifespans increase, but Japan and some European states face population decline.

There is no consensus on the reasons for the demography gap. This is not a circumstance for which different outcomes can easily be ascribed to institutions or policy. The ethnic makeup of the United States does not provide an explanation. Although Americans of European ancestry have lower fertility rates than Latinos and blacks, they have more children than Europeans.[13] Birth control is available in all these societies. Interestingly, in Japan the ban on oral contraceptives was lifted only in 1999, but even without the pill Japanese had fewer children than Americans. Several European societies had historically higher birth rates than the United States but now have lower ones. Roman Catholics used to have larger families than Protestants, but Lutheran Swedes now have more children than Catholic Italians. Women in poorer countries once had more children than those in richer countries, but Greek and Portuguese women currently produce fewer offspring than British and French

ones. As Massimo Levi-Bacci notes in his *Concise History of World
Population,* "The present-day lack of correlation between fertility
and income levels suggests that complex motivations, only slightly
connected with the availability of material goods, govern the fertility
decisions of couples."[14] Some analysts have noted the need to focus
on such anthropological characteristics of societies as, for example,
the tendency of Italian men to prefer living under their mother's care
than marrying.[15] Some think that the greater availability of spacious
suburban housing makes it easier for Americans to raise larger families. Others believe that the greater religiosity of Americans compared with Europeans may be the explanatory variable, while some
think that different traditions of family structure explain the higher
fertility rates in the United States, France, and Britain compared
with other European societies.[16] Whatever the causes, the fact is that
Americans have higher fertility rates than Europeans and Japanese,
and this demography gap ensures that the weight of the United
States in world affairs is likely to grow.

Immigration

Immigration makes a major contribution to U.S. demography
and to the American economy. It also creates U.S.-centered networks
of individuals who enhance the American position in the world.
Immigrants accounted for about 30–42 percent of the U.S. population increase in the 1990s and are expected to represent the same
share for the first decade of the twenty-first century.[17] In California
a quarter of the population is foreign-born.[18] Every year about
700,000 to 1,100,000 migrants arrive in the United States (statistics
vary, depending on accounting methods). Large numbers of illegals,
whose numbers can only be estimated, relocate to America as well,
perhaps as many as 400,000 to 700,000 a year in the late 1990s, for
a total undocumented population that may reach 6 or 9 million.[19]

Immigrants have thus had an enormous impact on the economy.
From 1990 to 2001, half of the 16 million new members of the U.S.
labor force were immigrants.[20] They contribute to the vibrancy of
American society and to its economy. As Samuel Huntington has
noted, "The continuing flow of immigrants into American society
reflects the opportunities it offers and contributes to its renewal.
Historically, first- and second-generation immigrants have been a
dynamic force in American society."[21] New arrivals have also been
crucial in revitalizing cities. The largest U.S. metropolis, New York

City, where 40 percent of the population was born in other countries, is a prime example. "Absent immigration, we would be seeing a very different New York, with neighborhood abandonment and depopulation."[22] Los Angeles (31 percent) and Miami (39 percent) are other major cities with large foreign-born populations.[23] From 1990 to 1998 both New York City and Los Angeles gained more than a million inhabitants through immigration.[24]

The qualitative aspects of immigration are as important as the quantitative ones. In the past four years, as Table 4.1 shows, twelve Nobel laureates born outside of the United States did their research in America. Over the years, seven Canadians who have moved south have won the Nobel Prize.[25]

Besides Nobel Prize winners, approximately 15 percent of scientists and engineers in the United States were born abroad, as were 21 percent of academic staff in higher education, 41 percent of engineers with doctorates, half of postdoctoral fellows, a majority of new mathematics professors, and more than a quarter of physicians, chemists, and economists.[26] Twenty percent of the employees of U.S. information technology companies are foreign-born.[27] In 1990 immigrants were 32 percent of Silicon Valley's scientific and engineering workforce, a percentage that has probably increased since.[28] Ten percent of the employees of Microsoft are of Indian origin.[29] Famous Indian-Americans in technology include Sabeer Bhatia, founder of Hotmail; Vinod Khosla, cofounder of Sun Microsystems and a leading venture capitalist; and Vinod Dham, the man behind the Intel Pentium chip. A study published in the journal *Science* revealed that individuals making an exceptional contribution to science and engineering in the United States are disproportionately drawn from the foreign-born.[30]

Although Chinese, Indians, and Taiwanese scientists are the most visible, the flow of scientific migrants to the United States is not limited to these countries. After China, Japan and Germany provide the most postdoctoral fellows in America.[31] There are tens of thousands of West Europeans working in Silicon Valley. A French institute lamented the brain drain of computer specialists to the United States.[32] About a third of German academics who go to the United States for research or further studies remain there for the long term. Another survey found that one out of seven young German scientists takes a post in the United States.[33] American universities employ around 5,000 German citizens, including 1,100 in the University of California system and 200 at the National Institutes

Table 4.1   1999–2002 Nobel Prizes Awarded to U.S.–Based
Foreign-Born Researchers

Field	Recipient	Place of Birth	Institutional Affiliation
		1999	
Economics	Robert A. Mundell	Canada	Columbia University
Chemistry	Ahmed Zewail	Egypt	Caltech
Physics	M. Veltman	Netherlands	U. Michigan (1981–89)
Physio./Medicine	Günter Blobel	Germany	Rockefeller U.
		2000	
Chemistry	Alan MacDiarmid	New Zealand	U. Pennsylvania
Physics	Herbert Kroemer	Germany	U. California
Physio./Medicine	Eric Kandel	Austria	Columbia University
		2001	
Physics	Wolfgang Ketterle	Germany	MIT
		2002	
Economics	Daniel Kahneman	Israel	Princeton U.
Chemistry	Kurt Wüthrich	Switzerland	Scripps Res. Inst.[b]
Physics	Riccardo Giacconi	Italy	Assoc. Universities
Physio./Medicine	Sydney Brenner	South Africa	MSI[a] Berkeley

[a] Molecular Sciences Institute
[b] Also Swiss Federal Institute of Technology

of Health.[34] In recent years, six Germans based in America have won
the Nobel Prize.[35] There has also been an increase in the number of
Japanese in the U.S. high-tech industry.[36]

Immigration will continue to make a major contribution to American science, thanks to the potential immigrants already in the
"pipeline" as foreign students. Excluding Canadians and permanent
U.S. residents, these immigrants account for 23 percent of graduate
students at Harvard and 32 percent at the Massachusetts Institute of
Technology.[37] As many as half remain in the United States following
graduation.[38] These students, and researchers who move to the
United States later on in their careers, guarantee a continued inflow
of foreign scientific talent to the United States.

This is not the first time that the United States has benefited from
imported scientists. The Manhattan Project to build the atomic
bomb during World War II relied on European exiles. Following the

American victory in 1945, the United States brought in German engineers, led by Wernher von Braun, to develop the American missile and space program. Earlier in the twentieth century, the "U.S. electrical industry benefited from educated European émigrés" who helped U.S. businesses become major players in this sector.[39] Other industries, as well as several academic disciplines, owe their beginnings in the United States to immigrants from Europe. What is new is that America now draws in individuals from all over the world rather than only from Europe.

Besides science, immigrants have been successful in business. Chinese, Indians, and Taiwanese started 27 percent of Silicon Valley's high-tech business.[40] Of the four hundred richest Americans ranked by *Forbes* magazine, seventeen were born in Australia, Canada, Egypt, France, Germany, Hungary, India, Iran, Israel, Korea, Poland, and Taiwan.[41] Companies that are, or recently were, run by immigrants include Altria (né Philip Morris), Chevron, Coca-Cola, Computer Associates, Eli Lilly, Ford Motors, and McKinsey.

Immigrants do more than supply America with scientists, billionaire entrepreneurs, and CEOs. They are an essential component of the labor force. The foreign-born account for more than three-quarters of all tailors in the U.S. labor force, as well as more than half of the cooks, taxi drivers, and farm laborers.[42] Mexican-born workers make up about 10 percent of the U.S. labor force.[43] Many of the small entrepreneurs who run newsstands, convenience stores, hot dog stalls, and motels come from overseas. They may not be business tycoons, but they do make an important contribution to the dynamism of the U.S. economy. Numerous farms, hotels, meatpacking plants, and restaurants would be bankrupt without migrants. One negative consequence of immigration, however, has been to push down the wages of the least-skilled members of the American workforce.

Another impact of immigration has been to shape new business networks centered on the United States. For example, Taiwanese who had studied and worked in the United States developed the Taiwanese semiconductor industry. AnnaLee Saxenian of the University of California, Berkeley, has documented how this "brain circulation" between the United States and Taiwan has fostered strong bilateral economic ties.[44] There is the beginning of a flowback of Indian professionals to the new Indian high-technology industry.[45] A similar phenomenon may occur between the United States and China, thanks to the Chinese scientists and engineers in America.

American businessmen of Central and East European birth have been active in industry and commerce in former Warsaw Pact states. Miami has become a hub of Latin American business due to its Cuban community. Over the coming decades similar developments could occur between the United States and Europe if some European professionals in the technology sector return home from the United States to establish businesses in Europe and in the process forge new ties between Europe and America.

In academia, too, this process is visible. Universities in South Korea, Taiwan, Hong Kong, and Singapore have recruited many of their nationals who were educated in the United States.[46] In addition, Asian-born faculty in the United States play an important role in disseminating information and helping build their native countries' science and technology infrastructure.[47]

These relations help the U.S. economy by fostering trade and investment with foreign nations. Thanks to immigrants, American and foreign businesses find it relatively easy to find employees who know both U.S. and foreign markets. For example, for every 1 percent increase in the number of first-generation immigrants, California's exports to that country go up nearly 0.5 percent.[48] But these new transnational business networks are more than profitable ventures. They create U.S.-centered personal and corporate linkages that demonstrate the gains that accrue to those who are in one way or another affiliated with the United States. As such, they serve to reinforce the ties that bind not only countries that are U.S. allies to America but also other nations to the United States.

Assimilation

A perennial worry of Americans has been that immigrants are not assimilating. Even in 1751, Benjamin Franklin was concerned that German immigrants would Germanize Pennsylvania.[49] In their seminal study published in 1963, *Beyond the Melting Pot*, Nathan Glazer and Daniel Patrick Moynihan argued that urban ethnic communities continued to avoid assimilation for generations.[50] But almost before the ink on their tome was dry, their conclusions were overtaken by events. Although the slogans of the past forty years have emphasized ethnic fission, the reality has been one of ethnic fusion.[51] Richard Alba, writing thirty-two years after Glazer and Moynihan, noted that assimilation—"the long-term processes that have whittled away at the social foundations for ethnic distinctions" and led ultimately to "high rates of ethnic intermarriage and ethnically mixed ancestry"—was proceeding rapidly.[52] Nearly three-quarters of younger Italian-Americans now marry someone with no Italian ancestry, exogamy is even higher for Polish-Americans, and outmarriage rates for Jews rose from 11 percent in 1965 to 57 percent in 1985.[53]

Non-European immigrants are being assimilated at a faster rate than the Europeans of a century ago who remained endogamous and congregated in their enclaves for generations. Roberto Suro noted that 30 percent of younger married Asian-Americans had a spouse from another ethnic group, a ratio that reaches 65 percent for Japanese-Americans.[54] Many of Los Angeles' most famous "ethnic" politicians are themselves of mixed background and/or married to someone from another ethnicity.[55] About a third of U.S.-born Latinos marry non-Latinos. From 1980 to 1998 the number of married couples from different racial groups almost doubled from 1.5 million (3 percent of the total) to 2.9 million (5 percent).[56] Cohabitation rates, a leading indicator of marriage trends, are higher. Even in the face of multiculturalist ideology, Nathan Glazer himself has more recently pointed out that "the forces of assimilation, operating through the economy, popular culture, and politics, are so strong that, even though they will have less support from the public schools and public agencies generally, they will still work their effects."[57] Continued migration will, however, create a condition under which there are always unassimilated recent immigrants, and within some communities there will always be holdouts who remain outside of the mainstream for generations.

Immigrants have also become economically assimilated. Within twenty years of arriving in the United States, 61 percent of immigrants live in owner-occupied housing, which indicates a high rate of economic integration.[58] After twenty years in the United States, immigrants have lower poverty rates than the native-born, though many recent immigrants are poor.[59] The large proportion of Asian-Americans in elite U.S. universities is another positive sign. They make up only 4 percent of the U.S. population, but their representation in the top colleges ranges from 10 percent to more than 25 percent.[60] They also account for 16 percent of new medical doctors.[61] Assimilation into the economic and educational mainstream has, however, been slower for Mexican-Americans, many of whom come from poorly educated families.

It is also noticeable that anti-immigrant arguments have changed, indicating a greater willingness to accept an ethnically diverse nation. In the early twentieth century, restrictionist views that led to the 1924 quotas reflected racial and religious prejudices against Irish, Italians, East Europeans, Jews, and Asians. In 1902 the head of the American Federation of Labor published *Meat vs. Rice: American Manhood vs. Asiatic Coolieism; Which Shall Survive?* Over the next decade Congressman Victor Berger of Wisconsin warned against the danger of a "yellowish black race" and of the "Slavians, Italians, Greeks, Russians and Armenians."[62]

Today, however, most of the rhetoric against immigration has focused on welfare, employment, and, as always, assimilation. Some restrictionists advocate more skills-based immigration, though such policies would bring in many non-white Asians. Foes of immigration, such as the British-born columnist Peter Brimelow, who seek to preserve a "white America," are an isolated group that has not found a way to generate support among elected officials.

It is nevertheless probable that many Americans dislike the arrival of large numbers of nonwhite non-Christians to the United States. The success of Patrick Buchanan's *The Death of the West: How Dying Populations and Immigrant Invasions Imperil Our Country and Civilization* is telling.[63] Despite its very low profile in the mainstream media, Buchanan's book was on the *New York Times* best-seller list throughout early 2002 and registered high sales at Amazon.com, showing that not all Americans are happy with the current situation. Opinion polls have always shown that Americans want less immigration. But whereas a century ago popular sentiment against immigrants was reflected in the views of politicians and journalists, this is not the case anymore. There are several reasons.

First, despite many citizens' doubts about immigration and foreigners, more American voters than before accept the reality of a multiracial society which also includes non-Christians. Second, racism is not acceptable in any mainstream political party any more. Congressman Victor Berger could warn against a "yellowish black race" in the early twentieth century, but when Republican Senator Trent Lott of Mississippi spoke favorably of Strom Thurmond's 1948 segregationist Dixiecrat presidential candidacy at Thurmond's one hundredth birthday party in 2002, he was swiftly ostracized by his colleagues, who removed him from his post as Senate majority leader. Neither does the press, with the exception of a few marginal publications, tolerate such discourse. It is thus nearly impossible for the defenders of "white America" to get airtime or press coverage, except for a few stories denigrating their views. Third, immigrants form powerful voting blocks in several states. The demise of the Republican Party of California after it embraced the anti-immigrant Proposition 187 in 1994 was a warning not only for Californian politicians but also for those of Texas, Florida, and other states with large immigrant populations and many votes in the Electoral College. The lesson for politicians was illustrated by the diverging fates of George W. Bush and Pete Wilson: the pro-Latino Texan became president; the restrictionist Californian not only failed in his bid for higher office but was succeeded as governor by a Democrat. Unions now support immigrants, even undocumented ones, in the hope that they will become new members. Finally, the American elite now has many immigrants or first-generation Americans from non-European or non-Christian backgrounds. This includes not only Asian-Americans and some Muslims of Southwest Asian background but also, in the realm of politics, several powerful Latino elected officials.

The aftermath of 9/11 revealed mixed attitudes toward immigrants and their families, especially Muslim ones. After the hijackings, some television stations and newspapers made an effort to portray the positive side of Islam as well as the fundamentalist extremes of the faith. Several journalists were openly critical of the racial profiling against Muslims by the FBI and the INS. Contrast this balance with the reactions of newspapers and radio stations after the Pearl Harbor assault. Racial epithets against Japanese were common. The American Civil Liberties Union, as well as a unanimous Supreme Court, supported the executive order authorizing the internment of American citizens of Japanese ancestry.[64] No respectable American after 9/11 suggested an analogous detention of Muslim Americans. One of President Bush's first acts after the attacks was to visit a mosque, though granted, this was really a foreign policy gesture: the president felt compelled to show Muslim nations that the United States was not waging a Christian war against Islam, in the wake of his provocative use of the word *crusade* shortly after the attacks. But even as the president voiced support for tolerance, several conservative Christian figures, some of whom were close to the Republican Party, made virulent anti-Muslim statements. Pat Robertson, a believer in Masonic and other conspiracies, spoke publicly against Islam.[65] The Reverend Jerry Falwell's web site "informed" its visitors that the Prophet Muhammad had taken a nine-year-old wife. The claim was amplified in June 2002 by the

Reverend Jerry Fines, past president of the Southern Baptist Convention, who called Muhammad a "demon-possessed pedophile."[66] On balance, however, politicians and public figures, with the noticeable and major exception of right-wing evangelicals, did not engage in anti-Muslim rhetoric, though shockingly few openly challenged the anti-Muslim statements of conservative pastors such as Falwell and Robertson.

There clearly was prejudice on the part of some Americans against Muslims, or those, like the Sikhs, whose unfamiliar attire leads some Americans to mistake them for followers of Islam. The average American was probably not convinced by the president's praise for Islam. Had the media tracked popular opinion more closely, their news stories on Islam and Arabs might have been quite different, though opinion surveys indicated that Americans were "scarcely readier to restrict the freedom of Muslims than of other Americans."[67] Some immigrants from the Middle East were harassed, and in at least one case Muslim-looking residents were murdered. (One of the killers was swiftly sentenced to death by a Texas jury.)

Although it was logical that most of those detained after 9/11 were of Southwest Asian background, innocent residents were arrested and harshly treated just because of their religious or ethnic background. Arabs, Iranians, and Pakistanis were detained or deported for minor immigration violations that would barely have been noticed had they been Chinese or Mexican. Many Muslims, in some cases American citizens, were treated far more harshly in questioning by authorities than is the norm in the U.S. justice system and were denied access to counsel, a basic American right. Had Americans been treated overseas in such manner, the U.S. government would surely have protested.

Nevertheless, taking into account the dark side of human nature, the aftermath of 9/11 revealed that, though far from perfect, the United States is more tolerant of ethnic diversity than in the past and than many nations are today. How long such attitudes would survive a prolonged war against Al Qaeda is unclear. Previous conflicts have shown that ethnic and religious hatred, escalating into mass murder, can develop even in societies, such as Bosnia, that were thought to be well-integrated and above such retrograde feelings. Measures that have targeted Muslims in the United States since 9/11 indicate how fragile ethnic tolerance remains during a crisis. Nevertheless, the United States is a more robust Liberal society than

Bosnia was and, it will probably remain a successful, though by no means perfect, multiethnic nation.

Immigration and U.S. Foreign Relations

Immigration spreads American ideals overseas. Immigrants who return home bring with them attitudes and ideas acquired in the United States. Those who stay in the United States influence their homelands through the ties they maintain with their country of birth. Yossi Shain of Tel Aviv University has noted, "To a large extent U.S. diasporas have emerged as the true marketers of the American creed abroad."[68] Hyphenated Americans "have contributed significantly, or have tried to effect, the eradication of dictatorial rule and the advent of some form of democracy in their native countries."[69] Formerly communist nations have relied on émigrés from the United States for senior positions: for example, Lithuania's former president Valdas Adamkus; cardinal Lubomyr Husar, head of the Ukrainian Greek Catholic church; and several senior military officers in the Baltics. When the interim government of Afghanistan took over from the Taliban, it was replete with men and women who had returned from the United States.

Obviously, not all immigrants adopt the American creed. In some cases their political activities in their homelands support causes that fuel conflicts and/or anti-Americanism overseas. The wealth they have accumulated in the United States can make their influence particularly nefarious. Irish, Hindu, Jewish, and Muslim extremists have received help from some of their American brethren, as have some of the warring factions in the Balkans. Moreover, groups linked to various ethnic lobbies have managed to exert influence on U.S. foreign policy that has not necessarily been beneficial to American interests. But overall, immigration to America is one of the many mechanisms through which U.S. ideology is spread to other nations.

As a result of the 1965 Immigration Act, which opened up the United States to immigrants from all over the world, there are now large numbers of Americans with roots in all continents. One effect, which Ben Wattenberg has noted, is that the many Americans who are not of European ancestry universalize America's message by demonstrating that Liberal democracy is not only for Westerners.[70] Another consequence, as Zbigniew Brzezinski has put it, is that the "multinational and exceptional character of American society has made it easier for America to universalize its hegemony without letting it appear to be a strictly national one."[71] American power and influence is no longer represented solely by American-born men of Northwestern European background. This diversification process is likely to accelerate because whereas in the 1950s more than half of immigrants came from Europe and only 6 percent from Asia, in the 1990s Asia accounted for 31 percent and the Americas (mostly Latin America) for almost half of new immigrants.[72]

Already, many prominent Americans were either born overseas or raised by immigrant parents from outside Northwest Europe. They include Central and East Europeans (for example, Madeleine Albright, former secretary of state, Czechoslovakia; John M. Shalikashvili, former chairman of the Joint Chiefs of Staff, born in Poland of Georgian, Polish, and German background; and George Soros, businessman and philanthropist from Hungary), Lebanese (Jack Nasser, former Ford Motor Company CEO, with Lebanese-Australian roots; such politicians as Spencer Abraham, George Mitchell, Ralph Nader, and John Sununu; and retired Central Command Commander in Chief Anthony Zinni); Asians (Elaine Chao, secretary of labor, born in Shanghai; Gary Locke, governor of Washington State, whose parents are from China; and Jerry Yang (cofounder of Yahoo, Taiwan), and the Caribbean (Colin Powell, secretary of state, whose parents are Jamaican). The Chinese-American I. M. Pei is one of the United States' most renowned architects, as was the late Japanese-American Minoru Yamasaki. Other Americans in senior positions in government or industry come from a non-European heritage, if not a recent immigrant background: Norman Mineta (secretary of transportation, Japanese-American), Condoleezza Rice (national security adviser, African-American), and Eric Shinseki (recently retired army chief of staff, Japanese-American), as well as the African-American chief executives Kenneth Chenault (American Express), Stan O'Neal (Merrill Lynch), and Richard Parsons (AOL Time Warner).

Immigrants have also played an important role as actors (as well as producers) in Hollywood, hence helping to project a multinational universal image of the United States. This phenomenon predates World War II (Rudolph Valentino, for example) and has continued ever since. In addition to several well-known African-American actors, several of Hollywood's top stars are from overseas, such as Pamela Anderson (Canada), Antonio Banderas (Spain), Jackie Chan (Hong Kong), Russell Crowe (New Zealand, raised in Australia), Arnold Schwarzenegger (Austria), and Jean-

Claude Van Damme (Belgium). One of Hollywood's top directors, John Woo, was born in China and raised in Hong Kong. The Taiwanese director Ang Lee lives in the United States. CNN employs numerous journalists who are not American. Several sports and entertainment icons, like Michael Jordan and Michael Jackson, also trace their roots to the non-European world. Tiger Woods, of European, Asian, and African ancestry, is a potent symbol of America's universalism.

The presence of immigrants and nonwhites in the American elite sends another important message. It demonstrates that the United States welcomes and rewards talent regardless of where it comes. In particular, it shows foreign nations that their nationals not only are well treated in America but can actually thrive. Immigrants who succeed in the United States are often more famous in their native countries than in America. Their fame is an effective tool to enhance the United States' prestige as well as to advertise the unique opportunities it offers.

Whereas the success of immigrants enhances the image of America abroad, it should also be noted that when the governments or citizens of another country think that their fellow nationals are not being well treated in America, relations with the United States suffer. This has sometimes been the case with Mexico and is now happening with several Muslim nations whose people see that U.S. authorities are mistreating their countrymen.

The United States Compared with Japan and Europe

The United States' success in absorbing foreign scientific and business talent and large-scale immigration contrasts with the performance of Europe and Japan. Given their low fertility rates, their difficulties dealing with immigration have important consequences for their future, because immigration is one of the ways in which they could reverse, or at least mitigate, population decline.

Japan takes in few immigrants. The total foreign population is 1.8 million, or 1.4 percent of the national total, and 680,000 of those are permanent residents, mostly ethnic Koreans and Taiwanese, generally born in Japan, whose families have been in the country for more than fifty years.[73] Given its low fertility rate, however, Japan needs to compensate for a dearth of Japanese babies. The United

Nations estimates that to stabilize its working age population Japan requires 615,000 migrants per year for 2000–2025.[74]

These figures are unrealistic. They imply that Japan, a country whose ethnic homogeneity has for centuries exceeded 95 percent, must by 2050 have a population that is one-third of foreign ancestry in order to keep its working-age population constant. So far, the country has tried alternatives to mass immigration, such as foreign direct investment overseas to export jobs rather than import workers. Other options include increasing the role of women and senior citizens in the economy. But these measures cannot fully compensate for the upcoming demographic collapse.[75]

It is possible that immigration will increase, though not at a rate as high as mentioned in the U.N. study. Even 100,000 or 200,000 annual arrivals would present Japan with a challenge. In the United States there is "a principled universalism (others can be like us), [whereas] the Japanese sense of uniqueness is a principled denial of any universal mission (no one can be like us)."[76] Even very modest levels of immigration in the 1980s, at a time of near zero unemployment, generated fears of crime, loss of social harmony, and other ills. How Japanese would react to more open borders is a difficult question the government would have to answer before moving on this front. At the same time, the collapse of Japanese fertility rates may force the country to open the door wider to immigrants, even though the political and social consequences may be problematic.

Europe's population challenge differs from Japan's. There is a long tradition of European immigration. European states have taken in refugees for centuries: Prussia welcomed persecuted French Protestants, Britain was the home of political exiles for centuries, and Switzerland provided asylum to more German Jews relative to its population than the United States.[77] Since 1945 waves of refugees from communism and other tyrannies have settled in Western Europe. European countries also have a history of bringing foreigners to contribute to economic development. The coal fields of the Ruhr and northern France were mined by Ukrainians, Poles, and Italians. Immigrants founded most of London's financial houses, including Barings, Cazenove, Lazards, Rothschilds, Schroeders, and Warburgs.

There has, however, been a major discontinuity in Western Europe. In a few decades it has become a continent of large-scale immigration. Foreigners represented 1 percent of the West German population in 1951, compared with 9 percent for united Germany in 1999, including about 2 million Turks.[78] Six percent of the French population now comprises foreign nationals, and an additional 4 percent is made up of naturalized citizens. Even Spain (720,000), Italy (1,250,000), and Greece (300,000), which have recently been exporters of surplus labor, have sizable migrant populations.[79] Immigrants are generally young adults in their reproductive years; in Germany foreigners and second-generation immigrants make up more than 15 percent of the under-ten age cohort.[80] In 1998 almost 12 percent of children born in France had either one or two foreign parents.[81] (In many cases where one parent was French, he or she was probably foreign-born or the child of immigrants.) Therefore, even without further intakes, the percentage of residents of foreign extraction will rise. Moreover, not since the late fifteenth century have such large populations of non-Europeans and/or non-Christians lived in Western Europe. There are now several million inhabitants of Muslim background in France and possibly as many as 3 million in Germany.[82] In a generation once relatively ethnically homogeneous European metropolises have attained religious and racial diversity on an American scale.

Given these facts, Europe has handled immigration fairly well. In 1968 Enoch Powell, a British Tory member of Parliament, warned of "rivers of blood" caused by racial tensions.[83] Thirty-five years later the closest to a "race war" in Western Europe has been the conflict between Catholics and Protestants in Northern Ireland. Europe, as Nicolas Eberstadt has observed, "populated as it has been by successive historical flows of peoples, possesses traditions and capacities of assimilation that are not always fully appreciated."[84] In the late 1990s Germany decided to grant citizenship to all children born in the country (jus solis), whereas previously only a child with at least one German parent was automatically a citizen (jus sanguinis). In 1999 German nationality was granted to 143,300 foreigners, of whom 103,900 were Turkish, and the numbers totaled more than half a million over three years.[85] Germany's naturalization rate is about half of the American one, a high level for an Old World country. (The statistics are not exactly comparable since some of Germany's naturalized citizens are native-born, whereas in the United States the native-born are automatically citizens and need not seek naturalization.)

In the future, Western Europe will continue to need immigrants. According to the United Nations, the European Union would require 1,380,000 immigrants a year to stabilize its workforce.[86] It is unclear, however, how many migrants would come from outside Europe. The rich Western European states have a hinterland in Central Europe whose labor force will be attracted to the West's higher wages. Immigration patterns into Europe, however, will be marked by the momentum of the past forty years. Current non-European foreign-born residents will continue to bring their spouses and relatives to Western Europe. Moreover, as we have seen, their younger population pyramid will cause the numbers of European residents of non-European extraction to further increase as a percentage of the total population.

Although Enoch Powell was wrong, immigration in Europe has not been without its problems. High levels of structural unemployment hurt Europe's ability to assimilate its immigrants, many of whom are unskilled workers whose children are poorly educated. Thus, whereas the foreign-borns' rate of unemployment in the United States is roughly similar to the national average, it is frequently twice that in Europe.[87] Some of these discrepancies between the United States and Europe are caused by the higher educational levels of immigrants to the United States, but labor-market mechanisms also play a role, as does discrimination.[88] In addition, immigrants in Europe are overrepresented in the prison population, whereas, adjusted for age and income, the percentages in the United States are comparable for immigrants and natives.[89] (It is unclear, however, whether the higher proportion of immigrants and their children in European jails is due to a higher propensity to commit crimes, to socioeconomic status, or to discrimination on the part of the police and judiciary in making arrests and convicting suspects.) At the same time, non-European migrants and their children, especially those from Muslim and African nations, are underrepresented in the middle and upper classes. The European Convention, the EU process which is to give Europe a constitution, had 105 members, none of whom are of non-European background.[90]

The success of extreme right-wing or populist politicians in Austria, Belgium, Denmark, France, Italy, the Netherlands, and other European nations indicates that large segments of the European public, and not only traditional supporters of the far right, are sufficiently uneasy with immigration to vote for parties who make opposition to immigrants, and often overt racism, the key plank of their platforms. In the future, Europe's problems with immigration may cause heightened social tensions and lead to more cases of extremist parties making inroads in the political system.

Outlook for the Future

The United States will continue to benefit more from immigration than its partners. First, as a New World society it is more open to outsiders than are Old World countries. Second, American institutions and laws are more effective at dealing with immigration. Its economic regulations help newcomers find employment. Noncitizens enjoy fewer restrictions for employment than in many other jurisdictions. The Constitution ensures that all U.S.-born children are automatically citizens, a procedure that allows faster assimilation than in nations that have more restrictive legislation. For those born abroad, there are few hurdles to naturalization.

Immigration not only contributes to American hegemony but also reflects it. Being a rich and powerful country, and having the added advantage of being English-speaking, the United States is well positioned to compete for the talent of skilled individuals who can choose where they want to live and work. Its large economy is a magnet for millions of laborers from Mexico and Central America as well as from other continents.

Though the United States has a successful track record at assimilating newcomers, the process is always challenging and never trouble-free. Data on the low rate of educational achievement of Mexican-American children show that a major effort needs to be made in this area.[91] Given the rising proportion of Americans of Mexican and Central American ancestry, improving their educational achievement must be a national priority for the United States. The boom of the 1990s undermined nativist sentiment, which often gathers steam in times of recession. The restrictionist climate of the early 1990s, epitomized by California's Proposition 187 in 1994, could reappear if the current economic slump is prolonged, especially if immigrants themselves decide that they would be better off by closing the border to further inflows. There is always the risk that a recession, combined with a fear of foreigners born out of the trauma of 9/11, could lead to a closure of America to new immigrants, as happened in 1924. Repeated terrorist acts on American soil can further the cause of those who wish to drastically curtail immigration. Already, the Qaeda attacks have made it much harder for Muslim would-be immigrants to gain admittance to the United States. On balance, however, such a development is unlikely. Immigration has made a critical contribution to American wealth and power and will probably continue to do so.

Women

The essayist Ralph Peters has identified the subjugation of women as one of the signs of a "noncompetitive society."[92] In many third world states, boys receive priority when food is scarce and medicines expensive, while girls are first in line for infanticide. In low-income countries fewer females get access to education than boys, though the situation is improving.[93] There are, however, enormous differences between underdeveloped countries; in some, women are treated barely better than animals, while in others, gender equality is more or less the norm.

Although much remains to be done, women's progress in the West has been remarkable in the past century. Several countries, including Britain, Finland, Norway, Switzerland, and Canada, have been led by women chief executives. The United States has not had a female president, but women are increasingly represented in Congress and in state government. About half of college students in the West, sometimes even more are women. Women have also made major inroads in the private and public sector managerial ranks. As Southern Europe has modernized, the gap between Western societies has narrowed. On average, American women probably have more access than European females to managerial positions, but there are major differences among European countries.[94]

Japan alone in the developed world has yet to bring women into the sociopolitical and economic mainstream. Although the status of Japanese women has also progressed in recent decades, there is still a paucity of women in positions of authority in the country. They are underrepresented in the best universities and in science.[95]

The news, however, is not entirely bleak. There has been a great increase in the percentage of Japanese high school girls going on to four-year colleges (12.3 percent in 1980, 31.5 percent in 2000), though it is still below the rate for boys (41.3 percent in 1980, 47.5 percent in 2000).[96] One-third of Japanese medical school students are now women. The percentage of women in elite colleges has also increased significantly. Thirty-six percent of students in Japan who earned bachelor's degrees in 1999 were women, compared with 45 percent in Germany, 56 percent in the United States, and 58 percent in France. Only 19 percent of advanced research degrees in Japan were awarded to women, compared with 33 percent in Germany, 41 percent in France, and 42 percent in the United States.[97]

The growing proportion of women who graduate from universities should change Japanese society, but it may be a slow process. It takes thirty-five to forty-five years for an age cohort to move from college graduation to the end of its professional life. Consequently, women's underrepresentation in higher education will reverberate for many decades even if the improvements of the 1990s continue. Moreover, getting an education is a necessary but not a sufficient step for a woman's career to flourish. There are many cases, not only in Japan, of women being denied employment opportunities commensurate with their qualifications.

Why is the Japanese economy denying itself much of the potential of half of its population? Japan is a modern nation, and its people are not in the thrall of some obscurantist religion. One reason is that Japanese women carry a heavy burden of caring for children and the elderly. Day-care facilities and babysitting services are less well developed than in the West. Children generally play a greater role than in the West in taking care of their elderly parents. With smaller families, more women find themselves the only daughter or daughter-in-law, thus making it impossible to split responsibility for the care of aging parents.

Culture is not the only explanation for the status of women in Japan. Japan has tight immigration laws. Thus Japanese mothers, unlike their American or European counterparts, cannot rely on foreign baby-sitters. There are few immigrant caregivers and nurses to care for the elderly, as they frequently do in the West. Moreover, the institutional arrangement of Japanese business is not woman-friendly. The rigidity of the corporate hierarchy forecloses the possibility of advancement from the clerical level to the professional, whereas it is possible—though not common—in the United States for a secretary or a clerk to ascend to a managerial position. Women are a large percentage of the clerical workforce and thus suffer the most from this lack of promotion opportunities.

In addition, it is hard to reenter the Japanese labor force. Women who want to work again after they have raised their children are likely to end up in jobs that "usually bear no relation to their education or abilities."[98] It is also more difficult for middle-aged individuals in Japan than in the United States to return to school, thus preventing women who might want to improve their credentials to study before returning to the job market. Moreover, the tax system deprives some married women of most of the financial incentives for working full-time.[99] Barriers to rejoining the workforce are particularly hurtful to women in Japan because it is still common for companies to "encourage" women to retire upon marriage.[100]

Greater opportunity for women is an economic imperative for Japan. Japanese demography is in a tailspin; thus all citizens need to contribute to their fullest potential to the economy. The relatively efficient use of the female labor force in the United States, in contrast, is one of the great sources of the strength of the U.S. economy.

Governments in free countries have difficulty implementing policies that lead to a higher birth rate. Banning contraception, criminalizing abortion, leveling confiscatory taxes on childless adults, and other draconian measures are, fortunately, unacceptable in Liberal democracies. And for a variety of reasons realistic policies aimed at fostering more births either are not effective or have not been devised by countries which are afflicted by below-replacement fertility rates. Moreover, it takes at least fifteen years for increased fertility to start to affect the supply of labor; higher birth rates therefore have a positive effect on the labor force only over time.

There are means to mitigate the impact of falling fertility rates. One is to raise the retirement age, which simultaneously expands the labor force and lowers pension expenses. This measure, however, can be politically detrimental to the politicians that enact it. (Employment rates for individuals aged sixty and over already are far lower in Europe than in the United States, though European governments are now committed to raising the retirement age.) But as life expectancy continues to rise, modest increases in the retirement threshold are compensated by higher longevity. Delaying retirement can make an important contribution to economic performance and is a measure which most governments now realize must be implemented.

Governments can alter funding mechanisms for pensions, switching from pay-as-you-go mechanisms that put the burden on current workers to funded schemes that force individuals to save for their retirement. There are, however, limits to the effectiveness of such changes, at least in the short run. Retirees and older workers who are not covered by funded plans will continue to be paid from tax revenues, possibly forcing one generation to pay both for its own retirement and for the pensions of the elderly. The politics, as well as the economics, of such reforms are complex and therefore changes are unlikely to be rapid.

To compensate for low fertility governments can seek to raise the labor participation rate of women. In many societies, however, women already actively participate in the workforce; in others, there are major institutional and cultural obstacles to overcome.

Countries can also increase their intake of immigrants, but there are limits beyond which this strategy is not palatable to voters. Moreover, due to the almost unlimited supply of poor third world residents, any nation can easily find millions of unskilled workers. But gaining highly educated ones is more difficult. The supply is limited and the best can choose where they want to go. This will be an added challenge to Europe and Japan. Their older populations will increase pressure on budgets, thus saddling citizens with higher taxes. The highly mobile elite potential migrants, most of whom know English, may thus prefer to relocate to the United States, where they also know that opportunities for the foreign-born are greater.[101]

One should not think that all demographic conditions favor the United States. From 1980 to 2000 the incarceration rate in the United States shot up from an already high 220 per 100,000 to 701 in 2000. This compares with 96 in Germany and 44 in Japan.[102] Along with the fact that the U.S. homicide rate stands at about 12.5 times Japan's, this illustrates one of the major failings of U.S. society.[103] That nearly half of prison inmates are black, though they make up only 13 percent of the population, is another aspect of one of America's biggest social failures.[104]

Growing obesity may also become a burden on the American economy as overweight citizens suffer from costly ailments and are sometimes handicapped in performing their jobs. An estimated 26 percent of Americans are obese, compared with 3 percent in Japan and 10 percent in France.[105]

Despite these weaknesses, America's demographic picture is better than that of Japan and Europe. The financial shock of adapting to an aging society will be less traumatic in the United States than in Japan and Europe. The United States faces only population *aging*, whereas Japan and many European nations are looking at both population *aging* and *decline*. The United States also makes better use of immigrants in its labor force than its partners and of women than Japan.

Overseas demographic trends, however, are a danger to the United States. Japan faces a threatening situation: well-below replacement fertility, underutilized women in the workforce, and major obstacles to immigration combine to paint a very frightening picture of the future. Europe's problems are worrisome as well, though less acute than Japan's. Japan and Europe are America's two major partners. The United States relies on them for its security and prosperity. Their demographic problems are therefore also America's.

5 The Economic Performance Gap

As noted in Chapter 2, the American empire accounts for approximately 70 percent of gross world product, and for an even higher percentage of the world's advanced industrial and service sector capacity. Figure 5.1 shows the enormous chasm between the developed nations and the rest of the world, which is unlikely to narrow significantly in the future and may well increase. As we explained in Chapter 1, the obstacles that economies bereft of Liberal institutions face are so enormous that wealth will remain concentrated in states that have such institutions, namely those of North America, Europe, Japan, and the smaller Pacific Rim Liberal market economies.

Within the American empire, the United States is in a leading position. With a $10.8 trillion gross domestic product (GDP), the U.S. economy is by far the world's largest, well ahead of no. 2 Japan's $4.2 trillion and no. 3 Germany's $2.1 trillion.[1] The combined GDPs of the European Union states are comparable to the American one. But despite the remarkable advances of European integration, Europe is still decades away, and maybe more, from being a fully integrated economic and political space. As we will argue in this chapter, the United States' economy is likely to continue to lead within the American empire and, at least for the coming decade, will probably outperform that of its major partners.

We will focus on the performance of the U.S. economy compared with that of Europe and Japan. This will shed light on the position of the United States within the American Liberal empire and help us understand the strength of the U.S. position in the world. Though our comparisons may make Europe and Japan look bad, it is worth repeating that their Liberal institutions are vastly more effective

Fig. 5.1. Per Capita GDP Current Prices

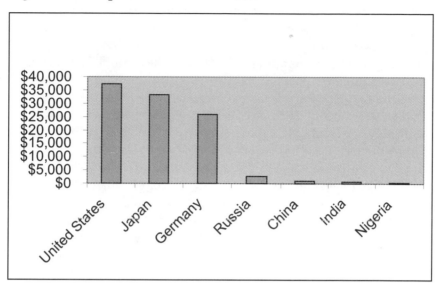

Note: We do not use purchasing power parities (PPP) because data based on current exchange rates give a better indication of relative power than PPP data.

than those of other, underdeveloped non-Liberal nations. Europe and Japan will thus continue to account for the bulk of the world's wealth outside of the United States. The widest gap in the world economy is between North America, Europe, and the capitalist Pacific rim on one side and the rest of the world on the other, not between the United States and its partners. Nevertheless, we compare U.S. performance with that of Europe and Japan because they all operate with functioning Liberal institutions; comparing the United States with third world non-Liberal states would make no sense, since these nations operate under totally different, and much less efficient, economic systems. Moreover, as long as the Liberal empire is based on American power and leadership, it is important to measure the relative strength of the United States within the nations of the community of Liberal states.

Historical Perspective on the American Economy

Before we look at the strengths of the American economy, we need to briefly survey how the United States reached its current status. America's position in the world reflects the combination of two factors: the United States inherited Liberal institutions from Britain, and it experienced much faster population growth than Europe. The combination of effective institutions and a rapidly increasing labor force made it possible for the United States to grow from a minor outpost of Western civilization into an economic superpower.

In 1945 most of Eurasia had been wrecked by years of warfare. With a few exceptions, such as Canada, the United States was the only self-sustaining industrial economy in the world. Therefore, in the 1950s and 1960s the relative weight of the United States diminished due to the reconstruction and development of Europe and Japan. By 1970 America had lost the undisputed economic position it had held briefly in the aftermath of World War II, but its relative decline then stopped, as illustrated in Figure 5.2. America's gross domestic product now accounts for approximately 30 percent of gross world product and has been in the 25–35 percent range for

Fig. 5.2. U.S. GDP Relative to the World, 1970–2003

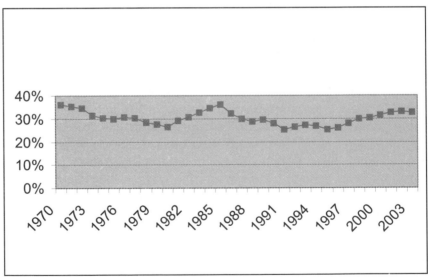

Note: As in figure 5.1, we do not use purchasing power parities (PPP) because data based on current exchange rates give a better indication of relative power than PPP data.
Sources: IMF, current prices.

Fig. 5.3. Relative GDPs 1970–2003

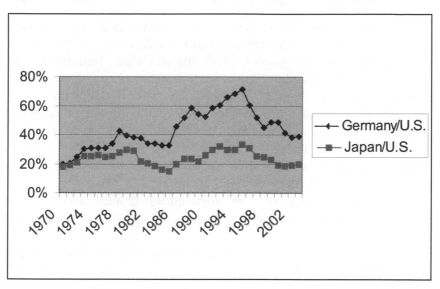

Source: IMF, current prices.

more than three decades, as illustrated by Figure 5.2. (Some of the more dramatic fluctuations have been due to exchange rate movements; note that the data excludes some minor economies.)

Figure 5.3 tracks the national incomes of the United States' leading allies, Japan and Germany, compared with the American income. It shows the Japanese economy growing fast relative to the United States in the 1970s, partly because Japan's post–World War II economic recovery was slower at the beginning than Europe's and it had a greater distance than Europe to cover to reach U.S. levels of prosperity. The Japanese "bubble economy" and a high yen in the late 1980s further allowed Japan to narrow the gap. In the late 1990s, however, Japanese GDP declined in relation to the United States' as the bubble burst and the cost of structural failures that had previously been kept under control started to hurt the economy. In the case of Germany, its years of high growth, the *Wirtschaftwunder,* occurred earlier than Japan's. Therefore, the post-1970 data show that, depending on business cycles and currency movements, the U.S.-German ratio has fluctuated but has remained fairly constant over several decades.

American Advantages

As we have seen, the United States accounts for about a third of the gross world product. But the true weight of the American economy is even greater, given the American leadership position in numerous key industries, such as computers, software, pharmaceuticals, and financial services, as well as in science and technology. To praise the performance of the American economy and its corporations is, however, to reflect on the past. Many of the businesses of the future are yet to be born. New industries will emerge in the coming decades, while some of today's biggest corporations may be history by 2025, or even 2010. We must therefore identify the institutional, regulatory, and structural advantages of the United States, those that will outlast the ephemeral movements of markets.

We will first focus on the most important factors that underpin the dynamism of the American economy. Economic growth requires—and the United States possesses—the institutional framework that fosters entrepreneurship. Finally, we will look at some of the macroeconomic consequences of these institutional and regulatory issues. We conclude by noting that the U.S. economy is not immune from decay and underperformance but that it is in a very strong position compared to other nations.

Innovation and Entrepreneurship

One of the salient features of the United States is its success in generating new businesses. The United States enjoys what the *Economist* labels an " 'innovational complex'—those thousands of entrepreneurs, venture capitalists and engineers—unmatched anywhere in the world."[2]

It is noteworthy that most companies set up in recent decades that transformed an industry, or created a new one, are American, the likes of Amazon.com, America Online, Apple, Cisco, CNN, Intel, Microsoft, Netscape, and, from an earlier era, American Express, AT&T, Disney, Ford Motor, IBM, McDonald's, and the commercial television networks. Although Europeans and Asians have made their contribution, the United States has accounted for a majority of innovative businesses. This American advantage at creating new industries is essential because it affects not only how the economy performs today but also how it will operate tomorrow.

The Legal and Regulatory Environment

To understand the roots of the U.S. institutional and regulatory development that support entrepreneurship, one must briefly take note of the legal and ideological basis of the American economic system. Businesses in the United States operate under a common-law regime. With the exception of the United Kingdom, Ireland, Australia, New Zealand, Anglophone Canada, Hong Kong, and Singapore, the other developed economies—that is, the nations of continental Europe, Japan, South Korea, and Taiwan—operate under code-law systems. "One of the principal advantages of common law legal systems," writes John Coffee of Columbia University Law School, "is their decentralized character, which encourages self-regulatory initiatives, whereas civil law systems may monopolize all law-making initiatives."[3] This is especially true in new industries where the absence of laws governing businesses leads to officials opposing new projects on the grounds that they are not specifically authorized by existing regulations. For example, some analysts have noted how U.S. law gives more leeway to create innovative contractual arrangements than German law.[4] Thus entrepreneurs, and businesses in general, are more likely to face legal and regulatory hurdles in code-law jurisdictions, where adapting the law to new technologies, new financial instruments, and other innovations is more cumbersome. Others have argued that common-law regimes are also better at protecting shareholders and creditors, hence facilitating the development of capital markets.[5]

U.S. entrepreneurs thus find it easier than their counterparts in code-law nations to innovate and operate. Because there are enormous transaction costs in switching legal systems, the United States, and the other nations whose laws originate from England, will retain the edge that their adaptable legal framework provides them for the indefinite future.

Common law sets the United States and other nations that trace their legal tradition to England apart from the rest of the world. The position of Liberalism in America differentiates the United States from other polities and provides a significant advantage to the economy. Liberalism in the United States, unlike in not only Old World societies but also other New World ones, has always enjoyed a hegemonic position free from serious competition from either anticapitalist conservatism or socialism. One aspect of this Liberal hegemony is that the American economy reflects the ideals of a society that praises individualism. This "dominant strain in American culture contrasts sharply with more ascriptive communitarian, and paternalistic cultures of European societies" (and also of Asian ones).[6] Therefore government policy and societal norms have been favorable to economic Liberalism, a fact that has helped American industry thrive in an environment less likely to be burdened by restrictive practices rooted in conservative or socialist anti-Liberal sentiment.

The combination of these legal and ideological factors forms the basis for the regulatory framework that gives American business an edge over its competitors. These include ease of incorporation, antitrust enforcement, bankruptcy proceedings, corporate governance, and capital markets regulation.

INCORPORATING A NEW BUSINESS

The advantages that Americans enjoy start with incorporation. An American can establish his own firm in a few hours by buying a kit at a local bookstore and mailing a few forms. In most other countries, setting up a limited liability company or even a sole proprietorship is a complex endeavor that takes time and effort and requires capital and a solid legal background or the help of a lawyer. As one commentator wrote, anyone wanting to start a company in Europe has to be patient and rich.[7]

It is cheaper, faster, and less cumbersome to establish a company in America or Britain than in Japan or continental Europe. Some countries require a significant amount of paid-up capital (more than $20,000 in some nations), whereas none is required in the United States. In some nations, it may take several months for a new business to obtain all the required documents for registration, whereas in the United States it generally takes less than two weeks. Several countries have preregistration requirements that aspiring businessmen must fulfill. Others demand time-consuming qualifications. For example, to open a bakery or a barbershop in Germany, one must be or employ a *Meister,* the holder of a medieval rank that signifies completion of a multiyear apprenticeship program (though the German government is attempting to remedy this situation).[8] In London it takes years to prepare for the taxicab exam. Some nations also have citizenship or residency requirements for the professions.

Some improvements are occurring overseas, where governments are trying to make incorporation easier, especially for sole proprietorships. But even if they want to, other countries are unlikely to streamline their procedures to U.S. levels. To eliminate or simplify regulations would strip officials and bureaucrats of their positions or of their prerogatives. Established businesses, having no interest in making it easier for others to compete with them, support the status quo.[9] Additionally, the underlying ideology of the state in Japan and continental Europe is that everything that is not explicitly allowed is forbidden, whereas in America all that is not prohibited is implicitly legal. Therefore officials outside the United States are more inclined to impose regulatory and bureaucratic burdens that make life difficult for those seeking to create their own businesses.

ANTITRUST

Antitrust legislation and enforcement constitute one of the most fundamental American economic institutions. Antitrust law is one of the major causes of the competitive character of the American economy and its ability to rejuvenate itself. Antitrust forces upon the economy a form of creative destruction. It removes obstacles to further economic growth by restructuring businesses that have achieved the means to stop competition. Without strict enforcement of antitrust laws, new businesses risk being stymied by monopolies that undermine competitors with better products.

Corporations that establish monopolies or cartels in the United States are more likely to be forced to refrain from anticompetitive behavior, through divestitures or other remedies, than in other jurisdictions. Historically, antitrust laws have helped American entrepreneurs enormously. For example, the 1956 restrictions on AT&T's activities outside of telecommunications and the consent degree mandating "liberal licensing" by IBM of its patents helped new technology businesses thrive.[10] In previous decades government action had broken up monopolies in the oil and transportation industries. Thanks to antitrust enforcement by the Justice Department, Americans are more likely to enjoy a level playing field to grow their new businesses free of monopolistic corporations. This is not to argue that American antitrust legislation is perfect. Despite major breakthroughs in the Carter administration, the airline industry is not immune to oligopolistic or even monopolistic behavior. Protectionism and other anti–free market actions have in several cases facilitated the survival of unfair practices. Businesses constantly use their influence over politicians to avoid prosecution for anticompetitive practices. Nevertheless, on balance, the United States is the economy with the most effective antitrust enforcement.

Europe and Japan historically not only failed to hunt down monopolists and cartels but supported them. One reason for fostering domestic monopolists was to create "national champions," large corporations that could compete on the international stage while holding the line against imports and foreign investors. With notable exceptions in the defense and aerospace sectors, American policy has never been to sponsor national champions. For example, when the computer industry was in its infancy, the United States did not support a national champion but actively prevented the emergence of monopolies. (In addition to American Liberalism, this policy reflected the fact that since the United States is the world's largest economy, American policy makers fear overseas competitors less than do their foreign counterparts.) In contrast, other governments tried to create dominant computer manufacturers. These policies on the part of Japan and many European administrations fostered businesses that grew in a national environment either free of competition or with special advantages due to subsidies or regulations. They were therefore unable to adjust to the competitive international scene. The data-processing industry overseas is littered with the corpses of firms that were going to challenge IBM and whose only achievements were to squander public monies while hurting consumers.

Most governments now recognize that trying to pick a winner and provide it with a domestic monopoly is ineffective. But it is difficult to entirely eliminate support for monopolies and cartels when they are embedded in the political economy. What William Overholt calls the "1940 system" of war mobilization in Japan, which was never properly dismantled, created an economy in which the allocation of capital and other resources favored monopolies and oligopolies.[11] Despite the events of the past decade, this dirigiste system has yet to be totally overhauled. The industrial policies of European states vary, and EU integration has forced them to liberalize their economies and dismantle some monopolies. Nevertheless, most European states have historically been, like Japan, quite tolerant, and often positively supportive, of monopolies, and sometimes continue to be so.

There are other obstacles to antitrust efforts overseas. In Japan, there is no effective right of private action, limiting the ability of individuals and corporations to sue competitors on antitrust grounds. In addition, various obstacles stand in the way of access to legal services, including restrictions on the numbers of lawyers in the country.[12] Reforms are taking place, but even when they are enacted, they take many years.[13] If cases are processed, the Japan Fair Trade Commission lacks the power and bureaucratic resources of the U.S. Department of Justice's Antitrust Division.[14] The European Commission's antitrust officials have grown much more powerful in recent years, but they are still not as well-organized as their U.S. counterparts. They always run the risk of being sabotaged by the member states. In addition, unlike American prosecutors, the commission lacks the power to jail individuals, and private action is still not as developed in Europe as in America.

The gaps in antitrust performance are not due solely to legal and technical issues, such as the differences in bureaucratic organization or rules governing litigation. Nearly all Americans hold monopolies to be undesirable. America's antitrust regulations date back to the Progressive Era. Their ideological roots in the American political tradition are even older. U.S. antitrust policies are upheld by classical Liberal economics, which dominates American economic thought, by the American populist distrust of Big Business, and by the hegemony of Liberalism in America. Americans legitimate monopolies only where regulations exist to protect consumers and prevent undue profits.

Outside of the United States, however, monopolies and oligopolistic firms are seen more as benign corporate citizens than as firms engaged in cutthroat competition. Monopolies are more stable, thus less likely to lay off employees. They are more willing to support "national goals," such as investing in depressed areas. In Europe and Japan the basic tenets of neoclassical economics, which form the intellectual basis for antitrust, are not universally accepted. In Europe, a strong socialist tradition views state-owned or state-influenced monopolistic enterprises as the allies of the working class. Many Japanese and Europeans officials, though fewer than in earlier decades, still believe that the state should guide markets. For them monopolies are therefore desirable. They also facilitate government influence over the economy, since it is easier for the state to direct an industry dominated by a single firm or a cartel.

Europe and Japan are taking more interest in antitrust enforcement but are unlikely to match the United States in antitrust efficiency. Even if their powerful statist and corporatist ideologies were eliminated, it would take decades for EU and Japanese antitrust practice to be as effective as those of the United States. The laws, regulations, lawyers, economists, bureaucrats, and consultants that are necessary for the smooth and efficient enforcement of antitrust policies are a highly complex intangible infrastructure that takes a generation to assemble. In Europe the co-existence of fifteen (soon to be twenty-five) sovereign states and the European Commission undercuts the efficiency of the antitrust process.[15] National governments will inevitably pressure the commission to protect their favorite monopolists. In addition, in smaller countries, it is not feasible to prevent the development of monopolies when the domestic economy cannot support more than one player, and economic, regulatory, or other obstacles limit the entry of foreign companies.

Will the United States continue to enjoy the advantages of a regulatory environment that is committed to preventing the emergence of monopolies? Antitrust enforcement is a never-ending process. Economic life and political decisions always create new monopolistic situations. Therefore, antitrust officials may win battles, but they never end the war. In addition, monopolies are, by definition, stronger than their fledgling competitors. It is easier for them to use their resources to influence, legitimately or through corruption, legislators, civil servants, judges, and the media. Consequently, there is always a risk that monopolies, by subverting antitrust legislation, will prevail.

BANKRUPTCY

Easy incorporation requirements and antitrust enforcement help American entrepreneurs, but laws governing bankruptcy are equally important. Excessively lenient bankruptcy legislation, besides deterring lenders, offers a fertile breeding ground for crooks. But regulations that make bankruptcy a lifelong mark of infamy hinder entrepreneurship by intimidating those who might start a venture and unfairly penalizing them should they fail. Even great entrepreneurs do not always succeed on their first try. The law must consequently not prevent them from making a second or third attempt. Bankruptcy proceedings in the United States, Britain, and Australia make it relatively easy for an entrepreneur to restart rapidly with a clean slate.[16]

American practices reflect the ideals of a society in which there is little shame in failing. Bankruptcy is seen as part of the learning process, but Europeans who go bust often do not get a second chance, as creditors are allowed to hound them for long periods.[17] In Japan, says an attorney specializing in the field, "if you go bankrupt, it's the end. . . . You cannot find another job," and "you cannot get married." Many Japanese mistakenly think they will go to jail if they file for bankruptcy. Consequently, many flee into hiding instead of filing.[18] The Japanese bankruptcy law was revised in 2000, but it will take time for traditions to change.

Besides its greater acceptance of failure, the American economy benefits from the size of the United States, which facilitates starting anew and reinventing oneself somewhere else. The structure of the banking industry also helps explain why it is easier to survive bankruptcy and rebuild a business in the United States. Historically, the banking and venture capital sector in America has been more competitive than those in Europe and Japan. Consequently, there are more loan officers and venture capitalists chasing opportunities than overseas, making it easier for an entrepreneur looking for a second chance to find funding.

Another aspect of bankruptcy that is relevant to this analysis is that, in the United States, most unviable businesses that fail go out of business. True, in some instances bankruptcy has been abused, allowing companies to operate under chapter 11 for many years, free from interest costs and thus enjoying an unfair advantage over their competitors. But in other economies there is a greater tendency to keep large failing businesses alive through government support. Small companies are generally left to face the rigors of the marketplace, but large ones are treated differently. The European Commission has sought to clamp down on these practices, and there has been a visible lessening of government rescue efforts in past years, but some member states still resist the commission's efforts. Europe has changed a lot in the past twenty-five years, but there is still more pressure than in America to protect unviable enterprises from the demands of the market.

In Japan, despite a long recession, many businesses that were clinically dead survived for years thanks to political support and to webs of relations with other companies, banks, and the government. As Richard Katz of the *Oriental Economist* has noted, in Japan, "Bankruptcy, far from being regarded as a cleansing shakeout of the inefficient, as 'creative destruction,' was considered a violation of an implicit social contract, a source of disorder and confusion."[19] There have been major changes since the late 1990s, with bankruptcies now engulfing large companies. But the government has sometimes continued to help, directly or indirectly, large firms that are no longer viable. Thus more Japanese businesses, and European ones as well, operate under a "soft budget" constraint: they are fairly secure in the prospect that the state will bail them out if needed.[20] Nevertheless, in Japan and Europe, there are fewer blatant instances of government-financed rescues, though the jury is still out on the willingness of the establishment to accept the collapse of very large corporations.

Rescue operations for failed companies that cannot survive on their own waste taxpayers' money but also affect the fortunes of their competitors. Money-losing firms that are forced to close their doors leave room for firms with better products and services, whereas failed businesses still operating thanks to government aid crowd out entrepreneurs and hinder the rejuvenation of the economy by blocking the Darwinian process of survival of the fittest. The United States is not immune to government bailouts, as shown by the rescues of Lockheed and Chrysler in earlier decades, the protection afforded to the sugar industry, steelmakers, and others, and the rush by countless corporations to receive billions of dollars in federal aid following the 9/11 attacks, but all in all, the United States is less prone to shielding companies from the consequences of their failures. As in the case of antitrust issues, however, there is no certainty that the American political process will always manage to keep such market-distorting operations under control.

CORPORATE GOVERNANCE

Corporate governance is another institution whereby American, or more accurately Anglo-American, legislation strengthens the economy. Good corporate governance is particularly important for new businesses. Anglo-American rules make it easier for entrepreneurs to acquire underperforming companies. By disciplining firms and providing reliable data to investors, the Anglo-American system ensures that capital is generally more likely to be allocated to the best-performing firms than in other nations. Anglo-American corporate governance thus provides greater incentives for managers to serve their shareholders.[21]

There have historically been wide gaps between Anglo-American and foreign practices of corporate governance. The key features of the Japanese or so-called J-type big business firm are (1) corporate insiders dominate the board of directors, with the possible inclusion of the main bank's representatives, (2) the firm belongs to a close network of affiliated enterprises *(keiretsu),* and (3) the capital markets play only a limited role in disciplining the firm. Another characteristic is government influence on management.[22] The J-Type model has been applicable to continental Europe as well, though with many variations on the theme. Germany's stakeholder model is considerably different from the British shareholder principle of corporate governance.[23] Arrangements that allow employees and other nonshareholders to sit on supervisory boards, such as German "codetermination," are another form of governance found overseas that diverges significantly from Anglo-American norms and, like the J-type, undermines the authority of stockholders.

Stephen Davis's Leading Corporate Governance Indicators ranks the corporate governance indicators of the main capital markets. The United Kingdom ranks number one with a score of 7.7 (out of 10); the United States' score (7.2) is lower for several reasons.[24] In the United Kingdom, it is more common to split the CEO and chairman position, preventing the consolidation of power in the hands of a single individual. In the United States, unlike Britain, few issues require the direct approval of shareholders. Moreover, there are more obstacles to takeovers in U.S. markets than in Britain, but far fewer than in continental Europe and Japan. Continental European markets earn significantly lower scores (Germany 4.5, France 5.8, Netherlands 4.9, Belgium 5.0, Portugal 3.1), and particularly low rankings on takeover barriers, which protect entrenched management by denying shareholders the opportunity to sell their holdings to the highest bidders. Japan is at the bottom, with 2.0 and with a zero score for accounting standards, board independence, and takeover barriers.

Mergers and acquisitions, greater foreign participation in the economy, and the unwinding of some cross-shareholdings have reshaped Japan and Europe. Recession and some measures to liberalize the economy have shaken up the cozy world of Japan Inc. European integration has done much to smash restrictionist practices that denied shareholders their rights. But continental and Japanese forms of corporate governance may be more robust than the exponents of "globalization" believe. Shareholder value is better for the economy, but alternative models serve established interests. Incompetent and superannuated directors would lose their positions if equity owners could demand more dynamism and independence from them. Entrenched managers would be fired if a new board or an acquirer brought in new blood. Unions benefit from continental practices, which provide for company-financed positions for their officials (such as the supervisory boards in Germany or the comités d'entreprise in France). Civil servants who look forward to life after retirement in a business they regulate and politicians who rely on the company to spend its resources on political rather than economic criteria are other powerful interests that would stand to lose under an Anglo-American system. German plans to force more businesses to include workers on their boards and the successful rearguard opposition by Germany in 2001 to scuttle a European takeover code that would have undermined managers' ability to block hostile bids were examples of the strength of enemies of change, though their successes may only be temporary.[25]

The resilience of the Japanese/continental type of corporate governance is also explained by ideology. Japanese and Europeans are more likely than Americans to believe that businesses must serve their "stakeholders" rather than only their shareholders. For example, the German constitution proclaims, "Property imposes duties. It should also serve the public weal."[26] Other European nations and Japan have similar institutional biases that give nonowners more influence over corporations than in Britain or America. Legal issues also play a role, because common law is generally deemed more favorable to the interests of investors than the continental European civil law traditions that are the basis of legislation in continental Europe and Japan.[27]

Over the past twenty years, however, the international gap in corporate governance has narrowed. The European Union's Single Market Initiative, the liberalization of investment flows, and the bursting of the Japanese bubble have forced Europeans and Japanese to do away with their more restrictive practices. Nevertheless, the differences between Anglo-American markets and continental European and Japanese ones remain significant. It is possible that over the coming years, European and Japanese norms will continue to move closer to American practices. It is also conceivable, however, that the profound differences between Anglo-American capitalism and its continental Europe and Japan versions will prevent a homogenization of governance practices. The differences between what Peter Hall and David Soskice call Liberal market economies (for example, the United States and the United Kingdom) and coordinated market economies (for example, Germany, Switzerland, and Japan) are deep and may be more resilient than many think.[28]

Do the Enron, WorldCom, Tyco, and other debacles of 2002 debunk the idea that American corporate governance is worth emulating? They certainly demonstrated that directors were either profoundly incompetent or dishonest. Those who favored improved regulation of auditors to force them to perform serious audits rather than to rubber-stamp accounts were proven right. The inability of regulators to deal with auditing firms' conflicts of interests showed that vested interests had become stronger than those of effective governance. But the strengths of American capitalism were also apparent. Enron filed for bankruptcy rapidly; there was no government attempt to rescue it or to compensate its employees. This will improve corporate governance as millions of employees who are stockholders through their pension funds realize that they must keep an eye on how their company is managed. The executives will face the courts, could lose all their assets, and may well spend years in jail. In most other jurisdictions, law-enforcement and regulatory agencies lack the power and resources, as well as the willingness, to punish fraud of the Securities and Exchange Commission and federal and state prosecutors.[29] Andersen was destroyed and forced to close down. Its partners stand to lose the capital they invested in the firm. Thus future auditors in partnerships will make a greater effort, out of self-interest, to sort out what their colleagues are doing. In many other jurisdictions, the government and the establishment would have found a solution to salvage Enron, and its employees, with taxpayers' money and spare the company executives and its auditors the fate that befell them. That both could go under so quickly was actually a sign that the U.S. system works. Unfortunately, a perverse impact of the scandals may be that they will be perceived overseas as indications that the American model is a failure and may dissuade countries from emulating Anglo-American norms of governance.

Nevertheless, the ability of American institutions, in this case corporate governance practices, to rejuvenate themselves has yet to be demonstrated by the fallout from the scandals. The challenge will be to devise new regulations, and the means to enforce them, to avoid a repeat of such catastrophes. Enron's failure in itself will create some incentives for better scrutiny, especially on the part of employee shareholders. But a thorough reform of the auditing profession and of other aspects of corporate governance is in order. Moreover, Enron has not been the only failure of U.S. corporate governance in past years. Numerous chief executive officers have enjoyed huge financial rewards from boards of directors even though they had done little to serve the interests of shareowners. Directors have been more concerned with pleasing the chairmen who provide them with their well-paid positions than with defending the interests of shareholders. The widespread abuse of options compensation has frequently aligned directors' and managers' interests differently from those of equity owners. An even more shocking practice has been repricing stock options to allow senior executives to enrich themselves even though they have failed to deliver for their shareholders.

INSIDER TRADING

In an area that is related to corporate governance, U.S. regulators have historically been less tolerant of insider trading than those of other jurisdictions. This makes investors more willing to trust the market, as they do not fear being swindled. New entrepreneurs with few connections are less likely to risk being defrauded by the establishment. Insider trading is not a "victimless crime" but a corrosive practice. Besides robbing honest sellers of capital gains that rightly should have been theirs or imposing losses on buyers who were on the wrong side of a shady transaction, the prevalence of insider trading corrupts markets, creating cliques of financiers, businessmen, and politicians who enrich themselves by trickery rather than through honest means. If left unpunished it creates a gap between the positive private rate of return of a transaction and its negative social rate of return that impoverishes the economy.[30]

It would be wrong to think that the entire world is awash in insider trading and that only the United States is pure. Leaks prior to the announcement of corporate acquisitions are common in the United States. Large investors find it easier to obtain data than small ones. Insider trading is also more likely to be prosecuted overseas than it was twenty years ago. But on balance, American markets are better-regulated and more protected from unethical practices. Since the Securities and Exchange Commission was created, regulators have generally taken a strong interest in outlawing insider trading and policing the markets. Insider trading has been punished severely in the United States, at least in some cases, with perpetrators being packed off to prison (though with sentences that seem disproportionately short compared with those of small-time thieves who languish behind bars for years).

Access to Venture Capital and Knowledge

The aspects of the American economy we have just surveyed are rooted in laws and regulations. Access to venture capital and to knowledge (via industry-academia relations) is also partly due to specific regulations. They are also the product of more than legislation, however, reflecting differences in the organization of the financial services industry and universities in America. We have grouped them together because capital and knowledge are two essential ingredients that successful entrepreneurs need to succeed.

Venture Capital

One of the first requirements of an entrepreneur is to find capital. In the United States there is an entire industry of venture capitalists that supports new enterprises. Although the volumes vary enormously depending on the business cycle, America not only has huge amounts of venture capital but also offers a large and diverse pool of investors, allowing businesses to market themselves to the institution or person most likely to be interested by their ideas, rather than being limited to only a few funding options. Moreover, venture capitalism is more than money. It requires a supporting cast of professionals to work effectively. In the United States, there are armies of consultants, accountants, corporate lawyers, and government and nonprofit bodies to provide the advisory services that entrepreneurs and investors require.[31]

Venture capital is not unique to the United States, and exact comparisons between different countries in this field are impossible to generate. Funding provided by venture capitalists can also be received from banks, industrial companies, or other sources. The difference between a "venture" and an existing business is frequently ill-defined. But most statistics indicate that the U.S. venture capital industry is several times larger than the European one.[32]

In addition, most venture capital funds in the United States are independent businesses, often partnerships founded by experienced investors. In Japan and Europe, venture capital frequently originates from the affiliates of banks and corporations. As a result these funders are more concerned with increasing the business flow of their parent company than with achieving the highest return on equity.[33] They are also unlikely to have professionals with as much experience in starting a company as American venture capitalists. Thus they may not be as effective in helping the professionalization of start-up firms as venture capitalists in the United States.[34] The situation has changed in recent years, but there remains a wide gap between the development of the U.S. venture capital industry and its foreign counterparts.

Business-Academia Linkages

Another strength of American entrepreneurship that has been particularly helpful in the technology field is the interaction of academia with private ventures. Silicon Valley, Route 128 near the Massachusetts Institute of Technology and Harvard, the San Diego biotechnology industry, and the Research Triangle in North Carolina, among others, exemplify the merger of academic research with business. American universities have served as incubators for innovations that "walked out the door" with individuals who commercialized them.[35] Cambridge Energy Research Associates, Cisco, Genentech, Intel, SGI (formerly Silicon Graphics), and others trace their origins directly or indirectly to universities. From 1999 to 2001 American universities spun off slightly more than one thousand start-up companies, filed more than twenty-five thousand U.S. patents, and collected about $2.5 billion in royalties. Although these numbers were boosted by the technology bubble, they do reflect the economic dynamism of American academia.[36]

Why is the U.S. industry-university relationship so productive? First, as we shall explore in Chapter 6, American universities are world leaders in nearly all disciplines. Most countries do not have a single university that would be in the top ten in the United States.

Second, U.S. academics operate in universities that often house business, law, and medical schools. These provide scientists with students and professors who are close to the private sector and can help them with the practical aspects of moving a concept from the laboratory to the market.

Third, private-sector culture permeates American universities to an extent that is unknown in other countries. They are in constant contact with the business world to seek contributions from it. They manage their own investment and real estate portfolios, a task that forces them to understand industry and markets. Some profit by licensing their brand names. American academics are used to dealing with the private foundations that fund their research. They frequently advise companies and sit on boards of directors, sometimes to the detriment of their teaching responsibilities. Moreover, a majority of America's best universities, though by no means all, are private institutions. The Bayh-Dole Act of 1980, which authorizes the patenting of discoveries funded by government grants, further facilitates the commercial exploitation of discoveries by American academics. Some countries have tried to replicate this law, but its success owes a lot to the unique American environment.

Fourth, the American academic labor market is more fluid, making it easier to switch between academia and industry. The civil-service culture of European and Japanese universities makes such moves more difficult, thus hindering the movement of talent between industry and university positions.

Other nations have made progress on improving university-business collaboration. Japan in 1998 abolished regulations that barred academics from accepting corporate funds. In 2000 public university professors were allowed to serve as consultants and to sit on corporate boards.[37] Decisions have been made to facilitate academia-industry collaboration, but the corporate culture of Japanese education, rooted in the centralized Ministry of Education bureaucracy and the tradition of academics as civil servants, will take time to melt away.[38] Europe faces similar problems in developing a strong university-business relationship. Most of its academics are tenured civil servants working in government-financed institutions. They have less contact with the private sector than do their American counterparts. The egalitarian culture of their universities makes it repugnant for academics and administrators to accept that some of their colleagues may become multimillionaires while others must live on their meager civil-service pay. It is also probable that some of Japan and Europe's scientists with strong business ambitions have already been lured to the United States.

Labor Market

The labor market provides American entrepreneurs yet another advantage over their overseas competitors. Its performance is the result of legislation and regulations but also of broader societal factors.

One of the most noticeable aspects of the U.S. labor market is that it is easier in the United States to move from one job to another. As a result, the percentage of unemployed in the United States who have been unemployed for more than six months has for many years been far lower than in Europe, indicating that most Americans who lose a job find a new one rapidly, though possibly one with lower wages and no benefits.[39] This fluidity in the United States helps new businesses, as employees of existing firms are less hesitant than their foreign counterparts to leave their positions, secure in the knowledge that if the new company fails, they are more likely to find new positions than would be the case abroad. One reason for this state of affairs is that in the United States workers can be fired relatively easily compared with the cumbersome procedures of other nations.[40] This helps entrepreneurs (and businesses in general) hire employees without making a costly commitment. In addition, America's relatively low minimum wage and limited welfare benefits ensure that most unskilled workers will seek employment.[41] This provides American entrepreneurs with a supply of relatively low-cost and flexible labor, making it possible to start a business with low labor costs.

The greater efficiency of the American labor market is clear when one compares it with the European one. Research by Hans-Werner Sinn and Frank Westermann showed that German social welfare provides an income that is similar to the average annual wage income after taxes and social contributions (generating what is known as an "inactivity trap"). Sinn and Westermann conclude, "It is impossible to run a market economy when the minimum income guaranteed through the welfare system is equal to the average net-of-tax wage income."[42] Not all economists would agree with their arithmetic, but there is a consensus that in many European nations the gap between public assistance and working in an unskilled job is narrow if not nonexistent, and surely narrower than in the United States, where unemployment benefits are far less generous.[43] (The adjective *generous* may seem callous. Life on the dole in a bleak crime-ridden European housing estate is not to be envied, but the economic consequences of welfare policies that undermine the incentive to work and to hire someone are inescapable.) The consequences of these labor-market regulations and other aspects of the welfare system are, as James Heckman of the University of Chicago, studying the system in Germany, notes, that "in the pursuit of social justice—which in actuality is a defense of protected enclaves of workers and firms—Germany has muted incentives to invest in ideas, skills, and new technology."[44]

High welfare payments are not Europe's only labor market problem. Many Europeans are stuck in a Malthusian thought process, conceptualizing work available as a fixed amount that is to be rationed (the "lump of labor theory"). As a result, during the administration of Prime Minister Lionel Jospin (1997–2002) France introduced thirty-five-hour workweek legislation designed to lower unemployment by preventing workers from stealing their fellow citizens' labor rations. The head of the German Labor Office, reflecting the same static outlook, argued in 2001 that one way to lower unemployment was to cut overtime.[45] Ideas about limiting the workweek or overtime hurt businesses, since it is generally more efficient to have one person do a job than to have two do half of it each.

In Japan, the labor market for professional-track positions in large corporations was based on the lifetime employment principle. College graduates joined conglomerates upon graduation secure in the knowledge that they would be employed and enjoy seniority-based promotions until retirement. This system had many advantages but also created major rigidities in the economy. It is significant, however, that in the past years the system has started to be dismantled under the pressure of Japan's decade-long economic slowdown. The Japanese labor market, however, remains deficient, as we outlined in Chapter 4, due to its relatively ineffective use of women. In addition, unless Japan opens itself to immigration, a shrinking supply of labor may drive up salaries for jobs that cannot be exported to levels that will hurt the economy.

The American educational system, which affects the quality of labor, is also favorable to businesses. Employees can retool themselves by going to college or graduate school, often at night or part-time, well into their forties. Individuals who decide to return to the job market later in life, such as women whose children are old enough to allow them to work again, can enhance their skills. Thus new businesses can access a workforce that has taken charge of its own training rather than have to train them in-house, a task that is feasible for large conglomerates but not possible for new fledgling enterprises.

Residential mobility is an important aspect of the labor market. Americans are more willing to relocate than most other nationalities.[46] The U.S. real estate market facilitates relocation thanks to its liquidity and the relative ease in obtaining mortgages. Moreover, American culture makes it easier to adapt rapidly to a new environment than is the case in the Old World. In Germany regulations governing rental housing give tenants an incentive to stay where they are.[47] In France transfer taxes increase the cost of buying a new home, and laws that protect renters make owners reluctant to rent out their properties.

Not all the aspects of the U.S. labor market are due to regulatory and institutional differences between the United States and other nations. Demography also plays an important role. The large population of the United States gives employers access to a huge domestic labor market. Europe's is as large, but language, cultural, and other barriers fragment it considerably. American businesses also benefit from a relatively open immigration policy that provides them with scientists and managers as well as semi- and unskilled employees (though post-9/11 restrictions have hurt many U.S. companies that need to bring foreign employees or contractors to the United States).

Will American entrepreneurs and corporations continue to enjoy the benefits of a more flexible labor market for a long time? Probably. Labor market reform is a time-consuming and arduous task, which many governments are unwilling to undertake. Thus it would take many years, and a willingness to confront powerful vested interests, for the European states to liberalize their labor-market regulations. Many of the strengths of the U.S. labor market are also related to product market regulations. Thus other countries would also need major product market reforms to improve their labor markets. Moreover, some of the advantages Americans enjoy—for example, the large size of the workforce—cannot be replicated by legislation.

Macroeconomic Implications

Though in this chapter we have focused on microeconomic issues, the institutional and regulatory questions we have covered have important macroeconomic consequences.

The regulatory regime and welfare policies of continental European countries have had perverse consequences on public finances. Taxes are a far greater share of GDP in continental Europe than in the United States, and the cost of running the state (government spending) is considerably higher.

State spending and taxes are not in themselves bad. Government must tax the citizenry to provide services. But there is clearly a point, albeit one that is difficult to quantify, at which the state is consuming too many resources. High government spending relative to GDP indicates that government has taken on tasks that would be better left to the private sector and/or that it uses resources inefficiently. When the state accounts for almost half of the economy, the consequences of its inefficiencies are burdensome for the society.

In particular, European policies in labor and product markets have resulted in large numbers of unemployed, whose benefits must be financed by taxing heavily those who work. For more than a decade, unemployment has consistently been significantly lower in the United States than in Europe.[48] Much of this unemployment is structural, thus unlikely to be reduced by economic growth.[49] Many European unemployed are hidden from statistics thanks to government-financed jobs schemes (like the youth employment program in France), disability (nearly a million Dutch residents, out of a working-age population of seven million, qualify for disability compensation), retirement as early as the fifties, or regions whose entire economy is underpinned by transfer payments (eastern Germany, southern Italy).[50]

On the one hand, some European unemployment may be overestimated due to the larger size of the "shadow economy"—economic activities not recorded in statistics, either to avoid taxes or because they are illegal. This underground economy is estimated to be almost twice as large as a percentage of GDP in Germany (16 percent) than in the United States (9 percent). But those employed in the shadow economy pay no taxes and make no social security contributions, thus increasing the burden on the "official economy."[51] On the other hand, real unemployment is higher than the official estimates since many Europeans citizens have opted out of the labor market. (An unemployed person is one who is seeking employment. Someone who is not looking for a job is not part of the labor force and thus not included in unemployment statistics.) Male labor participation rates in the United States are slightly more than 5 percent higher in the United States than in Europe, meaning that far fewer European men are in the labor market. (Data for males are more relevant than for women, who may stay out of the labor market to raise children or for cultural reasons. Almost all men, however, normally want to work.)[52] Older workers in particular (fifty-five to sixty-four years) are less likely to work in Europe (40 percent) than in the United States (60 percent).[53] The gap between European and U.S. unemployment and labor participation rates is partly due to asymmetric business cycles in the EU and U.S. economies, but it is sufficiently wide to depend also on major structural differences.

Besides the costs of unemployment and low labor participation rates, European economies suffer the consequences of economic systems that are less apt to let businesses thrive, thus hurting the ability of the economy to grow, and increasing the cost of financing the welfare state as a percentage of GDP.

Turning to Japan, government policies there also contribute to economic failures. As we have seen, the regulatory regimes that exist in Japan, such as corporate governance and antitrust, may have worked in the past but are now detrimental to economic growth. In a penetrating article Marie Anchordoguy identified other institutional weaknesses of the Japanese economic system, most of which are rooted in government regulation.[54] She identified the "institutional arrangements of Japan's system of catch-up capitalism," which others have called the capitalist developmental state, as the source of many of Japan's ills.[55] Under the aegis of the government and civil service, industrial policy, conglomerates based on cross-shareholding *(keiretsu),* bank-centered capital markets, and protectionism against imports and foreign investors have been used to ensure that the administration, senior politicians, and large corporations, rather than market forces, decide how to allocate resources. By banning, for all practical purposes, foreign direct investment until the mid-1990s, Japan made it easier to maintain a close-knit system based on exchanging favors and circumventing the market. (In 1998 Japan's per capita stock of foreign direct investment was $209, compared with $3,234 in the United States and $2,789 in Germany.)[56]

Equally problematic has been the cost of pork barrel politics. No nation is immune from this ailment. Comparative surveys are not really feasible. No spending bills start with the words "Congress is appropriating $10 billion to a useless road project." Deciding which items in a budget are pork is highly subjective. Nevertheless, Japan is arguably the leader in wasteful government spending. Japan's political economy has produced astonishing levels of subsidies for privileged industries, such as agriculture and construction. Construction accounts for 15 percent of Japan's GDP, twice the ratio in the United States, though the American population is expanding whereas Japan's is stagnant and soon to decline. In other cases, political influence prevents the rationalization of industry. For example, in Japan "mom and pop" stores account for 55 percent of retail employment, compared with 19 percent in the United States and 26 percent in France (a country with stringent laws to protect small outlets).[57] Politicians also bear a lot of responsibility for the inability to deal swiftly with the bad-loan crisis in the banking sector.

If Japan and Europe's economic arrangements are less efficient than those of the United States, why did they outgrow the American economy in the decades that followed the Second World War? First, Europe and Japan were devastated by World War II. This loosened

some existing social rigidities. European welfare systems stayed relatively lean in the early postwar years because there was no money
for expensive ones. In recent decades, a costly and counterproductive welfare system and labor market has become entrenched in Europe. In Japan the quasi-command economy that mobilized the
country in the early postwar era has become a value-reducing system. Second, until a few decades ago, Europe and Japan were playing catch-up to the United States. It is easier to achieve above-
average growth when an economy starts from a low base than when
it has reached a level comparable with the most advanced nations.
From 1979 to 1998, Europe's purchasing parity per capita GDP actually declined slightly compared with that of the United States,
whereas it had risen from 1960 to 1979.[58] Third, Europe and Japan
had far less costly population pyramids in the early post–World War
II decades than they do now. They must now simultaneously reform
their political economy and bear the burden of a graying population.

China, India, and the Third World

In this chapter we have dealt with the developed economies
of North America, Europe, and Japan. That emphasis may suggest
that we have forgotten the vast potential of emerging economies. In
particular, readers may ask, "What about China?" or "What about
India?" We will first survey China's prospects and then briefly address the issue of India's potential.

China has indeed made remarkable economic headway, becoming a major exporter not only of labor-intensive products but also of
more sophisticated manufactured goods. It is our contention, however, that China is not an emerging economic giant. To understand
our logic, it is necessary to go back to the points first outlined in
Chapter 1.

To be rich a country needs Liberal institutions. It can forgo democracy but not the stable property rights that guarantee and regulate private property, an independent judiciary capable of enforcing contracts, and personal freedoms. It also needs a strong state,
one capable of raising taxes and enforcing the law. The only rich
states bereft of a Liberal framework are underpopulated oil-rich
monarchies living off their petrodollars. Their situation is irrelevant
to China. Nazi Germany was wealthy without Liberal institutions,
but it inherited the resources of a Liberal society. Had the Third
Reich lasted longer it would have run the economy into the ground,

even without the war, due to its disregard for property rights, the judiciary, and basic liberties.

In China private property rights have developed in the past twenty-five years. But Chinese citizens remain subject to the arbitrary whims of the rulers or of functionaries rather than enjoying constitutionally guaranteed and enforced inalienable rights. A contract carries less weight than a good connection, lubricated by bribes, with a party official. As Sebastian Heilmann has written, "Chinese entrepreneurs are so utterly dependent on informal political and economic networks that there can be no real notion of entrepreneurial independence or of the inviolability of property and contracts."[59] Moreover, the Chinese Communist Party remains above the law, a situation that totally undermines the very concept of the rule of law.[60]

Some might argue that even though China is not Liberal, the fact that its economy has grown at a faster pace than America's in the past twenty years suggests that it can keep on growing under the present regime.

The reforms that have fueled Chinese growth since the late 1970s, such as letting farmers sell their products and enabling foreigners to run factories, did not require elaborate property rights. But to graduate to the next level of development, China will need a legal infrastructure like that of an advanced capitalist society. Otherwise, the more China's economy emerges from the Maoist Stone Age, the more it will suffer from its institutional weaknesses.[61] "Socialism with Chinese characteristics" may exist, but there is no such thing as "Liberalism with Chinese characteristics." Regardless of culture, economies that deviate most from Liberal principles perform less well over time.

Moreover, the Chinese state has become weak. It is not effective at collecting taxes. Prior to reforms, government-administered prices were a substitute for a taxation system, but with liberalization this mechanism has mostly disappeared.[62] Chinese tax receipts as a proportion of GDP are low, though they have been rising significantly.[63] Some libertarians who consider all taxes bad may think that this is a sign of progress. But a state needs to fund itself, and the capacity to tax is essential for a successful economy.

The absence of Liberal institutions is not only an obstacle to further growth. China's economic model has led to an accumulation of defects in its political economy that could cause severe economic setbacks in the future. These include massive corruption that has created a "clan economy" of mafialike functionaries feeding on the system, privatizing gains and socializing losses.[64] As Xiabo Lu has noted in an article on "booty socialism," Chinese bureaucracies themselves, rather than individuals, are the source of predatory corruption that distorts markets and weakens the state.[65] Thus, argues Lu, China is not a typical Asian developmental state, as South Korea and Japan were, because it lacks an effective bureaucracy to implement policy. The burden of corruption expands the amount of resources that have been misallocated due to bribery.

Moreover, China's political stability may be at risk. Traditional communist tyrannies provide for political stability. The party leader wields absolute power, dissidents are killed before they can even think of threatening the party, and the populace lives in fear of the omnipotent police. Economic welfare is low but regime stability is high. China, however, is not a totalitarian state anymore. Political repression in China is soft by Stalinist or Maoist standards. In addition, the private sector gives Chinese citizens the capacity to earn a living outside of the state-controlled economy and the financial resources to live where they want. Thanks to education abroad and the presence of foreign investors, many Chinese have contacts with outsiders. The Internet, foreign newscasts, and a relaxation of press controls allow some citizens media access beyond the government news monopoly. Thus the Communist Party's authority has decayed as a result of economic and other transformations.[66] The regime's weakness has been illustrated in recent years by Falun Gong, which the government has been unable to swiftly eliminate. Tax revolts by peasants and workers fighting layoffs are further examples. China faces many of the threats of societies in transition, in particular the inability of the political system to institutionalize peaceful and effective means to channel rising expectations and increasing social mobilization.[67] At the same time, the Chinese political system suffers from some signs of degeneration.[68] The Communist Party apparatus fails to attract the best talent in the country, a decline in ideological beliefs makes it harder to define the purpose of the current system, and an improperly institutionalized intrusion in politics of previously politically uninvolved groupings may destabilize the system.

In some authoritarian societies, the gradual weakening of the ruling group was accompanied by the willingness of those in power to allow an opposition to develop. In Taiwan, the Kuomintang slowly let other political parties emerge. The Chinese Communist Party,

however, has shown little interest in encouraging such developments. While freeing the economy, it has continued to insist on a
monopoly of political and ideological authority. This increases the
likelihood that if communist authority crumbles the transition will
be particularly messy.

Some assume that sooner or later the communists will be over-
thrown and replaced by a Liberal democratic regime. Therefore, according to that theory, China need only wait for the Communist
Party to be removed for the country to become Liberal. The transformation of illiberal polities into Liberal ones is, however, a very
rare occurrence, as we have seen in Chapter 1. Most regime changes
in illiberal societies see one set of illiberal officials replaced by another.

In the context of China's future, it is important to remember that
South Korea and Taiwan, the two Asian countries most frequently
cited as models which China will follow, made their transitions to
democracy in the 1980s, but they were already Liberal, though im-
perfectly so. Each, especially South Korea, had a strong state with
a bureaucracy that could enforce government policy. Their economic systems were based on private-property rights, they had
strong ties with the United States, and their regimes had been authoritarian rather than totalitarian.

Though it may sound like Western cultural arrogance to say so,
China faces another hurdle on the road to Liberalism: it is not a
Western society. Liberalism did not suddenly emerge out of thin air
in England and the Netherlands in the seventeenth century. It has
deep foundations in Western history. Civil law, which plays an essential role in the management of a Liberal economy, has more than
two thousand years of history in the West. In Imperial China, however, civil law never developed. The state opposed, rather than supported, the use of independent courts to resolve disputes between
private parties.[69] The totalitarian period of the Mao era was further
detrimental for the development of civil law, since communist systems restrict the area that falls under civil law and expand the reach
of the penal code.[70]

Feudalism is another essential contributor to Western Liberalism. It was rooted in law, with obligations but also legally enforce-
able rights for the vassal, whereas China did not develop a similar
institution of law-based feudal relationships.[71] Liberalism thus enjoys a long pedigree in the West. In China, however, there is no
Liberal tradition upon which to build.

Japan, South Korea, Taiwan, and Singapore demonstrate that Asians can establish successful Liberal polities that in some cases have higher per capita incomes than those of Western nations. But their Liberal transformation required the imposition of Western institutions (as well, obviously, as hard work and capable leaders). Europe and the United States in the late nineteenth century compelled Japan, through unequal treaties, to adopt their legal norms. Liberalism, however, was short-lived in Japan, collapsing in the 1930s. It was reestablished only after almost seven years of postwar U.S. occupation.

Korea and Taiwan spent forty and fifty years, respectively, in the first half of the twentieth century under Japanese rule.[72] During this period, the Japanese colonizers imposed on the Koreans and Taiwanese the Western legal and bureaucratic infrastructure which they had adopted from Europe. (Western institutions might have arrived in Korea without Japanese intervention had an independent Korean leadership survived, and foreign participation might have helped modernize the kingdom.)[73] Following Japan's surrender in 1945 both South Korea and Taiwan (a part of China until 1949) fell into the American sphere, allowing the United States to influence their destiny, though not as directly as Japan's. Finally, Japan, South Korea, and Taiwan have had strong military ties with the United States for more than a half-century.

As for Singapore, it was virtually empty until Britain took it over in the nineteenth century. The British shaped the island, giving it the laws, administrative procedures, bureaucratic culture, and European-educated cadres that are the foundations of Singaporean wealth. Singapore's rulers like to claim the uniqueness of their city-state, but its prosperity is first and foremost the result of the property rights, contract-enforcement mechanisms, and personal freedoms Singapore inherited from Britain and which have been wisely preserved by the British- and American-educated ruling class that runs the country (in English). Non–Western European countries that did not have the advantage of such close (and generally forced) interaction with the West—Russia, Turkey, and Thailand, to name a few—have failed in their attempts to emulate the Liberal states of the West. It should be noted, however, that Western influence itself in no way guarantees Liberal development, as evidenced by the sad fate of most of Western Europe's former colonial holdings.

The importance of the link with the West for Asian Liberal polities may diminish with time. As Liberalism has taken root in developed Asia, it has gradually become part of the native cultures and mores. It is wrong to believe that Liberalism is a Western monopoly. What is certain, however, is that to start on the path toward liberalism, non-Western countries need a long period of influence from Western nations or from non-Western states that have internalized Liberal institutions and values. The absence of a Western European tradition thus adds another difficulty to China's quest toward first-world status.

China will not be occupied or colonized by Taiwan, South Korea, Japan, the European Union, or the United States. Unlike Central Europe it cannot hope to acquire Liberal institutions by absorption into the European Union and NATO. It receives Western influences through foreign investment and cultural exchanges with the Western and Asian Liberal countries, especially Taiwan. But these interactions are no substitute for the radical transformations which European and American armies or Japan's colonial administrators imposed on other Asian nations.

Through a mixture of repression and co-optation the communist regime might survive longer than expected. Alternatively, the Communist Party might continue to decay until other groups are sufficiently strong to overthrow it or force it into a coalition. Regardless of the political evolution of China, we can make some forecast about its economic future. At best China will remain in the gray zone, with a strong mostly low- and mid-tech manufacturing base, a small but not insignificant more advanced industrial sector, an atrophied service sector, and hundreds of millions of poor peasants. Its growth rates will decline for three reasons. First, it is easier to grow fast from a small base than from a large one. Second, the absence of Liberal institutions will slow the emergence of more advanced industrial and service businesses. Third, the accumulating inefficiencies of the current system will create a continually heavier burden. Alternatively, the potential for political instability, the ideological vacuum generated by the absence of a credible postcommunist ideology, the rising cost of corruption, the plight of the state-owned enterprises, the weak financial industry, the possibility of military conflict with Taiwan (a major source of foreign investment), and the erosion of Liberalism in Hong Kong (one of the engines of China's growth) could lead to an economic crisis and derail China's modernization. To the extent that China can hope to avoid such a crisis, it will be by strengthening its ties to the Liberal democracies, who are a vital source of investment and markets, and eschewing a policy of confrontation.

India, as we noted earlier, is another nation that is now also mentioned as Asia's next giant, though less frequently than China. India does have the advantage of having inherited some Western legal and administrative institutions from the British colonial period. But it faces as many hurdles toward economic progress as does China. First, some of the institutions that Britain built have decayed since independence, thus negating the advantages of the Liberal system that was inherited.[74] Second, India was not Singapore. In Singapore the British occupied a mostly empty island, planting their flag on essentially virgin territory. Thus practically all institutions and administrative practices in Singapore are British. In India, British administrators ruled a vast territory inhabited by a large population with ancient and varied institutional and cultural traditions. Many of these were left untouched by the British, who left large tracts of India under the autonomous rule of local lords. In particular, the caste system has survived both British colonialism and Indian independence. Although the elite learned English, and continue to speak it to this day, the majority of the population speak a host of local idioms and cannot communicate in English, thus denying India the advantage of a lingua franca.

The multiplicity of languages, ethnic groups, castes, and religions in India is another obstacle for the country. As we pointed out in Chapter 1, successful Liberal polities which are multiethnic and multilingual are rare, and at most they have four languages and two religions (Switzerland). The EU may become a true state, but only after centuries in which separate Liberal polities have developed. The United States is a case apart, because, with the exception of native Americans and the descendants of African slaves, Americans made the conscious decision to immigrate to America; thus ethnic groups are different from Old World ones that are located in their ancestral lands and generally are in conflict with their neighbors. Moreover, the United States has one language, and though some urban ethnic enclaves survive, the territory is not divided along cantonal lines. For India, ethnic, religious, and caste conflicts have been causes of constant violence which shows no sign of abating. (Two thousand Muslims were slaughtered in Gujarat in 2002 with the tacit approval of the state government.)

India falls into the same category as the other nations which

Western European states colonized in Africa and Asia. In some countries, such as Congo under the personal rule of the Belgian King Leopold II, the Europeans exploited the natives with unspeakable brutality. In other cases, Western rule provided material progress and some institutional improvements. In almost all polities, however, when these countries gained independence they were left with weak institutions that were incompatible with Liberal politics and economics. In addition, the former colonial holdings were frequently afflicted by ethnic, religious, regional, and social cleavages that precluded the creation of a solid nation-state.

The obstacles to China's or India's transformation into first world economies apply equally, though with local variations, to the rest of the third world. Several poor countries, such as Nigeria, Russia, and Brazil, are democracies; others are autocracies, like Egypt or Pakistan. But regardless of their political regime, they all lack Liberal institutions. Property-rights regimes are ineffective, and the state is unable to enforce the law, which is itself frequently flawed. Lawless and unpunished violence, often sponsored or tolerated by the government or the police, is common. Some third world nations have made significant inroads in the past thirty years. There is obviously a vast difference between Nigeria, which is very poor and institutionally deficient, and Brazil, which is richer and better administered. Malaysia, Mexico, and Thailand are good examples of third world states that have made economic progress. But none has established a Liberal regime. There is always a risk of some upheaval that can wreck developing economies, as has happened to at least two countries that had been model emerging markets: Indonesia in the late 1990s and Argentina in the early 2000s. We can thus say that over the next twenty or thirty years, and probably beyond, the world economy will still be characterized by the concentration of most of its wealth and resources in Europe, North America, and the developed Western Pacific rim (Japan, Korea, Taiwan, Hong Kong, Singapore, Australia, and New Zealand). Technological progress should allow most nations, rich and poor, to get richer, but this will not affect the relative distribution of wealth. In fact, technological breakthroughs can widen the gap when, as happened during the Industrial Revolution, only countries with Liberal institutions can fully benefit from them.

Looking Forward

Previous books that marveled at the achievements of Japan (Ezra Vogel's *Japan as Number One*) predicted the decline of the United States under the unbearable burden of military spending (Paul Kennedy's *The Rise and Decline of the Great Powers*) or inferior institutions (Lester Thurow's *Head to Head: The Coming Economic Battle Among Japan, Europe, and America*) should caution us toward modesty in making forecasts.[75] It is not our contention that the gap between the United States and the European Union and Japan will increase inexorably. The United States is not immune from economic decay. For example, if the Enron, WorldCom, Tyco, and other scandals lead to a radical overhaul of auditing and corporate governance practices, it will demonstrate the ability of U.S. institutions to provide positive corrective feedback. If not, it will show that the United States is suffering from institutional decay.

American liability laws provide a good example of the ability of some U.S. institutions to decay. It is good for the economy that victims of negligent or malevolent businesses should receive compensation. The trend toward high awards in product liability cases, however, hurts the economy. Liability laws are often used by plaintiffs who either have suffered no harm or have only themselves to blame for their suffering. What is particularly disturbing is that state governments and the federal authorities have joined the fray by suing tobacco companies for tens of billions of dollars, in effect using their power, with the support of the judiciary, to confiscate assets of cigarette manufacturers. The litigation industry has also sought, sometimes with the support of local politicians and prosecutors if not of the federal government, to use the U.S. legal system to collect billions of dollars from European firms over Holocaust reparations (which have been lucrative for the American lawyers involved but not for Hitler's surviving victims) even though the cases should clearly have been dealt with in Europe without American interference.[76] Although many Americans are aware of the negative impact of these abuses of liability laws, there are enough winners in this game—not only trial lawyers but also politicians and others—to make reform difficult.

Nevertheless, we believe that over the next decade the United States is likely to continue to outperform the other major Liberal economies in the world for several reasons. First, as we noted in Chapter 4, the demographic position of the United States is stronger than that of Europe and Japan. Thus, all other things being equal, the U.S. economy will find it easier to expand than the European or Japanese ones. Second, the institutional and regulatory reforms that Europe and Japan need to undertake to improve their economic performance are not changes that can yield results in just a few years. Thus even if there is enough political willpower in Europe and Japan to take the necessary steps, the positive results of reforms are unlikely to be seen for years and in many cases decades. The British experience is telling. Margaret Thatcher assumed power in 1979. She enjoyed the benefits of a political system that centralizes power in the hands of the chief executive and had clear ideas about what needed to be done. Nevertheless, the benefits of her reforms were not reaped for a long time.

It is possible, however, that by 2010–15 Europe and Japan could outperform the United States. Unlike other regions of the world, they have the Liberal institutions and human capital necessary for great economic performance. Were they to implement the right sort of reforms, they could devise economic policies and regulations that are more efficient than those of the United States. Many of their current arrangements are so inefficient that reforms could generate significant additional growth. There are significant signs, albeit ambiguous ones, that the Japanese political economy is changing. European integration has helped the cause of economic liberalism. If major structural reforms are undertaken in Japan and Europe, these economies could hope to regain the dynamism they enjoyed in earlier decades. It is possible that observers, including us, have failed to notice the early signs of a reform movement that could gain momentum in future years. Nevertheless, the obstacles to successful reforms are significant, and they cannot be expected to bear fruit quickly. The political costs of reforms are high. Thus as long as Europe and Japan suffer from mild decay rather than from severe economic trauma, it is possible that entrenched interests will be strong enough to stymie reformist politicians.

Military might, which is essential for upholding the American empire, does not come cheaply. Therefore, a strong economy makes an obvious contribution to American power by providing the U.S. government with such a large economic base that the financing of its armed forces, on which the United States spends about one billion dollars *a day,* or more in a year than the entire GDP of Switzerland, represents only a minor fraction of U.S. national income.

Consequently, continued American economic success is a requirement for the continuation of the U.S. empire.

If America's success is good news for the United States, however,
the weakness of its partners is not. Samuel Huntington argued in
1993 that the United States and Europe "have deeply conflicting
interests over the distribution of the benefits and costs of economic
growth and the distribution of the costs of economic stagnation or
decline. The idea that economics is primarily a non-zero-sum game
is a favorite conceit of tenured academics. It has little connection to
reality."[77] Economics, he argues, becomes zero-sum because it is a
source of power, which is measured in relative terms. Richard Rosecrance made similar arguments in 1976, arguing that by focusing on
the Soviet danger "The American conception of interest [was] limited and naïve in that Americans could perceive no basic conflict
between their own interests and those of their European and Japanese allies."[78]

Huntington is right when thinking about balance-of-power relationships. The economic woes of the Soviet Union during the Cold
War served American interests. But the U.S. empire is different.
Power still plays a crucial role. U.S. hegemony would not be possible if the relative U.S. economic weight fell drastically (though,
one could imagine others running this Liberal empire and the
United States being a satisfied junior member of the alliance). But
if Europe and Japan decline economically, is that good for America?
The answer is a resounding No. First, Americans would be poorer
because the richer Europe and Japan are, the richer America becomes thanks to trade and investment. Americans, as noted earlier,
own more than $7 trillion worth of assets abroad, and foreigners
hold more than $9 trillion worth of U.S. assets.[79] American exports
and imports amount to more than $2 trillion.[80]

Second, the United States now has partners that contribute to
the cost of the upkeep of the American empire rather than impoverished clients who live off the generosity of the U.S. Treasury.
America's allies annually devote around $240 billion to the common
defense and to international assistance programs that serve American interests. [81] Europeans have contributed billions to reconstruction in the Balkans besides housing and feeding hundreds of
thousands of refugees from the former Yugoslavia. They provide the
majority of NATO peacekeepers in Southeastern Europe. Japan un-
derwrote $13 billion worth of the 1991 Gulf War costs and pays
billions of dollars every year toward the upkeep of U.S. bases in

Japan. Europe and Japan provided men and materiel to the war effort in Afghanistan following the 9/11 attacks.

Third, Europe and Japan could become less stable due to economic discontent at home if they grew poorer. Their electorates would conclude that American hegemony is undesirable since their standard of living is going down. Voters would consequently support parties that favor pulling out of the American empire. European and Japanese wealth sends a message, which Central Europeans have clearly understood: Joining the American empire pays; its members are rich, other nations are poor. Samuel Huntington wrote in 1982 that "the disappearance of liberty in Britain or France or Japan would have consequences for the health of liberty in the United States."[82] The same applies to the fate of prosperity.

6 The University Gap

The developed world has practically all the leading research universities in the world. But whereas economic power is well-distributed within the American empire, with the combined gross domestic products of Europe and Japan greater than America's, the majority of the best universities, though by no means all, are in the United States. They provide America with an unsurpassed science and technology base, employ the most Nobel Prize winners, lead the world in journal publications, and attract more than half a million overseas students. Scholars at Harvard publish more articles in the top economics journals than those of any continental European country.[1] As Philip Altbach of Boston College, an expert in the field of higher education, wrote: "The American university stands at the center of a world system of science and scholarship and is the largest producer of research and scholarly publications."[2] Although U.S. universities have their weak points, the top tier of the American professoriat "is the arbiter of many of the scientific disciplines for much of the world."[3] Britain's *Financial Times* noted, in an editorial on Britain's higher education, that U.S. universities are "magnets for the world's talent and sources of much of its intellectual innovation."[4]

In this chapter, we will first introduce some parameters for measuring the extent of the primacy of American higher education. We will then provide some explanations for the dominance of U.S. universities and conclude by analyzing the role that the university plays in sustaining American hegemony, not only as a contributor to American power but also as an international public good.

Some Measures of the Primacy of U.S. Universities

Quantifying the performance of higher-education institutions is difficult. Fluctuations in share prices, net income, and other parameters facilitate the comparisons of businesses. Judging universities is far more subjective. There are few obvious yardsticks to use. In some scientific disciplines, there are some generally accepted objective benchmarks, such as bibliometrics and prizes. In the social sciences and humanities, the task is more difficult and can fall victim to personal or ideological biases. Nevertheless, we can demonstrate with hard evidence that the American higher-education system is the most successful in the world. Our comparisons are with the university systems of other developed nations. Other countries, obviously, have competitive higher educational systems. Some, like China and India, graduate first-rate professionals, especially in the hard sciences. But large research universities, with the ability not only to train undergraduate and graduate students but also to carry out original research, are almost all located in the rich countries of the American empire.

Bibliometrics

One measure of achievement is bibliometrics—that is, the analysis of publications in scholarly journals. This quantifies two important parameters. One is the number of citations—that is, how many times articles in academic journals cite the work of a particular individual or institution. This weighs only that research output which is strong enough to be cited by others in the field. The other, more qualitative, datum is the impact factor. It is the number of times a particular article is cited in other articles. For example, if a scientist's article is quoted in twenty papers by other researchers, it has an impact factor of 20. A high impact factor indicates that an article was cited frequently by other researchers.

The data, gathered between 1988 and 1996, covered several disciplines (hospital-based clinical subjects, biochemistry, biology, physics, mathematics, mechanical engineering, economics, politics, and accountancy). U.S.-based researchers accounted for between 51 percent and 81 percent of the articles cited in the journals surveyed from scholars in the United States, Canada, Britain, France, Germany, Japan, and Australia (which together account for a large majority of the world's advanced research).[5] Moreover, in all fields but one, authors from the United States had the highest impact factor. Although in some cases the share of papers published in the United States has declined because of an increase in publications from Asia, the United States remains well ahead.[6] Not all of the research included in this study came from universities, but without its universities the United States would not be in such a dominant position.

The research firm of Evidence Ltd designed another comparison, covering only four leading countries in research: Canada, Germany, the United Kingdom, and the United States.[7] In biology, medicine, physics, engineering, and mathematics, American universities occupied on average 3.6 of the top five slots in citations of articles, and four out of five times a U.S. school was number one.

Another more recent survey is summarized in the National Science Board's comprehensive report on science and engineering, which showed a decline in the percentage of scientific and technical papers written in the United States, from 38.5 percent of the world total in 1986 to 30.9 percent in 1999, but found the relative prominence of U.S. scientific and technical literature had remained almost constant from 1990 (at 1.36) to 1999 (at 1.35), well above the Western European (0.98 in 1999) and Japanese (0.83) levels.[8]

These various surveys indicate that the United States is in the lead in bibliometrics. Its position has somewhat declined in recent years, but not to an extent that threatens its preeminence.

Scientific Prizes

Scientific prizes are another indicator of success. Researchers affiliated with U.S. institutions, mostly universities, won 70 percent of the Nobel Prizes over the past two decades. Stanford scholars alone received eight Nobels from 1980 to 2000.[9] A high proportion of other prestigious awards—the Kyoto, Crafoord, Wolf, Volvo, Draper, Bower prizes and the Fields medal—also go to recipients from the United States.[10]

For many awards, especially the Nobel, there is a long time lag between a discovery and official recognition. But even though they may be lagging indicators statistically, prizes help attract able young scholars who look forward to working with Nobelists and other famous scientists. Thus those universities with many laureates can recruit high-caliber junior researchers.

International Impact of U.S. Social Science Academic Output

Another indicator of the success of U.S. universities is that American academic publications in the social sciences and humanities enjoy an international following that is second to none. In economics, Americans dominate the market for textbooks all over the world. Paul Krugman's *Pop Internationalism* has been translated into eleven languages and Paul A. Samuelson's *Economics* into forty-one.[11] When American economists talk, the world listens. Krugman's critique of Asian productivity, published in *Foreign Affairs* in 1994, caused major reverberations. Singapore's trade and industry minister recalled that "everyone in the region was very upset" about the article.[12] Another example of the influence of U.S. economists is the mobilization of antiglobalization activists in favor of the "Tobin tax," named after the late James Tobin, Sterling Professor Emeritus at Yale University. Joseph Stiglitz, who became in 2001 the third Columbia University professor to win the Nobel Prize in economics, is another globally influential American economist and critic of the "Washington consensus."

History is another a field in which Americans are influential. *Hitler's Willing Executioners,* written by Daniel Goldhagen of Harvard University, fueled a major debate in Germany.[13] New York University professor Jan Tomasz Gross's *Neighbors,* about a World War II pogrom, prompted reactions by Poland's president, prime minister, and Roman Catholic primate.[14] Columbia University's Robert Paxton, an expert on Vichy France, was invited by French prosecutors to testify at the trial of a former official, Maurice Papon, who had been charged with complicity in crimes against humanity.[15] In South Korea, the writings of Bruce Cumings of the University of Chicago have had a significant influence on Koreans' perceptions of their history.[16] *Embracing Defeat: Japan in the Wake of World War II,* by John Dower of the Massachusetts Institute of Technology, sold 122,000 copies in Japan in a few months after coming out in translation.[17] The *New York Times* noted that attitudes in Belgium toward its colonial past were changing, "but no book had the impact of Adam Hochschild's *King Leopold's Ghost: A Story of Greed, Terror and Heroism in Colonial Africa* (Houghton Mifflin, 1998), which appeared in translation in Belgium in 1999."[18] Hochschild is affiliated with the University of California at Berkeley.

The debate about post–Cold War world paradigms in academic circles is another illustration of how Americans shape ideas. This discussion developed around the ideas of Samuel Huntington (Harvard, posited the clash of civilizations), Francis Fukuyama (George Mason, then Johns Hopkins, the end of history), and Michael Doyle and Bruce Russett (Princeton and Yale, democratic peace). U.S. intellectual influence is felt by the practitioners of foreign policy as well. Hubert Védrine, then France's foreign minister, published a book-length interview in 2000.[19] His interviewer, at the start of their discussion, refers to Fukuyama's end-of-history thesis and Védrine, who is known to resent American power, replies by citing Huntington's clash of civilizations. Forty years ago French journalists and officials would have quoted Aron, Camus, Sartre, or maybe Marx, but today they seek guidance from American professors.

Americans provide much of the contemporary conceptual framework for international relations specialists in other countries. In philosophy, a field that was reinvigorated in the West by Germans in the nineteenth century, more than 20 percent of the articles appearing from 1998 to 2001 in the prestigious *Deutsche Zeitschrift für Philosophie* were written by academics affiliated with American universities.[20] The list of books cited in the *Philosophische Rundschau,* another leading German journal, includes many published in the United States and the United Kingdom but only a few in languages other than German and English.[21]

Thanks to European Union initiatives, studying in another European country is now routine for elite European students. This will train scholars with pan-European credentials and interests, but so far the United States and Britain are the dominant providers of foreign materials for Europeans in the social sciences. Similarly, East Asians are more likely to refer to American publications than to those from other Asian nations.

Not all the flow of ideas is from America to the rest of the world. Literature studies in the United States have been inspired by European, particularly French, concepts of deconstruction and other novel ways of analyzing writings. In the humanities, American academics continue to be influenced by Europeans in many fields. Nevertheless, on balance, the traditional intellectual flow, from Europe to the rest of the world, has been replaced by an America-centric diffusion of ideas and publications to other nations.

The English language dominates in the natural sciences. In the social sciences and humanities, authors may know English, but most publish in their native tongue. Therefore in these disciplines, the output of Asians and continental Europeans may be ignored not because of lower quality but because other scholars cannot read it. It is consequently unfair to assert unequivocally the superiority of American and British social scientists based on their overseas readership. Still, regardless of the causes, it is the output from universities in the United States and, to a lesser degree, the United Kingdom that is most read and that most influences other scholars. Antonio Gramsci suggested drawing "the intellectual and moral *map* of the country" to chart the movement of ideas.[22] Such a map today sheds light on the extent to which American thought provides the lenses through which the world is understood.

Foreign Students

Analyzing international flows of students and scholars highlights which countries' universities have the best reputation. In the United States, as of the academic year 2001–2, there were 582,996 foreign college and university students enrolled, accounting for 4.3 percent of the total U.S. enrollment.[23] There were also 86,015 overseas scholars in the United States. (Scholars in this context are postdoctoral fellows and others who have completed their studies but have come from overseas to be affiliated as researchers with universities and colleges.)[24] Students at U.S. colleges and universities come from all over the world, including around 82,000 from Europe, 68,000 from Latin America, 67,000 Indians, 60,000 Chinese, 49,000 South Koreans, 47,000 Japanese, and 29,000 Taiwanese.[25] The foreign scholars are from the European Union (more than 17,000), China (15,600), India (6,200), Japan (5,700), South Korea (5,800), and many other nations.[26]

Some students come for science and engineering, some for the social sciences, but large numbers are also attracted to business programs. About a third of their students at such prestigious business schools as Wharton and Harvard are from abroad.[27] U.S. managerial education enjoys an unrivalled reputation. Of the ten top programs for the master of business administration (MBA) identified by the *Financial Times*, eight were American, including all the top five.[28] The *Economist* Intelligence Unit, using a different methodology, put nine U.S. institutions in the top ten, and yet another survey by the *Wall Street Journal* had ten American MBA programs in the best ten.[29] These are subjective league tables, but they accurately reflect the impressions of students and employers. In the legal profession, as well, American universities have a growing international student body. There has been a noticeable increase in the number of foreign students in one-year master of law (LLM) programs.

America does not have a disproportionate fraction of the world's foreign students. At 30 percent of the total, the U.S. share is commensurate with the size of its population in the developed world.[30] The United Kingdom and Australia have larger proportions of foreigners in their universities. The position of the United States in international education is, however, much stronger than this percentage would indicate.

First, it appears that the best students, and those who belong to the privileged classes, prefer the United States for foreign study. Consequently, foreign graduates of American universities tend to be very successful when they return home. For example, 65 percent of Taiwan's cabinet members hold American degrees. International corporations' senior ranks are replete with holders of U.S. MBAs. Of the elite-track Japanese civil servants who are sent abroad for graduate studies, 71 percent have attended school in the United States since the program started in 1966. In 2000 the percentage enrolling in American institutions was 83 percent, not including the numerous midlevel and senior officials from Japan who are visiting fellows in American think tanks and universities.[31] Several countries are governed by alumni of American universities: Bolivia, Chile, Colombia, Peru, the Philippines, Singapore, and Thailand. The secretary general of the United Nations, Kofi Annan of Ghana, is also a graduate of American universities. France's Jacques Chirac attended Harvard summer school. Canada, Israel, Jamaica, Mexico, Pakistan, Taiwan, and Turkey have in recent years been governed by American-educated leaders. The former heads of state of Brazil (Fernando Henrique Cardoso, visiting professor at Stanford University), and South Korea (Kim Dae-Jung, who spent some of his years in exile at Harvard University) had affiliations with American academia. The future kings of Spain and Norway are also U.S.-educated, as is the Japanese crown princess.

Second, American universities attract scholars and researchers from the world's wealthiest and most developed nations. The United States hosts more than 200,000 students and more than 37,000 researchers from the developed world. There are, for example, about 5,000 German scholars in the United States who are, according to a well-researched report, the crème de la crème of the country's research cadre.[32] Of the students and scholars from the third world, many are from the more dynamic developing regions, such as China, India, and Latin America.

Continental Europe, by contrast, fails to draw large numbers of students from the other developed regions, North America and Northeast Asia, or from the most economically vital areas of the less developed world. More than half of the foreign students in continental Europe, excluding other Europeans, are from Africa (45 percent) and the Middle East (8–15 percent), regions which play a small role in the world economy.[33] There are ten times more Japanese studying in the United States than in the EU's continental European states. There are 7,300 South Korean students on the Continent, compared with 49,000 in the United States. Only 12,000 Americans study in EU states on the Continent. Britain, it should be noted, performs better, attracting more Japanese students (6,100) than all the continental states combined and almost as many Americans (11,100).[34] The United Kingdom benefits from two major advantages over the continental nations. It is English-speaking, thus attracting Japanese and other non-Anglophones who want to improve their English language skills and Americans who prefer to learn in their own language. In addition, its flagship universities, Cambridge, Oxford, the London School of Economics, and a few others enjoy worldwide reputations that are unrivaled on the Continent.

Japan increased its foreign student head count to slightly more than 95,000 as of 2002, up from 31,000 in 1989. Those students are mostly from a few Asian countries, however, with China accounting for 61 percent; very few are from Europe or North America.[35] Whereas Chinese studying in America are the nation's brightest or wealthiest, frequently attending elite American universities, many of the Chinese in Japan enroll in institutions of doubtful reputation, sometimes to gain residency in Japan to work in menial jobs there instead of studying.[36] At Peking University, China's most prestigious, those who travel abroad for graduate study go to the United States or Britain; few go to Japan, and most of those who do enroll in one-year exchange programs.[37] South Koreans with Ph.D.s are more than three times as likely to have earned the degree in the United States than in Japan, even though Japan is much closer and its language easier for Koreans to learn.[38] Japan's most prestigious undergraduate programs, the core of the country's elite training system, have very few non-Japanese.

Third, statistics overstate the number of foreign students outside of the United States. In America a "foreign student" is a noncitizen who moves to the United States from abroad for the specific purpose of studying. In many nations, immigrants already in-country are counted as foreign students. In Germany and France the parents of about 40 percent of the so-called foreign students live in the country.[39] For all practical purposes, they are locals rather than foreigners. They have chosen a German or French education not because they think it is better but because they reside there.

Europeans, the Americans' main competitor in the international educational market, recognize how far ahead the United States is. The rector of Switzerland's flagship Federal Institute of Technology in Zurich lamented, "Everybody knows about studying in the United States. But who in the rest of the world thinks about studying in Europe?"[40] Another European noted, "The fight over students, young scientists, and scholars from all over the globe is finally on, and Europe—aside from Britain—is not on the winning side."[41] The Erasmus World program, modeled on the U.S. Fulbright scholarship, is part of Europe's efforts to close the gap, but it remains to be seen how successfully Europe can compete.[42] The smaller English-speaking nations, Britain, Canada, and Australia, educate many foreigners, but the numbers are lower than in the United States because their educational systems are much smaller than America's and, except for a few British establishments, they lack universities with the reputation to attract star students and faculty.

The United States could do even more to strengthen its position in international education. American consulates often deny visas to bright students from developing countries on the assumption that they want to emigrate, a doubly counterproductive move which denies America the opportunity to educate poor but intelligent foreigners and in many cases deprives the U.S. economy of dynamic immigrants. The United States generally refuses to let in children from nations such as China to attend U.S. boarding schools, again on fears of immigration, leaving these children to choose other English-speaking nations that then often keep them for their universities. Restrictions and regulations applied after the 9/11 attacks have raised additional barriers to foreign students and scholars who wish to come to the United States. Given how much elite graduate programs, especially in the sciences, depend on foreign students and faculty, this could seriously affect not only the international character of U.S. universities but also the quality of the education which they offer.

The presence of so many foreigners in American universities indicates that U.S. schools enjoy an unparalleled reputation. But we should note that this influx also depends on other factors.

First, the United States is the world's largest economic and military power, which makes it attractive regardless of the quality of its universities. American schools give MBA candidates the advantage of proximity to Wall Street, Silicon Valley, and a $10.8 trillion economy, something no other country offers. America gives computer science students the possibility to be close to the world's leading computer and information technology businesses. Those focusing on international relations in America get the additional opportunity to learn firsthand more about the world's only superpower. Military officers from all over the world are also obviously very interested in studying in the United States for this reason.

Second, foreign students frequently seek not only an education but also a job. Of all major labor markets, the American one is the most open to immigration. It is also a place where migrants can hope to reach well-paid and prestigious positions. After Elias Zerhouni graduated from Algiers Medical School in 1975, he went on to a residency in radiology at Johns Hopkins. By 2002 he was executive vice dean of its medical school when President Bush nominated him to the directorship of the National Institutes of Health. Had he chosen another country, he is unlikely to have had such an outstanding career. (Unfortunately, were an Algerian man of similar talent to attempt to study in the United States, his Muslim background might now deny him a visa and deprive the United States of his potential contribution to American science.) Polish-born Zbigniew Brzezinski, who arrived from Canada to attend graduate school at Harvard, rose to become President Carter's national security adviser, another example of the opportunities America affords. America's diversity further contributes to draw foreign students, since they know that they will find compatriots already in the United States who can make their stay less lonely.

Third, English is by far the language that is known by the largest number of students interested in studying abroad and able to do so. Thus English-speaking schools have an edge in selling their services internationally. Moreover, improvement of their English is often a significant additional benefit for foreign students—sometimes even the main one—of going to America. Thus they opt for the United States, or other Anglophone lands and eschew universities in non-English-speaking nations.

How American Universities Became Dominant

How did the United States achieve such primacy? There are organizational explanations, as well as economic, demographic, and linguistic ones, but first we have to turn to the historical events that precipitated the rise of American academia and the decline of Europe's.

Historical Background

The Western world's earliest universities arose in Europe in the Middle Ages, but the modern research university dates from nineteenth-century Germany. "Until about the 1870s, German universities were virtually the only places in the world in which a student could obtain rigorous training in how to do scientific or scholarly research."[43] Between unification in 1871 and Hitler's ascension in 1933, German scholars turned their country into an academic superpower. To this day, many disciplines rely upon German research from this period for the foundations of their scholarship. Johns Hopkins University and the University of Chicago were founded along German lines, forcing older American schools, such as Harvard and Yale, to reform themselves to remain competitive.[44] Many Frenchmen identified the superiority of German education as one of the cause of their defeat by Prussia in 1870–71. Thus the French University Law of 1895 was considerably influenced by the German model. In its drive to catch up with the West, Meiji Japan (1868–1912) dispatched many students to Germany while inviting German professors to teach in its fledgling universities.

Unfortunately, the Nazis vandalized universities. By 1939 one-third of Germany's tenured faculty, twenty-four of whom were or would become Nobel laureates, had emigrated.[45] Fortunate intellectuals fled while the unlucky ones were murdered. The persecution of German Jews, who accounted for twenty-eight Nobel Prizes from 1905 to 1978, was particularly costly to the country's intellectual life.[46] In addition, the damage inflicted by the world wars, Nazism, and communism to the nations of Mitteleuropa destroyed a region which had contributed much to Germany's intellectual vigor, depriving the country of its eastern cultural hinterland.

As the United States grew economically and demographically in the twentieth century, it was already gaining ground in academic pursuits. The destruction of much of Europe's intellectual capital by the world wars and totalitarianism accelerated the rise of American universities by wrecking much of Europe's educational institutions and bringing European academics to the New World. The exodus of Germans to America in the Nazi era "amounted to a sea change in the international location of research and scholarly work."[47] Great men, such as the Albert Einstein and Hans Bethe, another physicist who won the Nobel Prize, were exiled. Younger scholars and children who could have grown up to be leading German academics became American professors instead, among them Hans Gatzke, Peter Gay, Hajo Holborn, Henry Kissinger, Hans Morgenthau, Henry Rosovsky, Fritz Stern, and Leo Strauss. Besides Germans, Italians (Enrico Fermi, Nobel Prize winner), Poles (Richard Pipes, Adam Ulam), Hungarians (John von Neumann, Leo Szilard, Edward Teller), Frenchmen (Claude Lévi-Strauss, who returned to France after the war), and others fled to America. Most are now dead or retired, but their legacy lives on in America, where their students and their students' students now teach.

Institutional Advantages

The economic growth of the United States in the past century and Europe's intellectual suicide in the twentieth century do not by themselves explain the achievements of American universities. Institutional and organizational factors have also contributed to the global primacy American schools have achieved in the past decades.

GOVERNANCE

U.S. universities enjoy a better management system than their foreign counterparts. Henry Rosovsky, former dean of the Harvard Faculty of Arts and Sciences, described in *The University: An Owner's Manual* how the unitary governance system makes American education different. The president and managers are appointed to run the school under the supervision of "relatively independent trustees [who] serve both public and private schools, giving considerable protection from political interference even to state universities."[48] Thus U.S. schools are unique in enjoying a professionalized administration.[49] By private-sector standards, U.S. university management is sclerotic, weak, and excessively decentralized. No business school would hold up a university as an example for aspiring managers to follow. But compared with other countries' university systems, the American system excels.

Although there is pressure overseas to follow the U.S. example of professionalized management, other countries have less effective methods to run academia.[50] In Germany "the only formal authority above the level of the professor is the ministry [of education of the Land]."[51] Because that administration "is far away, [it] does not monitor the professor's day-to-day activities," letting academics enjoy unsupervised "self-government." The 1968 revolts "added a system of governance by committees of professors and students." These mechanisms foster a state of "organized irresponsibility" and unaccountability.[52] An elected administration that gives representation to students and nonfaculty employees guarantees weak and highly politicized leadership. In France, students—or, more accurately, their unions—and support staff play a role in university management.[53] Some European states initiated reforms in the 1990s and limited student power, but the European system is still vastly different from the American one.[54] Nevertheless, European universities should not be summarily dismissed as mediocrities; many European institutions do undertake world-class research, but their management structure acts as a brake on their performance. Japan as well suffers from governance problems. A commentator noted that faculty councils make the key personnel decisions. Thus "when it comes to naming a president, faculty members tend to pick some harmless-seeming figure from among their own ranks." This observer contrasted this system with that of the United States, where "the people at the top, such as the president and deans, are executives in the true sense of the word."[55]

The efficiency of management in many foreign universities is further undermined by the large proportion of employees and teaching staff who are unionized civil servants devoted to fighting reform and defending their privileges.[56] Recent moves toward unionization of academics in America could hurt U.S. education by increasing rigidities and making it even more difficult for the administration to manage the teaching staff. Unionization of some teaching assistants may indicate the start of a change, but so far the United States has not had to deal with powerful unions among the instructors.

Ineffective governance explains the difficulties in dealing with the transformation of higher education from the pursuit of a small elite to the mass production of graduates. American universities adapted remarkably well to the massive intake of students in the decades that followed the GI Bill and the baby boom. (The number of university students grew from 1.5 million in 1940 to 14.8 million in 1999.)[57] Europe and Japan, however, were less successful in coping with the "massification" of university education. In Germany this failure to adapt created "unbearable studying conditions—such as lecture classes with over 1,000 students—unavailable professors, and incompetent administrators [that] caused major student strikes in 1998."[58] In Japan the government allowed the "burden of expansion to be picked up by private institutions," some of which became "virtual degree mills" of doubtful academic credentials.[59]

Foreign governments are aware of these problems. Reforms have enhanced the power of rectors and deans in Germany, but there are many obstacles to a successful transformation.[60] In Japan the government plans to make universities autonomous entities, but it is not clear that they have the required internal governance mechanisms necessary to successfully manage devolution.

FACULTY MANAGEMENT

Governance is not the only American asset. U.S. schools trade in a competitive environment. Administrators, trustees, alumni, and state governments want their schools to excel. Schools fight for faculty, students, research funds, and recognition. The labor market for faculty members is therefore liquid, with professors hired away from their positions by other universities, sometimes by the lure of much higher salaries. Even elite schools compete to keep their best professors.

Seen from an American perspective, the functioning of the academic labor market seems flawed. Scholars who disagree with the fad of the day are often sidelined even though they may be excellent, while a few others are hired to fill affirmative-action quotas. The tenure system allows some professors to enjoy a thirty-year paid holiday. In some schools teaching is perceived as a humiliating chore that is not properly rewarded. Firings of academics, even non-tenured ones, for incompetence are shockingly rare. But compared with the rest of the world, the U.S. market is very competitive. In most other countries, universities are organized like civil services, with little competition and immobile hierarchies. Foreign universities cannot bid in the academic market the way U.S. schools can when they offer premium packages to the best professors. Firing employees, professors or nonacademics, is even harder than in the United States.

In some countries, such as Germany, there is a strong egalitarian ethos which is inimical to the best and the brightest. A brilliant academic would rather be in an elite institution than be confined to an environment that wants to keep all schools equal. As a result, some first-rate German scientists have moved to the United States, prompting the German minister of education and research to plead before a gathering of Germans at Stanford in 2001 for their return home.[61] "A debate is under way" in Germany concerning the lack of differentiation of schools and other issues.[62] But it will be arduous to switch to a U.S.-style system under which some universities are prestigious and wealthy and others much less so. German universities and research centers do retain some excellent scientists, however. The "brain drain" has not sent all of the best talent to the United States.

The management of junior faculty is another difference between the United States and other countries. The American way is not a perfect system by any means. Creativity suffers when young academics are concerned less with breaking new ground than with pleasing the senior professors who make tenure decisions. The "publish or perish" ethos of research universities induces them to neglect teaching. Nevertheless, compared with other nations, the U.S. system fosters innovation and dynamism because American assistant professors pursue their research independently even as their lack of permanent employment encourages them to work hard to earn tenure. In Germany, in contrast, the habilitation requirement puts recent Ph.D.s "under the thumb of senior professors for 10 years or more," letting them emerge as independent scholars only in their early forties.[63] This long apprenticeship bordering on serfdom hinders innovation. Projects are in the works that would create junior professor positions and replace habilitation with other criteria, including publications in referred journals.[64] But even if these reforms are implemented, they will take time to have an impact.[65]

In the sciences, Japan's public universities keep junior professors under the authority of the *koza* (literally "department chairman," but in fact a senior professor). Historically the young Japanese scientist was "indentured to a professor who controls the meager funds and dictated the research program," and was little more than a "bonded servant."[66] Measures are being instituted to correct this situation. Postdoctoral fellowships have been created to give resources and autonomy to junior scholars while the *koza* system is gradually dismantled, but these reforms will not yield results immediately.[67]

Another strength of American academia's faculty management is that departments always comprise professors who obtained their degrees in different universities. In several other nations, however, prestigious establishments suffer from inbreeding, functioning in a closed-air circuit where most of the faculty are graduates of the same school and stay in place forever. For example, at Waseda, one of Japan's top universities, 66 percent of the professors are alumni.[68] Such a percentage would be unimaginably high for a U.S. university but is not unusual in Japan, where "academic inbreeding has become characteristic."[69] The custom dates to the founding of modern Japanese universities in the nineteenth century.[70] At Seoul National University (SNU), South Korea's premier institution, "professors are almost always SNU graduates."[71] In France's *grandes écoles,* teaching and admissions are frequently entrusted to alumni. In contrast, American universities are much more open to the outside world. The large number of visiting and adjunct professors, including foreigners, fosters further cross-fertilization. American academia also has its form of endogamy, with cliques of like-minded academics undermining the tenure and promotion opportunities of dissenters by hindering them from publishing their research. But the large number of quality universities and the liquid job market lessens the impact of this pathology.

Yet another strength of the American faculty is its international dimension. When a major university has an opening for a senior professorship, especially in the natural sciences, it scans the entire planet. In other nations hiring is frequently limited to locals. In some countries, such as Canada, the government discourages the recruitment of foreign professors. In nations where faculty members are civil servants, bringing in outsiders, especially as full-time tenured professors and academic administrators, can be complicated. In many countries, linguistic obstacles make it difficult to integrate faculty and students from abroad. Foreigners are also attracted by the opportunity to interact with people from many different countries in America, an experience that is difficult to replicate outside of the United States, except in Britain.[72]

STUDENT MANAGEMENT

Another advantage that American universities have is that each college or graduate program sets its own standards for admissions. The process is competitive for universities; even the top ones must make efforts to recruit the best students. Regulations to favor in-state residents in public institutions and affirmative action for the children of alumni, benefactors, and some minorities constrict the freedom of action of admissions officers. Nevertheless, each university can, to a considerable extent, allocate available slots according to its own needs. Overseas, there are frequently no means to regulate the influx of students. In Germany, with the exception of a few fields such as medicine, gymnasium graduates who passed the *Abitur*—terminal examination, analogous to the French *baccalauréat*—are free to attend any university. "As a result individual universities have had little control over their total size or the size and balance of their departments."[73] In France most universities, in contrast to the *grandes écoles,* are open to anyone with a baccalauréat. In other countries, such as Japan and South Korea, entrance examinations test a narrow set of skills and memorization that require rote learning, whereas American students are judged on a broad set of criteria. To be fair, the East Asian approach forces minimum standards of literacy and numeracy often lacking in America. Moreover, some Japanese universities are now using more imaginative and diverse methods of selecting candidates for admission.

Once students are admitted, the American system provides them with much flexibility. They can transfer fairly easily from one school to another. The foreign-educated can easily adapt and excel in American universities. In many other countries, switching between universities or arriving from abroad is far more difficult if not impossible. At community colleges, Americans can earn a two-year degree or move on to a B.A. program, whereas in many other nations non–university track post–high school programs cut off participants from the possibility of a university education later on. Opportunities for part-time study for those already in the American workforce are numerous. Moreover, high school graduates can work for several years and enter college well into their mid-twenties. It is not rare for Americans in their late thirties or forties, or even older ones, to be enrolled in graduate programs. In other nations, however, it is more difficult to reenter the educational system after several years in the workforce. This flexibility in the American system is due not only to institutional differences but also to the fact that Americans see very clearly the link between education and better employment opportunities; they are inclined to attend a university and even to borrow if needed to get a degree. Thus they demand the option to get an education part-time or at night after their workday and at any age.

One weakness of American students that affects universities, however, is the abysmal quality of some public American high schools, though Catholic and private establishments are generally better. Colleges offer remedial courses that would shock professors in other nations. The performance of American primary education in math and science is good, though below that of East Asia, but by the end of secondary school American students are among the lowest scorers on standardized tests. According to a 1995 survey of twelfth-graders, U.S. students were 4 percent below the international average in science and 8 percent lower in math. Even America's most advanced science and math high school pupils rank below the best of other countries.[74]

Statistics may be skewed because most Americans attend high school, whereas in other countries only college-bound students do. (Only 29 percent of German children are enrolled in gymnasium.)[75] Obviously, if American high school education were universally bad, it would be impossible for the United States to have such good universities. But the numbers from international comparisons are nevertheless disturbing. International surveys of reading proficiency and math and science literacy in the developed world conducted by the Organization for Economic Cooperation and Development (OECD) in 2000 of fifteen-year-olds show that American students are at about the average, not a particularly impressive achievement for Americans given that several OECD countries are considerably less rich than the United States.[76] The high proportion of immigrants in math and science is a testimony to the openness of American society but also a reflection of the failure of American primary and secondary schools to instill a knowledge of and interest in mathematics and the physical sciences. When professors in ten countries were asked whether their undergraduates were "adequately prepared in mathematics and quantitative reasoning skills," the United States was at the bottom, with 64 percent of respondents answering in the negative.[77]

DIVERSITY OF ORGANIZATION

One characteristic of American education is its great diversity of institutional arrangements. This facilitates breaking new ground and innovation, in contrast to countries where all institutions of higher education are similarly organized and managed. Some U.S. universities and colleges are secular private organizations, while others fall

under the aegis of one of the fifty states. Many trace their roots to
Protestant churches, though most schools in that category are now
secular. More than two hundred institutions are Catholic in origin
and tradition, including such major establishments of higher learning as Boston College, Fordham, Georgetown, and Notre Dame.[78]
Brandeis University in Boston and Yeshiva University in New York
are the only important Jewish-sponsored universities outside of Israel. The Department of Defense has a large network of undergraduate and graduate schools that, in effect, educate civilians as well
because many officers resign or retire early in their careers to join
the private sector. At the same time, the U.S. system is sufficiently
homogenous for faculty and students to move easily from one school
to another, thus creating an enormous single educational market unmatched anywhere in the world.

Diversity in funding sources also differentiates the United States
from Europe. In the United States about one-third of higher-
education students are in private schools and about half of the funding originates from the private sector.[79] In Europe the state dominates higher education.[80] There the vast majority of students are in
public institutions, where tuition is paid by the government. In Japan more than three-quarters of college students are in private colleges, but except for a few elite schools, such as Keio, Sophia, and
Waseda, private establishments are for those who fail to gain entrance in the more selective public universities.[81] When the higher
education framework was designed in the Meiji era, the authorities
discouraged private institutions.[82] To this day, formal and informal
regulations make Japanese private universities more state-
dependent than their American counterparts. Moreover, not having
substantial endowments, most of them are unable to invest in expensive facilities on their own.[83]

Thus the United States is unique in having rich and prestigious
private universities largely free of government control operating
alongside autonomous public schools, some of which—for example,
the flagship universities within the California, Indiana, Michigan,
North Carolina, Ohio, Texas, Virginia, and Wisconsin systems—are
first-rate. Europe is developing greater diversity, thanks to the rapid
increase in transnational European exchange programs, but such remaining limits on cross-border movement as costs, segmented labor
markets, and language will make it impossible, at least for the next
two or three decades, to establish a single educational space.

FUNDING

During World War II and the Cold War, the U.S. government invested huge resources in higher education, which made the United States the first country where going to college became a mass phenomenon rather than an upper-class privilege. Although other countries later followed the same path, the United States led the way. Americans continue to spend more on higher education than citizens of any other country in the OECD, and U.S. education spending (public and private) is one of the highest as a percentage of GDP.[84]

Moreover, the top American universities are at a great advantage thanks to financial assets that provide them with large resources and partially free them from depending on the government. The five largest endowments range from Harvard's $17.2 billion to Stanford's $7.6 billion (though they fluctuate with the stock market). Small elite liberal arts colleges are also rich relative to the size of their student bodies. (Amherst's and Williams's endowments are about $500,000 per student; Harvard's endowment is about $900,000 per degree candidate, but the figures are not comparable due to dissimilar cost structures.)[85] Gifts are continually added to the asset base. Higher education collected a total of about $24 billion in private contributions in the 2000–2001 academic year and again in 2001–2.[86] Some recent donations show the extent of the commitment of individuals and organizations: $400 million pledged in 2001 by the William and Flora Hewlett Foundation to Stanford University, $600 million pledged to the California Institute of Technology by Intel cofounder Gordon Moore and his wife, and $150 million bequeathed in 2002 by a 101-year-old man to New York University.[87] Eleven universities collected more than a billion dollars in multiyear fund-raising campaigns in the 1990s (admittedly, an exceptionally good decade).[88]

The institutional framework of American education partly explains this wealth. Requirements for money are great: private schools need to raise funds to remain competitive, and a public university must widen its resource base beyond the state's coffers. The ability to raise money arises from the American philanthropic tradition. For various historical and religious reasons, as well as tax-code encouragement, Americans feel a greater sense of duty to participate in philanthropy than do citizens of other wealthy nations. Moreover, giving is one of the most important ways in which Americans and their families can establish their social credentials. Having an endowed chair or university library named after him or her is for the successful American entrepreneur the equivalent of receiving a peerage from the queen for a Briton. As a result, charitable giving provides about 50 percent of funding for the American cultural/ recreational sector, compared with 5–13 percent in other major developed nations; and the share of GDP going to such philanthropy is three to fifteens times as large in this country as in other rich nations.[89]

American foundations illustrate the strength of American philanthropy. The assets of the wealthiest ten charitable foundations range from the Bill and Melinda Gates Foundation's $32.8 billion to the Pew Charitable Trust's $4.4 billion. Together these ten institutions gave away $4.5 billion in 2001.[90] By comparison, the total assets of Japanese foundations as of 31 March 2001 were at about the same level as those of America's second-largest foundation alone.[91] American charities give to numerous causes, but many support colleges, universities, and academic researchers. In the 2000–2001 academic year, foundations gave $6 billion to higher education.[92] Charitable contributions to museums, which are equally impressive— New York's Metropolitan Museum of Art raised $450 million in 1994–2000—also serve universities by providing art historians with the cultural institutions they need.[93] Music programs gain from donations to orchestras, zoology departments benefit from philanthropy that goes to zoos, and other academic departments are the indirect beneficiaries of gifts that do not directly go to them.

Another aspect of American universities' funding is that in the United States, unlike Europe, students who can afford it pay for their studies. This situation, though it creates unfair situations when colleges cannot provide scholarship to needy students, gives students—and their parents—a feeling that they are fee-paying customers who can demand good service from their schools. In Europe, however, since education is generally free, students do not have the same sense of ownership, and thus are less likely to be as demanding as American students.

Foreign universities can, of course, rely on public funds. But American schools' diverse sources of finance give them more freedom to innovate and escape uniform government regulations. Private money has the additional advantage of allowing elite universities to gather enormous resources, something that is difficult in foreign state-funded systems that are more egalitarian. Moreover, by engaging in fund raising, universities develop ties with corporations and businesses, a process that integrates academia with the rest of the economy.

RESEARCH FOCUS

In the United States and Europe many universities perform basic research, though in several European countries it is often done in conjunction with nonuniversity public institutions (the Max Planck Institute in Germany, for example, or the Centre National de la Recherche Scientifique in France). In Japan, however, universities have historically not been research oriented. In the late nineteenth century, pressed to build a modern state and a strong army, the government ordered the newly chartered universities to train a cadre of managers and serve the state rather than produce great scholars.[94] The Imperial Rescript on Education of 1890 further ensured that Japanese education would not infuse a spirit of experimentation and original thought. Japan has changed since the Meiji period, but aspects of the original system survived. Some of the research tasks that are carried out by universities in the West are undertaken by private-sector businesses in Japan. But the universities' deficiencies in basic research undermine their international competitiveness.

Demography

Not all of the advantages of American colleges and universities accrue because of institutional differences from other countries' systems. One of the major assets of U.S. schools is the scope of their internal market.

The college-age population of America is more than twice that of Japan and more than three times that of the German-speaking world.[95] The English language further expands the scope of the market since so many foreigners know it. The setting in which American academia operates is therefore much bigger than that in other societies. India and China have more young people, but poverty limits the resources they can devote to education, though they do have a few outstanding colleges whose graduates are found in large numbers in America's best doctoral institutions.

The United States supports a large number of universities and colleges: 1,643 public institutions of higher learning, 1,681 nonprofit private ones, and 617 for-profit ones, including 261 doctorate-granting institutions.[96] The United States has 13 million higher-education students compared with 4 million in Japan and 2 million each in Germany and France.[97]

The United States is consequently the "largest market for new academic 'products' of all kinds."[98] The European market as a whole is comparable, but it is fragmented along language and national lines.

This quantitative advantage generates a qualitative edge for the United States. The pool of potential students and faculty is larger. Specialized institutions or departments that cater to a small fraction of the student body can survive, since even a low percentage of the U.S. market is large in absolute terms. Moreover, many first-rate universities can coexist in America, whereas in smaller countries monopolies or oligopolies arise due to their inability to sustain more than a few players. The size of the U.S. education industry (and the even larger English-speaking one) makes it less likely that a few textbooks will dominate a discipline. The economic base upon which U.S. education is built is also much bigger than that of other countries, as U.S. national income stands at $10.8 trillion, with more than $3 trillion generated in other English-speaking nations. This compares to Japan's $4.2 trillion and well under $3 trillion for German-speaking Europe. The American higher-education industry alone is as large as Austria's GDP.[99]

The American population of young adults is growing, constantly widening this demographic gap. By 2025 there will be nearly 3 million more twenty- to twenty-four-year-olds in the United States than in 2000, but almost 550,000 fewer in Germany and an incredible 2.5 million fewer in Japan.[100] In addition, as more people learn English, the recruitment pool for students and faculty further increases.

English

English is the lingua franca for original research papers in the sciences, and increasingly for economics; it is one of the working languages of nearly all international academic congresses (and often the only one). The humanities and some of the social sciences remain multilingual, but even in those fields those who do not know English are marginalized. This has some negative consequences for Americans. Under little pressure to learn a foreign language, too many American academics and students lack fluency in a single one, let alone two or three. But the growing dominance of English has, on balance, helped the Anglophone nations. Recruiting of foreign faculty and students is facilitated. Americans, Britons, and other native speakers of English find it easier to write and read articles in English and to speak in symposia. American and British academics also benefit from the presence of most of the top academic journals in the English-speaking United States or the United Kingdom. All this increases the visibility of Anglophone scholars and helps their careers. A few schools and some national university systems outside of the English-speaking world now use English as a medium of instruction, but these programs are limited and are not without problems, such as a lack of instructors with good English skills and students who have difficulty understanding.

Although English first gained its international role thanks to the British Empire, American wealth and power have done much to contribute to the primacy of the language.[101] And as English-language dominance increases, so do the returns from knowing the language; equally important, the cost of not knowing English has risen to such levels that in many disciplines, not only scientific ones but also in the social sciences and humanities, it is now impossible to conduct research without at least the ability to read in English.

The Future of U.S. University Primacy

America's advantage in higher education has been increasing and will not be challenged by other nations for many decades. It is possible that U.S. universities could decay, but if that happens it is likely to be a slow process and will not, at least for a long time, imperil the U.S. claim to primacy in higher education. Foreign competitors are slowed by the fact that a great university takes decades to be established. To do so requires not only money but also institutional arrangements to attract good students and teachers and dismiss bad ones, management structures to run the university efficiently, effective funding mechanisms, and a host of policies and procedures to ensure excellence. Even in a society as fast-moving as America's, rankings move slowly. Some schools have improved and others have declined, but, of the top ten universities in America, most were already preeminent fifty years ago and all are at least one century old. In the original thirteen states, some of the best colleges, such as Harvard, Yale, and Columbia, date from the colonial era.

Japan and Europe could challenge the United States' preeminence in higher education. They have the money, cultural resources, and the educated population that are required for such an endeavor. They already have some excellent universities. To successfully challenge American leadership, however, they would need to implement dramatic reforms that would be opposed by many vested interests, including powerful education ministries, academic administrators, unions representing faculties and administrative staff, and students and their parents. To revitalize their university systems, these countries would need to set up new institutions free from the rules and regulations of the current systems. In any case, success is unlikely to be rapid in this field.

The U.S. lead in higher education should therefore continue well into the twenty-first century. The dramatic reversal in the balance of university and research power between the United States and Europe in the twentieth century had several causes. First, the U.S. population and GDP grew at a much higher rate than Europe's. The United States could consequently devote ever-greater resources to education compared with other nations. Second, wars and dictatorships eviscerated the German cultural sphere. Third, the United States benefited from the enormous investment of the federal government in university education for defense-related research during World War II and the Cold War and from the GI Bill, which gave millions of Americans the opportunity to attend college. Fourth, the United States developed institutions that were more effective in managing universities and nurturing excellence. Fifth, the openness of the United States to the outside world and the dominant position of the English language have given American education a global reach unmatched anywhere else. Sixth, American universities benefit from the effects of path dependence and increasing returns. The more that U.S. universities dominate academia the more costly it becomes not to be familiar with research carried out in the United States, and thus the more overseas students and scholars seek to come to the United States, further enhancing the U.S. position as the center of academic work in the world.

American universities reflect U.S. power and institutional advantages, but do they accentuate American power? In some ways they obviously do. They provide the United States with well-trained scientists and engineers who are the backbone of American high technology. Not only do universities train scientists, they also educate managers, accountants, lawyers, and the other professionals. This "soft power" of universities contributes to American "hard power." It is, however, difficult to quantify the economic loss for

Europe and Japan that results from having university systems that are not as good as the United States'. Much of the research performed in the United States is disseminated overseas, so foreign nations benefit from the output of American-based scholars. Other countries also use corporations and nonuniversity research facilities to undertake some of the training that is performed in universities in America. Foreign states can also compensate by sending students to the United States. Moreover, despite their shortcomings, European and East Asian universities are not cultural deserts: they do educate millions of students and train outstanding researchers. The advantage that accrues to the United States from its lead in universities is significant but probably not as dramatic as the gaps between American and foreign universities would make it appear. Still, universities constitute an important component of America's international prestige. They highlight to the world's elite U.S. achievements and, thanks to their internationalism, demonstrate to non-Americans the rewards of the American empire.

Besides its service to the U.S. economy, American academia is an international public good, acting as the world's university. It provides students and scholars from all over the world the opportunity to work in the best colleges and universities and to interact with other researchers from every country on the planet. The influence the U.S. academic system wields on global intellectual developments lowers transaction costs by making it easier for professionals in the worlds of business, medicine, law, academia, and government to communicate. Around the world, officials, business executives, academics, journalists, and others are linked to one another through U.S. "software," having studied in the United States or read American publications as part of their education. In business, American MBA programs have graduated a significant percentage of the international business managerial classes. American public policy schools (for example, the Kennedy School at Harvard and the Woodrow Wilson School at Princeton) and economics departments have trained many foreign officials. Graduate-level military schools (war colleges and the National Defense University, for example) have educated numerous foreign officers who have gone on to become generals and admirals in their home countries. Thus the United States, thanks to its universities, provides part of the world's elite with its lingua franca.

American academic primacy, however, does not prevent international disputes. Studying in America does not necessarily convert students to economic Liberalism, political pluralism, and support for American policies. Moreover, the increasing "Americanization" of the world's elite is a relative phenomenon. A growing number of individuals have been educated in America or been influenced by U.S. ideas. But even after several years' education in the United States, most foreign students retain their idiosyncrasies, and many remain, at least partly, unfamiliar with American values. In some cases, studying in the United States fosters hostility on the part of those who react with jealousy and anger at the United States' success. Some foreign students return home to work for hostile governments. But still these nefarious consequences can easily be kept under control as long as American unipolarity and military hegemony are maintained. On the whole, American universities make international dialogue easier. In business, science, and diplomacy, the world's decision makers and officials work better together because they share the same U.S. experience. This phenomenon has been useful for America as the U.S. empire has expanded from its homogeneous World War II English-speaking core of the United States, Britain, Canada, Australia, and New Zealand to include more than twenty European and a few Asian states. The "U.S. software" also helps the United States in dealings with countries outside of its empire whose elites are U.S.-educated.

As the provider of this international public good, the United States has obligations that go beyond its narrow national interest. Other nations would find it difficult to accept American academic primacy were the United States to restrict access to its universities to Americans or exclude foreigners from its research centers and laboratories. America therefore has to maintain the international openness of its educational enterprise.

7 The Science Gap

Many industries, such as computers, aerospace, motor transportation, oil and gas, chemicals, pharmaceuticals, and telecommunications, rely on scientific advances, as do defense contractors. Thus a prosperous economy and a powerful military require strong science.

The United States, which accounts for two-thirds of Nobel Prizes awarded and almost half of OECD-area research-and-development spending, is the world's number one scientific power. This reflects the wealth of the United States and the quality of its universities. In turn, American science makes it possible for the United States to lead in most technologies, strengthening the U.S. economy and guaranteeing the U.S. military a technological advantage. American scientific discoveries, however, are widely disseminated overseas, and many foreigners work in American scientific establishments. Thus the American science enterprise is not only a U.S. asset but also, like universities, an international public good, especially for the nations of the American empire that are tied to the United States through economic interaction and military alliances.

Although mankind has studied science for millennia, the institutionalization of research for technological and economic progress is a recent phenomenon. The Industrial Revolution's innovations were the work of gifted men who excelled at tinkering with machinery but lacked formal scientific education. By 1900, however, a paradigm change had occurred. A thorough and methodical scientific training certified by an advanced university degree became a requirement for scientists and engineers who devised new technologies and built new industries.[1] Scientific education itself became more institutionalized. Laboratory usage was perfected in Germany, where it was integrated with teaching procedures, "making it a key part of a combined research and instructional program leading to the doctorate."[2] Due to the increased reliance on institutionalized science in industry, Germany's superior academic research and its unparalleled universities altered the industrial league tables in Europe in its favor when it overtook Britain in the years before World War I.

The role of scientific research for new developments in industry and commerce is now taken for granted. Science plays a key role in inventing new manufacturing processes and products, but the service sector is equally dependent on state-of-the-art research. Logistics, telecommunications, and many financial services would not be possible without the modern data processing made possible by the semiconductor and software industries. Medicine, which relies on the tens of billions of dollars spent annually on scientific research, is also highly dependent on scientific advances for progress. Mathematics plays an essential role in fields as different as medical magnetic imaging devices, weather forecasting, the design of new financial instruments, and cryptology.

The developed world has a quasi monopoly when it comes to scientific research. Almost all Nobel laureates in the natural sciences and economics are affiliated with institutions from the rich countries. Approximately 90 percent of the winners of other prestigious scientific prizes come from the developed nations of North America, Europe, and Japan.[3] Nearly all the leading graduate programs in the sciences are in the developed world, as are the best corporate research laboratories and scientific journals. Sophisticated private-sector research is very rare in poorer nations.

The research and development that takes place in developed countries is also more advanced, and there is much more of it. For example, data on U.S. patents for all sectors show the domination of OECD nations.[4] Similarly, scientific and technical articles in major international journals are predominantly written by authors based in North America, Europe, and the Pacific rim Liberal economies.[5]

As a result of this scientific imbalance, and of other obstacles as well, technology-intensive activities are generally located in the developed world. Thanks to the legacy of the Soviet military-research complex, Russia has an established scientific establishment. But the Russian government, which can barely raise taxes, cannot direct massive resources to research establishments on a scale comparable to the Soviet regime that exercised total control over the economy. Russia suffers from other handicaps. First, many of Russia's best scientists have emigrated to the West or to Israel. Second, the most advanced region of the Soviet Empire, Central Europe, is now within NATO, and Moscow also lost the Baltics and Ukraine. Third, even before its collapse the Soviet Union was losing the scientific race in areas that are of growing importance to the economy—for example, electronics—and failed to invest in sectors that were not relevant to military power, such as biology and medicine. China now has some first-rate research programs, but not on a scale comparable to those of the world's richest nations.

An advanced research establishment necessitates sophisticated logistical arrangements, ranging from intellectual property law to grant-making processes. The institutional gaps that undermine the economic performance of the third world (as we saw in Chapters 1 and 4) thus hinder the development of its scientific base. Moreover, a strong scientific infrastructure requires a rich economy to thrive. The dominance that first-world nations enjoy in science and technology will therefore remain strong in the decades to come. The Soviet Union demonstrated that totalitarianism could partly compensate for poverty if the regime decided to invest massively in science. But even a totalitarian state would require a long time to develop a strong scientific base, and the Soviet experience showed that it could maintain a first-rate scientific cadre only in a few areas related to military research. The autocratic centralized nature of totalitarian states allows them to focus on a few specific areas but makes it impossible to develop a broad-based science and technology base.

Given the handicaps of the third world, the world at large looks to the developed nations—primarily in Europe, North America, and the rich countries of the Pacific rim—for scientific achievements. By the second half of the nineteenth century, the United States was already ahead of Europe in many process technologies, such as small-arms manufacturing, and by the 1880s the United States was the largest and most efficient steel producer, though "most of the key discoveries and inventions bearing on steel production were made in Europe."[6] The United States was thus strong in applying science to manufacturing and industrial engineering but lagged behind Europe in basic research. At the start of the twentieth century, most of the world's greatest scientists were still in Europe. As of 1920 only three researchers based in the United States had ever been awarded Nobel Prizes in science or medicine.[7] American industry had the advantage of a strong cadre of technicians and engineers, but not until the massive inflows of European scientists fleeing Hitler and World War II did the United States reach the pinnacle of science.

American scientific preeminence is undeniable. Bibliometrics indicate that American institutions lead the field in most disciplines, both in numbers of articles published and in impact factor. In science and engineering, as we observed in the section on universities, American scientific articles enjoy a high degree of relative prominence (1.35, compared with 0.98 for Western Europe), and the United States is also by far the largest source of published papers in scientific journals.[8] Besides writing many articles, researchers from the United States lead in most scientific prizes. Foreign scholars study in the United States because that is where they can undertake pathbreaking research. An illustration of the reputation of American science is that "some German researchers jokingly add 'iAg'—in Amerika gewesen (been in America)—to their abbreviated titles" to enhance their credentials.[9]

Another way to measure scientific achievements is to analyze patenting activity. Patents generally require scientific research and are frequently the intellectual-property building blocks of high technology products or services. The American share of patents registered in the United States has grown slightly, after bottoming out around 1990, and stands at more than 50 percent.[10] The United States accounts for 42 percent of the patents filed with the World Intellectual Property Organization, well ahead of Germany's 13 percent and Japan's 10 percent.[11]

In the pharmaceutical sector, an industry that lives on scientific discoveries, the United States is the world leader. The modern pharmaceutical industry originated in Europe, especially in Germany and Switzerland.[12] But today the United States leads in pharmaceutical research and discoveries. The United States also holds a preeminent position in math.[13] This is demonstrated by the many foreign-educated holders of bachelor's degrees who move to the United States for graduate math education.[14] Nevertheless, it should be added that the American position in math is not as strong as in other disciplines and that it could decline in the future.

The United States scientific enterprise is backed by massive financial resources. During the Second World War, the United States invested heavily in military-related research. The Manhattan Project to develop an atomic bomb was the most famous, and costly, of these programs, but by no means the only one. Since 1945 government funding has continued, though scientists would like even more generous government support.[15] In the 1990s the United States accounted for about 45 percent of OECD-area spending on research and development, and since 1982 the U.S. share relative to the other G7 nations—Canada, France, Germany, Italy, Japan, and the United Kingdom—has been relatively stable.[16] Thus almost half of the rich world's research and development takes place in the United States; second-ranked Japan accounts for only about 20 percent of OECD research expenditure. Although Japan spends a higher proportion of GDP on research and development (3.01 percent) than does the United States (2.63 percent), the United States devotes a greater share of national income to this purpose than its main European partners (from 1.04 percent for Italy to 2.38 percent for Germany).[17] In sum, the United States spends as much on research and development as Japan, Canada, the United Kingdom, Germany, France, and Italy combined.[18]

What accounts for America's leadership in science? The wealth of the United States obviously plays an important role. Good science is expensive, and U.S. national income is by far the world's largest. The scale of the U.S. market further ensures a large pool of customers and suppliers for the commercialized output of scientific research. The United States accounts for 50–70 percent of the global market for many high-technology products and sets the standards for the rest of the world.[19] The U.S. scientific enterprise enjoys other advantages. First, it has more world-class universities than any other country. Second, the large number of actors in every field ensures a diversity of sources of funding and a competitive environment for researchers. Third, the openness of the United States to outsiders has brought tens of thousands of highly skilled foreign scientists and engineers.

The European Union has an economy the size of the United States' but is still not a fully integrated economic area. Government-funded research and development there frequently suffers from duplication, or triplication, among fifteen separate nation-states (twenty-five starting in 2004). Factors detailed in other chapters, especially differences in university performance, play a role in explaining America's lead in science. Moreover, the greater difficulties in creating a business and the lack of solid university-business ties limit the ability of scientists to commercialize discoveries. This in turn may deprive European scientists of the economic incentive to innovate that their American counterparts enjoy.

Japan is by far the world's second-largest economy, and the Japanese economy and population are much larger than those of any European state, but bibliometric surveys and comparisons of laureates in scientific prizes put Japan roughly at the same level as the big European countries. This can be attributed to Japan's having "never built up a publicly funded R&D infrastructure comparable to" the American and European ones, as well as to the lack of research focus of its universities.[20] Moreover, research in Japan has been much less reliant than that in the United States on competitive merit-reviewed funding.[21] Funding in Japan had historically been granted regardless of achievement, a process that hurt the quality of research.[22] In the past few years Japan has made efforts to strengthen its scientific capabilities, but it is still weaker in that regard than a country with an economy of more than $4 trillion, 127 million well-educated citizens, and some of the world's best performing industrial giants might be.

Nothing is more international than science. Many discoveries today cannot be claimed by a single country; research may have been conducted in laboratories in several different nations by scientists from an even larger number of countries. But some countries contribute more than others to this global enterprise, and no nation makes a greater contribution than the United States. The preeminence of American scientific research is a reflection of American wealth and power but also contributes to it. One reason the United States is the only superpower on the planet is that it has the world's most powerful science base. Scientific power directly upholds American military might by providing the Pentagon and its suppliers with the advanced weaponry that modern militaries require. Scientific excellence also serves the American economy, giving American businesses access to new technologies. Less tangibly, American science contributes to the prestige of the United States because U.S. scientists and laboratories are held in high esteem throughout the world.

Nevertheless, as in the case of the "university gap," we should realize that the "science gap" does not relegate Europe and Japan to second-class status. Scientific discoveries made in America are exploited by businesses in Europe and Japan through several mechanisms. First, foreign corporations can set up American research facilities to tap into U.S. scientific capabilities. Second, overseas investors can acquire U.S. technology companies. Third, American patents and technology can be bought or licensed by foreign corporations. Fourth, overseas students and researchers working in American laboratories can take advantage of the country's research facilities. A strong science base is an asset to the United States, but it does not automatically ensure a wide gap in economic performance between America and the rest of the developed world. Japan, despite its relative paucity of scientific achievements, has some of the world's leading electronics and automotive firms. Japan's economic problems have many roots, but weak science is not among them. Europe may not be the equal of America in science, but is a major player in aerospace, from launching satellites to building commercial airliners. Italy, which plays a minor role in scientific research, has some of the most competitive small and medium-sized industrial firms in the world. But given the importance of military power for the United States' role in the world, a superior science base is essential because it is not possible to maintain a position of technological dominance in military affairs without conducting a vast amount of research and development in the United States itself. Consequently, in order to remain the world's only superpower, the United States requires an indigenous scientific capability that is second to none. Retaining it requires sustained funding and effective—as opposed to sclerotic—organizations. It may be that, as some have argued, government support for scientific research should be significantly increased to allow the United States to retain its position.[23]

But besides making America strong, American scientific excellence is an international public good, especially for the nations of the American empire that enjoy close ties with America's scientific establishment. This is illustrated by the research and development undertaken across national borders. About $37 billion of research and development is performed either by American firms overseas or by foreign corporations in the United States.[24] Science as an international public good is not a uniquely American phenomenon. Although the United States is the science leader, there are numerous outstanding laboratories and researchers overseas. Thanks to the international regime maintained by the American empire, Americans can benefit from the research of these foreign scientists. Thus American science helps foster progress throughout the world, while non-U.S. research contributes to the welfare of the American economy as well.

It could be argued that the openness of American science undermines the United States. Unfriendly nations use American science to develop military projects aimed at thwarting American power. American scientific discoveries are also used to strengthen the economies of unfriendly nations. But on balance, the international dimension of American science strengthens American goals. It is particularly important for the United States because, due to the relative lack of interest on the part of American youngsters in science, America relies on a large influx of foreign-born students and researchers to maintain its scientific primacy.[25] Restrictions that make it harder for foreign scientists to visit the United States and work in America are therefore particularly detrimental to U.S. interests. Moreover, U.S. science serves to make other countries rich, thus helping the United States through trade and investment with these nations. The openness of American science also shows that the U.S. imperial framework is open to anyone who wants to participate in it, rather than a closed system that is hostile to outsiders. American science brings individuals from all over the world to the United States or puts them in contact with the nation's scientific and intellectual achievements. Because the overwhelming superiority of the U.S. armed forces deters challengers to the American empire, the fact that some unfriendly countries get a small fraction of the benefits of the American scientific enterprise system is not a threat to American primacy, especially compared with the vital role of American science in serving the needs of its allies.

8 The Media and Mass Culture Gaps

American hegemony manifests itself not only in the military and economic arenas but also in the field of news media and mass culture. In both cases the worldwide role of American news outlets and popular culture does not necessarily increase American power, but it reflects breadth of American preeminence, which extends from the military field to mass culture.

Media Gap

For several decades American publications and broadcast have attracted a large foreign audience. The *International Herald Tribune, Newsweek,* and *Time* all have large foreign readership. In the world of business, *Business Week, Forbes,* and *Fortune* are widely sold outside the United States. The *Wall Street Journal* has dedicated European and Asian editions. *Le Monde,* France's leading newspaper, regularly includes some articles, in English, from the *New York Times.* English-language newspapers published in foreign countries, such as the *Japan Times,* the *Korea Herald,* and the *Nation* (Thailand's English daily newspaper), carry opinion pieces from American columnists. In electronic media as well, the reach of U.S. conglomerates is considerable. Not everyone tunes in to CNN, but the network Ted Turner founded is watched overseas, especially by individuals whose professions in government and business call for keeping abreast of breaking news. Besides television, American electronic media are also present worldwide through American Internet sites.

American dominance, however, is not total by any means. The *Financial Times,* published in London, is one of the world's most influential dailies and a must read for many executives. The *Economist,* also published in London, is the world's premier newsweekly. No public broadcaster enjoys the brand-name recognition and reputation of the British Broadcasting Corporation's World Service. But overall, the global reach of American journalism, ranging from daily newspapers to quarterly publications, is greater than that of any other country's media industry.

The export of American media is not limited to English-language material. *National Geographic,* for example, is available in Chinese, French, German, Greek, Hebrew, Italian, Korean, Polish, Portuguese, and Spanish editions, with more than two million copies sold outside the United States. *Reader's Digest* has editions in more than thirty different countries. *Business Week* provides articles to the French newsweekly *Le Point* and has a Chinese-language edition. *Newsweek* is issued in Arabic, Japanese, Korean, Polish, Russian, and Spanish. *Aviation Week and Space Technology* has a Chinese-language partnership. The *Miami Herald* has a Spanish-language edition (for Latin Americans as well as Spanish-speaking U.S. citizens), and *Wall Street Journal Americas* is published in Spanish and Portuguese as a separate section of local Latin American newspapers. Chinese readers can find stories in their language on the *Asian Wall Street Journal* web site. *Foreign Affairs* recently started a Spanish-language edition. CNN also has a Spanish-language division and Internet sites in various languages, including German, Italian, and Japanese. Bloomberg TV provides international viewers with programs in several languages besides English. The penetration of U.S. journalism is particularly striking in Japan, the world's second-largest economy. *Forbes, Foreign Affairs, Fortune,* the *Harvard Business Review, National Geographic, Newsweek, Time,* and *Scientific American* are available in the Japanese language. Those who do not understand English can watch many CNN programs live with a Japanese-language voice-over or can tune in to Bloomberg TV in their own language. They can also enjoy some broadcasts from the Discovery Channel and the Golf Channel in Japanese or with Japanese subtitles. Japanese citizens therefore have access to a wide section of the American media without needing to know English.

The diffusion of American media also extends to book publishing. As we observed in the chapter on universities, U.S. academic publications enjoy a global following. But nonacademic books, on business and management, for example, are translated into numerous languages and widely disseminated overseas. A survey of the

"What the world is reading" section in the *Economist* indicates that most best-seller lists abroad include one or two American authors.

As U.S. media have expanded overseas, they have adapted to local conditions. Editors adjust to regional tastes, and broadcasters hire news anchors with accents and looks that blend better in the target market. Thus the product that is read or heard abroad is partly or even mostly indigenized, but its contents still rely at least to some extent on what is written or produced in the United States. The United States is unique in projecting its media output in so many foreign idioms. No other country has been able to generate enough demand for its journalism to justify the translation of so much of its production into other languages in addition to a large export of native-language material. And non-English-speaking nations' output in their local idioms is limited since few people outside their home regions (or former colonies) know their language. For example, the international circulation of the *Frankfurter Allgemeine Zeitung,* one of Europe's leading quality daily newspapers, is a quarter of the sales of the *Wall Street Journal Europe,* and most readers of the paper outside Germany are probably Austrian or Swiss, or German expatriates.[1]

Besides these private-sector ventures, the United States government supports several networks that broadcast abroad, including Radio Free Europe/Radio Liberty, Radio Free Asia, Radio Martí, and the Voice of America. These broadcasters transmit their messages in more than fifty languages and reach audiences of millions abroad through radio waves or audio webcasts. The United States, however, is not unique in devoting resources to government-funded international broadcasting. And since these broadcasts are freed from the discipline of the marketplace, it is far more difficult to judge the demand that exists for them.

The National Archives is an interesting example of the success of American media broadly defined. Its collections are mined by foreign scholars researching their own nations, because the United States declassifies documents more rapidly and thoroughly than do other governments, and the extent of American diplomatic activity ensures that data on almost every country can be found in U.S. archives. For example, Japanese researchers investigating their country's defense policy rely on American documents because the Japanese authorities are more restrictive in releasing files to the public.

Why is the international reach of American media so extensive? English is one obvious reason. By a wide margin, no foreign language is more studied. Technology has also played a role. Modern telecommunications allow American newspapers to be printed simultaneously in several facilities in Asia and Europe, making same-day delivery possible in most markets. Satellite and cable systems enable television signals to reach many more homes and businesses than before. The Internet further facilitates the penetration of foreign markets, as anyone with a connection can read a U.S. newspaper or listen to American radio broadcasts. Broadband connections allow some U.S. television programs to be watched overseas from a computer screen (though this is still a developing technology).

But language and technology do not by themselves explain American media's ability to reach foreign audiences. Many other countries have English-language media. Technology enables every outlet, not only American ones, to gain international exposure. But thanks to the unique role the United States plays in world affairs— be it in business, finance, war, or entertainment—American journalists have an enormous edge in competing for readers and viewers. Consumers of news are interested in what is happening in the United States, whether on Wall Street, in the White House, at the Pentagon, or in Hollywood. This induces them to read American newspapers or magazines or tune in to U.S. television.

Foreign leaders know that by talking to the American media they can achieve two goals. First, they can influence the American public and through it the U.S. government. Second, they can reach a wide international audience. Thus presidents and foreign ministers sometimes issue their most important statements to American journalists and are eager to be interviewed by them. This in turn gives American journalists better access to decision makers. (The *Financial Times*, which is for finance ministers, central bankers, and some corporate chiefs the vehicle of choice to circulate their views, is the only non-U.S.-based media institution that enjoys the same status.) This phenomenon has a reinforcing effect. The more American outlets become the newspapers and networks of choice for the world, the more leaders will grant them interviews, thus increasing the numbers of readers and viewers who rely on them.

Moreover, American journalism benefits from economies of scale. The large scale of the U.S. market makes it possible to generate revenue streams that publishers and broadcasters cannot achieve in smaller countries. An additional one hundred million native English speakers in the rich world outside of the United States allow for large foreign sales without the need for translation.

Mass Culture

U.S. popular culture is everywhere—films, music, clothing, food, and sports icons. From Hollywood to McDonald's, mass culture is mostly American-made. Japan's cultural exports are also prominent. With its video game consoles, Pokémon, Yugiyo manga, animation movies (anime), sushi, and karaoke, Japan is the only country to have emerged as a global mass-culture producer in the past decades—a remarkable feat for a nation as culturally isolated as Japan. But Japan's foray into international popular culture remains limited to a few items. Japanese anime has a worldwide following, but Japanese actors, singers, or sports figures do not have global fame, though Japanese pop culture enjoys a vibrant following in Northeast Asia, and baseball player Ichiro Suzuki has many fans in the United States. Latin American soap operas have also successfully penetrated foreign markets, but these are the only cultural exports from the region. Outside the United States, only Britain— thanks in part to sharing a common language and heritage with its former colony—produces world-renowned stars, including actors, singers, athletes, and the Windsors.

The strength of U.S. mass culture increased during the twentieth century. The movie industry originated in Europe; "throughout the first decade of the 20th century French film production led the world, and Charles Pathé created the first international film empire."[2] A few decades ago, most of the most renowned filmmakers were from outside the United States: Bergman, Chaplin, De Sica, Eisenstein, Fellini, Godard, Hitchcock, Kurosawa, Lang (who fled Nazi Germany to the United States), Renoir (who also moved to America during the war), Rossellini, Truffaut, and Visconti, among many others. Today the number of non-Hollywood directors who succeed outside of their domestic market has dwindled, though some non-U.S. filmmakers have managed to gain a global reputation. Most world-famous actors who are not American are those (of whom there are many) who work in America. American productions have almost all the top slots in the charts of the top-grossing films in the world.[3] In popular music as well American singers have been very successful exports. Tens of millions of Michael Jackson albums sold overseas.[4] Until recently, with few exceptions—Jesse Owens, for example, after his performance at the Berlin Olympics in 1936, and later the boxers Joe Lewis and Muhammad Ali—American sportsmen were rarely internationally recognized. Today several American basketball players enjoy enormous name recognition overseas. The international success of such companies as McDonald's, the Gap, or Nike is another phenomenon that has developed only in the past decades.

Tourism might also be considered a form of mass culture, although it depends on what the goals of the trip are. With the exception of Canadians, forty years ago only those of considerable means could afford an American holiday. Today millions travel to the United States. In 1975 there were 746,000 visitors from Japan; in 1999 there were more than 4.8 million. For Germany the figures were just under 300,000 in 1975 and almost 2 million in 1999. French tourists numbered fewer than 160,000 in 1975, but more than 1 million in 1999.[5] An interesting aspect of U.S.-bound tourism is the rapid growth in the number of teenagers from overseas who attend summer camps in the United States.[6] International tourism, it should, however, be noted, has increased throughout the world. More travelers come to the United States, but the numbers of those visiting other destinations have also increased dramatically.

Why is American popular culture so successful? Being the world's richest nation, growing demographically, and speaking English have done much to help the United States disseminate its mass culture. Many smaller nations lack the economic base necessary to maintain a strong mass-culture industry, thus they find it more effective to import American productions. The image overseas of the United States as a place of boundless opportunities has also contributed to the appeal of American mass culture. Even the less desirable aspects of the United States, such as its high crime rate and violent streets, generate an appeal to youngsters that more orderly societies lack.

Moreover, the U.S. regulatory environment helps the mass-culture industry. In other countries, regulations such as restrictions on advertising, as well as competition from heavily subsidized public television and radio networks, hurt private-sector media producers. The United States is the only major nation in which the private sector, as opposed to state-owned broadcasters, took the lead in creating the television industry. Marketing principles—a devotion to pleasing consumers—have dominated U.S. electronic entertainment from the start. In other nations political interests or the cultural tastes of the establishment set the goals for the television industry. Thus when the international market for television programs developed and private channels were allowed overseas, Americans were ready with a host of crowd-pleasing miniseries and films. In recent years, however, many non-U.S. producers of TV shows have managed to successfully compete with U.S. offerings, leading to a decline of the American share of TV series overseas. In the case of fast food, less restrictive zoning regulations and a more flexible labor market facilitated the growth of an American industry that relied on low-paid workers who could work flexible hours.

Is the role of American media a source of power for the United States? Some would argue that it gives the United States the ability to influence the world. In fact, though, media dominance does not contribute directly to American hegemony. American journalists are not propagandists for the U.S. government. Many disagree with American policy and are critical of U.S. society, though most of them disseminate American political and cultural values. Moreover, readers of American newspapers may find them interesting without agreeing with their editorial views or with those of the American administration. In a broader sense, American media may contribute to the U.S. empire by creating an international class of decision makers in the private and public sectors who are brought closer together by reading the same newspapers and magazines and watching the same newscasts. This is a process, however, whose importance cannot be quantified and may contribute to American power only to a very small extent.

As for mass culture, is American primacy additive to American power? One can argue that it is, but only marginally. U.S. mass culture increases familiarity with the United States from an early age before other forms of American culture make their influence felt. Thus before they can read *Time* or *Newsweek* young foreigners get used to America through movies and music. The image of the United States through movies, singers, clothing, and sports is distorted, but it helps bring the world's next generation into a global community arranged around the United States. Moreover, audiences get a positive impression of the United States from these cultural exports. In most American movies—the strongest U.S. mass culture export—the United States is portrayed as a great country, full of opportunities, and a place where the good guys usually triumph.

But the impact of U.S. popular culture is not as great as some would think. Watching American movies and listening to American singers does not transform every foreign teenager into an American. The weight of local cultures and traditions is much stronger than many hope—or fear. Superficial signs of Americanization, such as clothing, should not be overrated. Moreover, the appeal of U.S. culture often enrages local cultural elites. If the masses have no interest in indigenous cultural offerings, anti-Americanism born out of jealousy can arise among members of the native intelligentsia. In countries with cultural norms that are radically different from those of the United States, American culture also generates feelings of anger at the "corruption" brought in by American influences.[7]

Conclusion

Returning to Lincoln's framework, "where we are and whither we are tending," we should now see clearly "where we are." The United States did not set out to create this new international regime. Its aim was the economic and political reconstruction of Western Europe and Japan based on Liberal political institutions. The result, however, was the inadvertent creation of a new regime, one that has gained the somewhat misleading label of "empire." Cold War competition with the Soviet Union obscured the capacity of this international regime to survive the end of the bipolar distribution of power in the world. If we recognize why it did so—because of the Liberal institutional arrangements at both the international level and the domestic level in most of the member states—then we can also recognize the confusion that informs much of the foreign, defense, and economic policy debate over the past decade.

Examples are easy to find. To suggest, as both pundits and political leaders periodically do, that the United States should retreat to isolation is to advocate the diminution of the wealth of both the United States and its allies. To insist that the United States conduct its foreign policy mainly on the basis of unilateralism is to promote the destruction of the American empire. To pursue the expansion of democracy without first achieving constitutional breakthroughs is to increase the prospects for tyranny. To assume that international markets can work without governance is to invite economic decline in international trade and investment. To fail to recognize the many different roles that military power plays in sustaining the American empire, especially as a substitute for supranational political-military authority, is to risk unhinging the present international political and economic order.

So much for "where we are." Now we must deal with the rest of Lincoln's formula by looking forward.

"Whither We Are Tending"

Exploring two major issues is the best way to learn "whither we are tending." The first is the durability of the internal structure of this new international regime, and the second is how its relations with the large part of the world outside the empire will affect its durability.

Internal Factors

If sheer quantity of power is the measure of how long the American empire will last, the answer has to be for a long time, perhaps several centuries, using past empires as a measure. None has enjoyed such a preponderance of power, not just regionally but also globally. Nor has any been able to create the economic growth that the American empire has over the past half-century, not just within the United States but also in most of those states claiming some kind of membership or association with the empire. If one falls back on theories of "realism" in world politics to predict the durability of the American empire, then one can make an argument that it is unstable and will soon be "counterbalanced" by other powers; or, using the same theory, one can argue that it will endure for a long time.[1] The latter conclusion has much more evidence to support it, if only quantitative measures of power are considered.

As we have shown throughout this book, however, other factors, particularly institutional arrangements, contribute to the stability of the American empire, in particular the nature of the economic system, universities, elite and mass media, and some aspects of culture. Unlike in traditional empires, the member states in this new Liberal empire have a strong stake in its durability. The United States cannot be indifferent to their welfare without endangering its own. The resulting centripetal forces are peculiar to this new type of empire, allowing it to avoid the costs of coercion to contain centrifugal forces that have characterized all traditional empires.

Demography, as we explained in Chapter 4, also favors the durability of U.S. leadership within the empire. The birth rate and immigration create population growth in the United States that is not matched either in Japan or in Europe. Although Liberal institutions are key to economic growth, so is a population that increases in numbers and is educated and thus efficiently utilized, and that is the case in the United States. Population growth without education and efficient utilization can be a detriment, as is the case in parts of Africa, India, and China. Barring a major catastrophe, the favorable trends in the United States cannot be altered quickly; nor can adverse demographic trends be changed quickly in other countries except by massive migrations or plagues.

When we go beyond these quantitative and paramechanistic institutional factors, however, we begin to see that the role of voluntarism in the behavior of American leaders is critically important. The United States faces no serious challengers for its leadership position in the world, but that does not prevent U.S. leaders from destroying the empire.

The American constitutional drafters assumed avarice and ambition on the part of all Americans, especially political leaders. Thus they used the device of separating executive, legislative, and judicial powers to provide checks and balances. They inherited another device—ideology. It derived from the Protestantism that early Americans brought from Europe, and it was perpetuated both in churches and public education on civic virtues. The American scholars James Q. Wilson and Edward C. Banfield called them "public regarding values" in contrast to "private regarding values."[2] In other words, the ethic of making personal sacrifices for the public good helps restrain avarice and ambition. To be sure, separation of powers has carried far more of the load in checking the destructive behavior of leaders than has the ideology of public-regarding values. Moreover, Wilson and Banfield observed that the large immigrations into the United States at the beginning of the twentieth century brought in people whose ethic put private-regarding values and ethnic-group interests before public values, increasing the levels of corruption in the politics of the urban centers to which they came. Over a generation or so, however, the offspring of these new immigrants absorbed some of the public-regarding ethic, easing the clash of political cultures.

Today, some observers warn that recent immigrants are being taught to resist the old American ideology by fashions of "political correctness" and fads of "cultural diversity." They identify what can be described with Huntington's phrase, a domestic clash of civilizations.

Both devices, separation of powers and public-regarding ideology, are vitally important to the constitutional stability of the United States. They are barriers to the abuse of public power that could lead to tyranny. What are the devices at the international level that sustain the quasi-constitutional character of the American empire? What keeps U.S. leaders from abusing the vast power at their disposal?

The American empire is by no means a replica of the U.S. federal government. There is no clear balance among three governing branches. Power has been checked not by separate branches of government but by the willingness of American leaders and voters to put international Liberal institutions ahead of narrower U.S. national interests. American presidents have, for the most part, acted as though they were checked by some kind of international legislature and high court.

Here we confront the most serious danger to the American empire. The power of its leaders is limited primarily by their ideology—that is, by the Liberal norms that guide their use of that power. No other means exists of checking them. Nor can a set of rules be devised to assure that leaders do not misuse that power, either by intent or poor judgment. In any case, the best of intentions are not always a sound guide to such rule-breaking policies, and good intentions have justified policies damaging to the empire.

Probably no other variable will prove as significant for the durability of the American empire as leaders' decision making. Other variables may surprise us: an ecological disaster, a massive nuclear weapons attack, or a meteor from outer space might trigger the decline of the United States. While overcommitment of military forces is not nearly the danger that many observers believe, gross misuse of military power in parts of the world that promise little return for the effort could erode U.S. hegemony in the world.

President Bush's invasion of Iraq in 2003 and all of the diplomacy related to it appear to constitute a severe test of this proposition. If the eventual outcome of that war is constructive for the norms of the American imperial system, then the president's unilateral actions will have been justified. As we explained in Chapter 2, his father's strong-arm diplomacy in 1990, leading to the reunification of Germany within NATO over the adamant objections of several NATO countries, especially Britain and to a lesser degree France, proved highly constructive for Europe. The same was true of the Persian Gulf War in 1991, though in this case U.N. Security Council support and broad international assistance in the forms of money and forces reduced the costs of that war to the United States to a trivial level and ensured that it was not perceived as a unilateral U.S. action, even though the war effort was managed by the United States.

The 2003 war in Iraq, by comparison—still ongoing as of this writing—has already cost well over $100 billion and will undoubtedly cost much more. Moreover, whether it will ever be won in the sense of transforming the politics of Iraq—the president's stated goal—is doubtful. The war also makes a long-term conflict with a large part of the Arab and Muslim world virtually inevitable. One may argue that Osama bin Laden's attacks on the United States in September 2001 made it so in any case, but one cannot claim that strong support from most of the members of the American empire— abundant for the war in Afghanistan against bin Laden and his Taliban supporters, including from many Arab states—was forthcoming for the invasion of Iraq. Nor can one argue that the war in Iraq has improved transatlantic ties within NATO. On the contrary, repairing the damage the Bush administration has done to those ties will take years of sustained effort.

The final outcome, of course, could disprove these assessments. If Iraq were to emerge as a stable state with a moderate regime willing to cooperate with the United States, and if other regional states such as Syria and Iran were to do the same, the American empire would emerge even stronger.

On the transatlantic front, a number of states that opposed the invasion of Iraq have already begun struggling to restore good ties with Washington. That demonstrates a major proposition of this book: U.S. power is so overwhelming that trying to counterbalance it simply does not pay. But it does not prove that the administration's policy in Iraq and its handling of relations with NATO from the day it came to office has been wise or constructive for the American empire. On the contrary, it warns that U.S. leaders can, through demagoguery and poor strategic judgment, deal the empire highly damaging blows, even fatal ones.

Some observers may believe we dismiss too easily the possibility that the European Union will challenge U.S. leadership in the world.[3] Possibly it will, but it must first achieve full political integration. To date there is no example of the successful integration of two dozen nationalities, each with its own territory, in a Liberal regime. If, however, the EU were to achieve integration against such odds, it would, as explained in Chapter 3, still face obstacles to becoming a first-class military power. As suggested in Chapter 2, full political and military integration of the EU, if it leads to a Liberal regime, should not be a threat to the American empire but rather a complement to it, a leader of the empire in the event the United States falters. That need not be bad for Americans.

Another kind of uncertainty confronts predictions about the durability of American power. The rate of economic development and technological advancement in premodern times was low and irregular. Powerful regimes have existed for long periods in several regions of the world over the past five thousand years. Some of them achieved remarkable feats of engineering construction and administrative reach that required considerable scientific knowledge and technology, but they soon faded away, taking their advances with them. Since the 1400s scientific and technological knowledge has advanced steadily, not just arithmetically but geometrically. As pointed out in Chapter 1, economic development followed a similar path until the sixteenth and seventeenth centuries. Since that time, it has proceeded at remarkable rates. Joseph Schumpeter explains capitalism as propelled by innovators, not by market equilibrium, and much historical evidence supports his theory. His capitalism is revolutionary, constantly tearing apart older economic enterprises and bringing growth through new and more innovative ones.

Will this exponential economic growth and scientific advancement continue indefinitely? Will it be accompanied by the same creative destruction of the past four centuries? If so, the rates of change may even be hyperbolic. Thus linear extrapolations about the durability of American power are indeed hazardous. They are bound to miss the timing. Without nearly as great a power monopoly as the United States has today, other empires lasted for several centuries. The destructive nature of economic and technological change today could bring the erosion of power at faster rates than it was created.

A more optimistic way to look at the durability question is with the concepts elaborated in Chapter 1 about an increasing returns process causing institutional lock-in and thereby creating path dependence for countries with poor levels of economic performance. Liberal regimes, as Douglass North describes them, provide third-party enforcement that reduces transaction costs, prompts corrective feedback information from markets, and yields much higher rates of economic return. Do such regimes also experience a lock-in to Liberal institutions? If so, then the fortunate few Liberal regimes within the American empire have a lock on their economic lead that is unlikely to be broken over the next century or so.

The historical evidence that path dependence yields poor economic performance extends back many centuries. The evidence for Liberal regimes is much shorter, since they first began to appear in the late sixteenth century (excepting, of course, small city-states like Venice), initially in Holland, then Britain and North America. Much of Western Europe followed in the late eighteenth and early nineteenth centuries; Japan joined in the late nineteenth century. Although the economic lead has shifted somewhat among these Liberal states, it has remained exclusively within their three regions— North America, Europe, and Northeast Asia.[4]

Less sanguine about the durability of these Liberal economies is Mancur Olson's theory of why nations decline. He examines the economic performance record of many countries, concluding that all suffered economic decline over time.[5] Although their markets work effectively at first, small groups organize to gain advantages through laws and regulations that bias markets in their favor. As such interference with competitive pricing accumulates over time, it undercuts the market's efficiency, causing economic decline.

This analysis suggests that Liberal regimes with competitive markets are not locked into path dependence in the way that poorly performing countries are. Political competition in Liberal regimes produces rules that distort corrective feedback from markets. Decline, therefore, is certain.

David Cameron has challenged Olson's theory on both logical and empirical grounds, throwing considerable doubt on the reliability of the theory for generalizing about economic decline.[6] Olson is really arguing that corrective feedback slowly but surely dries up in market economies as a result of the political behavior of small groups. Cameron shows that significant corrective feedback leaks through even where the social and organizational rigidities appear to be strong.

Perhaps "business cycles" offer a way out of this seeming paradox. The down phase of a cycle destroys some of the rigidities and restores corrective feedback from markets. Still, the quite different results from business cycles in East Asia, Europe, and the United States suggest that social rigidities are not cut back to the same degree everywhere. The savings and loan scandal in the United States in the 1980s prompted action to remove the advantages these institutions had enjoyed and abused. In Japan, such action has not been taken although the banks' nonperforming loans are vastly larger. Sooner or later Japan will have to act if it is to forestall economic decline. The more recent business failures in the United States— Enron, Arthur Andersen, Global Crossing, WorldCom, Adelphia Cable, and so on—are corrective of the accumulation of inefficient capital investments, as well as of accounting fraud, made in the 1990s. In other words, they are signs of corrective feedback in the U.S. market, even if they seem excessively tardy. In many other countries in Europe and Northeast Asia, governments often subsidize unprofitable firms rather than allow them to fail. Thus periodic failures and bankruptcies are an indication of a stronger market system in the United States than in those countries.

While the record shows that business cycles can correct inefficient allocations of capital investment, it does not prove that governments are compelled to restore the health of their corrupted third-party enforcement performance. Olson's theory explains how better-organized and powerful minorities intervene in the legislative process to bias third-party enforcement. If business cycles have the effect of catalyzing political action to remove those biases, then economic decline can be averted. If they do not, then it will not be averted in the long run. If the U.S. government acts to improve third-party enforcement, accounting rules, oversight for auditors, and resources for regulatory agencies, then its economic vitality will be sustained after a period of corrective recession. If it does not, then its economic performance will be poorer.

In the context of the institutions of the American empire, outside pressures are sometimes brought to bear to impose corrective feedback on economic policy making. The IMF and the World Bank have leverage they try to use for that purpose. Serious disagreement exists, of course, on whether IMF and World Bank pressures actually impose corrective policies (negative feedback) or error-exacerbating policies (positive feedback).

It is therefore impossible to say whether path dependence for Liberal countries is stronger or weaker than for non-Liberal countries locked into ineffective institutions, but to hazard a guess, it is probably weaker. Long-term economic effectiveness, the sine qua non for the durability of the American empire, depends a great deal on policy makers. Third-party enforcement, once established, cannot be taken for granted thereafter. Sustaining it is a constant battle because businessmen persistently organize and scheme to undermine it for their personal and corporate interests.

Although no confident predictions are possible about the durability of American power, conditional ones can be made. If reasonably effective third-party enforcement can be sustained, not just where it concerns U.S. domestic economic activities but also at the supranational level within the American empire, then U.S. power can endure for a long time. This means, of course, reinforcing the quasi constitutionalism embodied in the international organizations established by the United States. When military power is required, multilateral military coalitions are always preferable for the added legitimacy they provide in backing supranational third-party enforcement.

External Factors

At least two sets of major threats from without confront the American empire, and critics suggest that these might be capable of undermining or catalyzing the empire's decline. First, some claim that the United States has paid insufficient attention to terrorism, proliferation of weapons of mass destruction, information warfare, and other such so-called asymmetric threats. Second, other critics cite the political and moral tensions created by the empire's possession of three-quarters of the world gross product for consumption by less than a fifth of the world's population. They also point to what they feel is an inadequate U.S. response to such health crises as the spread of HIV in Africa, Asia, and elsewhere in the third world. These global social problems, the theory goes, stir the moral and political indignation that motivates terrorist groups.

We do not deny these threats and dangers, or the fact that they can cause pain and damage to the United States and its allies. But the salient question is whether these issues present a threat serious enough to cause the decline of the American empire.

Consider the terrorist threat. Al Qaeda's attacks on the World Trade Center and the Pentagon were tragic for the approximately three thousand victims and their families—cataclysmic for many of them. For the strategic position of the United States, however, the attacks did only minor damage. Moreover, the U.S. military reaction, carrying the war to Afghanistan, where Al Qaeda and its Taliban sponsor have been decimated with little loss of U.S. military personnel, has reinforced the world's understanding of the immensity and reach of U.S. military power. The campaign certainly reinforced for the Russian and Chinese general staffs the impressions they got from the Persian Gulf War in 1991. An indirect consequence of the 9/11 attacks has therefore been to enhance the image of American power in the world by accenting some of its capabilities.

Additional Qaeda attacks may occur, but they cannot destroy the American empire. Terrorist organizations, even if they acquire and use weapons of mass destruction, can be no more than painful nuisances. They do not even rival ordinary crime or drug trafficking in the United States as problems.

They can, however, prompt U.S. leaders to make unwise decisions in pursuing military operations against them, in treatment of American military allies, and in management of both the U.S. and the global economy. The serious threats in the post–9/11 era were also present in the pre–9/11 era.

As pointed out in the introduction, terrorism is a tactic and not an enemy. This observation clarifies the dangers of wars against terrorism. The United States, by any legal definition of terrorism, has been among the largest sponsors of terrorist operations since World War II. It has supported liberation movements in Afghanistan against Soviet occupation and against communist regimes in Central America, Southeast Asia, and elsewhere. From the American viewpoint, the forces carrying out these operations were "freedom fighters," not terrorists.

This elementary point needs repeating because of the vast amount of misleading rhetoric in the United States since 11 September. Al Qaeda is an enemy, and it can be either defeated or reduced to trivial levels of operation. To trumpet terrorism as a worldwide scourge, however, is to confuse the public and misdirect diplomacy. U.S. leaders need to stay focused on specific countries and groups ("nonstate actors" is the misleading new jargon), not on emotionally loaded terms and slogans.

So-called terrorist groups will certainly try to exploit weapons of mass destruction, especially biological and nuclear. The spread of technology has never been stopped more than temporarily in the modern world. If terrorists succeed in carrying out an attack with weapons of mass destruction, then the United States and its allies will have to deal with the damage, but such a successful attack would not mean that the attacking group had defeated the United States or even caused strategically significant damage. Only imprudent U.S. reactions to such actions can do that, especially those that could split the United States from its military and political allies, the members of the empire.

The second external source of challenges and uncertainties arises from the very large portion of the world's population living in countries outside the empire, about 83 percent, who consume less than 30 percent of the world gross product. Moral indignation about this inequity will continue to be a major factor in world politics, as it was throughout the Cold War and even earlier. Liberal societies have developed and tried many kinds of welfare transfer programs, private and public, over the past two centuries, all inspired by the broadly shared desire to soften the plight of the impoverished.

A critique of the issues involved and the validity of the popular assumptions about global poverty cannot be provided in a few paragraphs, but a few disturbing facts can help us avoid illusions about "what to do and how to do it" in dealing with such vast inequities.

In the postwar era, government foreign aid programs were initiated by the United States. Japan, Western Europe, and several other countries soon followed with programs of their own. Churches and religious organizations have a much longer record of missionary work that has continued and expanded. A few secular organizations that provide aid to the world's poor predate World War II, but in the postwar era the number of such nongovernmental organizations has risen rapidly. International organizations within the United Nations, the World Bank, and several regional international banks have also contributed to welfare transfers, but in many of these the aim has been to promote economic development.

For all of the wealth transfers through these many programs, public and private, the record of improving life and economic performance among the 83 percent of people living outside the American empire is poor. Humanitarian aid programs to regions afflicted with wars often have the effect of prolonging conflicts by unintentionally feeding the armies of one or both sides. Economic development aid, the great hope of several American presidents and many American economists, has a disappointing fifty-year record. It has, of course, helped victims of famine and provided shelter to some of the world's poor, but it has not put them on the road to sustainable development.

The explanations of economic growth in Chapters 1 and 5 make the reasons for this poor record obvious. Capital assistance to countries without constitutional orders and governments that provide third-party enforcement cannot sustain economic growth. In fact, it makes matters worse. Moreover, where effective institutions exist, direct economic assistance to governments is seldom needed. Commercial banks and international capital markets readily supply capital.

How will the American empire cope with this morally disturbing reality? As we emphasized in Chapter 1, modern Liberalism has deeply religious roots in the Protestant Reformation. The same moral impulses that defend the autonomy and inalienable rights of the individual also inspire sympathy for the world's poor and downtrodden masses. The American public has repeatedly refused to sit by while such poverty existed. It has shipped hundreds of billions of dollars of aid in many forms to third world countries since World War II. At the same time, it has also seen very little result for that large transfer of wealth. While the average income level in South Korea, starting at the same level of several sub-Saharan African states, has increased by a factor of twenty-five, income has not appreciably grown in any of those African states. Latin America and Southeast Asia have a better performance record but no promise of reaching first world levels.

The cruel fact is inescapable: aid programs have assuaged the consciences of the publics in wealthy Liberal countries, but they have done little or nothing for the world's poor. The major cause of this sad outcome is as evident as the failure of the aid programs itself: indigenous political institutions that stubbornly sustain perverse path dependence. No amount of aid will overcome the capacity of such institutions to squander it.

The third world's greatest shortage is not food, clothing, and capital. It is effective government. Effective government would encourage the production adequate food, clothing, and capital savings. Meeting this shortage has to be among the greatest challenges facing the American empire in the decades ahead. The United States has long tried to cultivate effective government in many countries but with little success except where its military forces have remained for many decades and U.S. officials have effectively imposed Liberal institutions on the local society. This expensive method is simply not feasible for such a large part of the world. Moreover, the United States could better help the third world by merely abolishing all of its tariffs than it has with all its economic aid.

Some observers insist that this inequitable distribution of income inspires groups such as Al Qaeda. Perhaps it plays some role, but the causal linkages to poverty turn out, on closer examination, to be tenuous if they exist at all. Vast wealth from oil production did not mitigate radical groups' behavior in the shah's Iran, nor does it dissolve political radicalism in the Arab oil-producing states. Moreover, Osama bin Laden is from one of Saudi Arabia's wealthiest families, and all of the hijackers on 9/11 were from relatively privileged backgrounds.

The clash between traditional values and modern ones brought by Western influences and wealth provides a better explanation. While it is tempting to say that if wealth were equitably distributed, anti-Western groups like Al Qaeda would decline and disappear, it is simplistic to believe so. We know well that reactions against modernization are unavoidable, and we know that the political leaders who exploit those reactions often include beneficiaries of that modernization.

There is a strong objective case for concluding that it would be wiser to ignore the third world's impoverished masses. The impact, however, both domestically and internationally, on the United States' moral reputation would be unacceptably damaging. But to continue the same old ineffective aid programs is not a promising alternative, either, because their fecklessness, once acknowledged only by a few serious scholars, is ever more widely recognized.[7]

This issue has come to embrace more than economic development in the poor regions of the world; now it also includes ecology, demography, globalization, and other such problems. American hegemony does not make such problems easier to solve, but it does make them increasingly unwise for the United States to ignore.

"What to Do? How to Do It?"

As Clausewitz pointed out, "Everything in strategy is very simple, but that does not mean that everything is very easy."[8] The things "to do," therefore, are simple to point out, but that does not mean that "how to do them" is obvious or easy. The following list emerges conspicuously from our analysis. The first four recommended policies are in priority of importance, and the fifth is critical for accomplishing the others.

1. Guard, maintain, and sustain America's Liberal institutions. They are the key to American power because they promote trust, give citizens a stake in the state, reduce political and economic transaction costs, and provide corrective feedback for adjusting and improving government policy making and private-sector economic

decision making. The periodic upheavals and changes they promote are the price we must pay for avoiding decline.[9]

2. Maintain and steadily improve U.S. military power. As long as U.S.
economic performance remains healthy, the cost of sustaining U.S.
military global hegemony is easily bearable. It should be considered an overhead cost, not just for the security of the United States
but also for the security of the twoscore states within its Liberal
empire.

3. Cultivate Liberal institutions—political, economic, and military—
as the organizational context and ideological standard for international relations. Foremost, consider America's allies, especially
the majority that are mature constitutional states, as full stakeholders in the empire. That means allowing them to influence U.S.
policy making and strategy, though not always to make policy and
strategy. If U.S. allies back Liberal international institutions, the
far more numerous states outside the empire will find it difficult
not to abide by them as well. The resulting drop in transaction
costs for sustaining the empire is a key source of its immense and
widely shared wealth. It is especially important for the United
States to support and abide by international economic rules, such
as those of the WTO.

4. Rethink the promotion of democracy in countries that have not yet
achieved Liberal breakthroughs. Encouraging "waves" of new democracies has not brought "waves" of new constitutional regimes,
and it may have blocked the emergence of a few. Violence and
civil war are more often the precursor to Liberal breakthroughs
than are regular elections. A period of direct U.S. military rule
followed by a few decades of continued military presence is the
only way we can be reasonably sure that a Liberal regime will take
root. Collaborative peacekeeping under which the United States
does not provide the majority of the military forces and make the
rules, as in Bosnia, Kosovo, Afghanistan, and Iraq, is a formula for
failure. It fails to deracinate extant illiberal institutions, encourages illiberal democracy, and ensures political and economic stagnation.

5. Recognize that the U.S. government is not just responsible for the
United States but has also become a metropole for many other
countries. Overwhelming wealth and power bring equally large responsibilities. In the decades since 1945, Washington has become
the focus for many foreign states seeking to be heard, to gain American support, to influence foreign and domestic policy, and to
share the protections and benefits of the American empire. The
unbridled emotions of American patriotism are easily provoked
against this larger governing responsibility; yet those emotions re-

flect the psychological component of U.S. military power, without which it declines to nothing. The two competing demands, however, pay handsomely if both are met in a balanced fashion.

The durability of the American empire cannot ultimately be predicted, but the resources and other advantages at U.S. disposal and the unique character of this international regime provide an encouraging prospect that it will be long lasting.

Appendix
The Debate to Date

Forecasts about the rise and decline of the United States in the postwar era are not peculiar to the end of the Cold War. They go back several decades.

In 1967 Jean-Jacques Servan-Schreiber, one of France's most brilliant minds, predicted in *The American Challenge* that by 1980 the United States would "hold a monopoly on the technological and scientific components of modern power" in a world where the Boeing 2707 would rule the supersonic skies above while American industry in Europe would dominate local manufacturers below.[1] Although the United States was indeed the world's leading technological power in 1980, as it has been ever since World War II, Europe in 1980 was not some underdeveloped continent in the shadow of the American colossus. On the contrary, the European states in 1980 were rich, technologically advanced, and politically stable.

While some, like Servan-Schreiber, predicted America's rise, it has been more common, especially in the United States, to think that American dominance in the immediate post-1945 decades was caused by the exceptional situation resulting from the devastation of Europe and Japan during the world conflict. Gradually America's relative power would decline as Europe and Japan recovered. By 1975 Robert Gilpin had already taken into account, in *U.S. Power and the Multinational Corporation,* the "relative decline of American power and the emergence of new centers of economic power in Europe, Japan, and elsewhere."[2] Richard Rosecrance, in *America as an Ordinary Power,* noted in 1976 that "America has become an ordinary country in foreign relations." Still first among equals, "her role as maintainer of the system is at an end." Like others, Rosecrance focused on the "foreign policy deficits" of the United States, which left it bearing the burden of empire while Japan and Europe devoted their energies to economic development.[3] Henry Kissinger's vision, during his service in the Nixon administration, that the world was moving toward a pentapolar system—the United States, the Soviet Union, China, Japan, and Europe—reflected this belief in the gradual decline of American power.

The concern expressed by Rosencrance that the United States could not fund its foreign and military polices was a recurrent theme in the 1980s. James Chace, in his 1981 book *Solvency,* also argued that the United States, partly because of its overseas military commitments, had underinvested in its economy compared with other nations.[4] In 1982 Mancur Olson designed a theory in *The Rise and Decline of Nations* to explain why countries decline. Special interest groups organize to pass legislation and regulations that create "rigidities" that obstruct market forces and hurt performance.[5] Over time, the cumulative effect is national decline. While Olson addresses the general problem of decline, his theory's relevance to the United States drew public attention, along with two pessimistic books published in 1987. The first, Yale historian Paul Kennedy's *Rise and Fall of the Great Powers,* concluded that, like many previous great empires, the United States was suffering from "imperial overstretch" and could not maintain its imperial status, in part due to the unsustainable cost of its military establishment.[6] The second, David Caleo's *Beyond American Hegemony,* also saw a declining America: "The United States is markedly weakening in relation to its own allies, the Soviets, and the rest of the world." Caleo, like Kennedy, pointed the finger at America's large military expenditures and argued that though "America is not sinking, the rest of the world is rising," forcing America to accept a more "plural structure" in international relations.[7] Joseph Nye, a Harvard professor who served in the Clinton administration, wrote in 1990, "There is no doubt that the United States is less powerful now at the end of the twentieth century than it was in mid-century."[8]

Others argued that hegemony was unsustainable in the absence of major wars. In 1984 Robert Keohane explained in *After Hegemony* that after World War II, "Henry Luce's 'American Century' was under pressure after less than twenty years." Keohane predicted, along lines familiar to proponents of "realism," that "hegemonic leadership is unlikely to be revived in this century for the United States or any other country. Hegemonic powers have historically only emerged after world wars; during peacetime, weaker countries have tended to gain on the hegemon rather than vice versa."[9]

Most declinists, however, believed that the Cold War masked America's relative loss of strength. The primacy of the East-West confrontation and U.S. military power kept other capitalist states in a position of weakness and dependence on the United States. But once the Soviet Union broke up, American hegemony even within the Western community would be rapidly challenged. Robert W. Tucker and David Hendrickson explained in 1992 in *The Imperial Temptation* that American power had diminished because the security dimension of the U.S. alliances was less relevant with the demise of the Soviet Union. The U.S. economic position had declined, with "little evidence that this decline might soon be arrested, let alone reversed," and thus the United States was becoming less powerful.[10]

Others argued that the competition had moved from the political-military realm (United States vs. Soviet Union) to the economic one (United States vs. European Union vs. Japan), in which the United States was in a weaker position. Lester Thurow of MIT proclaimed in 1992 in *Head to Head* that "without a pause, the contest has shifted from being a military contest to being an economic contest" and that "in the next century the United States will be just one of a number of equal players."[11] Thurow saw the United States as particularly ill-equipped in its competition with its new European and Japanese rivals. The MIT Commission on Industrial Productivity had in 1989 warned about America's poor industrial performance.[12] Paul Kennedy, in his 1993 book *Preparing for the Twenty-first Century*, explained that the United States had weakened itself because "while engaging Moscow in an expensive arms race, America has had to compete for world market shares against allies like Japan and Germany which have allocated smaller percentages of the national resources to the military, thus freeing capital, personnel, and R&D for commercial manufacture that has undermined parts of the American industrial base."[13] As mentioned previously, Samuel Huntington in 1993 foresaw that economic conflicts between rich countries would undermine U.S.-led alliances. He wrote that the United States and Europe "have deeply conflicting interests over the distribution of the benefits and costs of economic growth and the distribution of the costs of economic stagnation or decline" and noted that economic power would gain in importance as military conflict between major states became less likely. Being relatively weaker in the economic field than in the military one, America's weight in the world would thus decline. Huntington concluded that "the threat to American primacy from Japan is serious," and warned against a future challenge from Europe, too.[14] Ronald Steel, the author of several books on U.S. foreign policy and biographer of Walter Lippmann, wrote in 1995 that with the end of the Cold War the new contest had moved to the economic plane. "With our chronic deficits, weak currency, massive borrowing, and immense debt," Steel wrote, the United States was not much of a superpower in that realm and he predicted that U.S. influence would consequently decline.[15] Chalmers Johnson, an iconoclastic observer of Japanese politics, made an even more forceful argument, explaining that Japan's "capitalist developmental state" had defeated the American economy, based on classical free-market principles. "The Cold War is over and Japan won," proclaimed Johnson.[16]

It became clear in the late 1990s that American primacy had survived the collapse of the Soviet Union. But for some observers it was a brief "unipolar moment" that would soon be eclipsed by the rise of China, India, Russia, a united Europe, and others.[17] Some, like Charles Kupchan, called for gradual switch to multipolarity and also questioned whether American voters would continue to willingly foot the bill for an arrangement that "saddles the United States with such a disproportionate share of the burden of manning the international system."[18] William Pfaff, a noted American columnist based in Paris, also predicted the end of America's hegemony. In his essay "The Question of Hegemony," he argued that with the end of the Cold War and China's transformation into a relatively benign power, "the alliance system lost what had been its compelling rationale, along with, potentially, its legitimacy." Thus, sooner or later, the American position would be challenged because "it is in the nature of an hegemonic system to generate opposition, as well as its own eventual replacement."[19]

Others, however, saw the United States' preeminence as more than a brief unipolar apotheosis. Even before the formal end of the Cold War, Samuel Huntington, in a *Foreign Affairs* article in the winter of 1988–89, noted that the United States was a uniquely powerful nation, endowed with a "peculiarly multidimensional" strength that ranged from population size and economic development to military might and ideological appeal.[20] Ben Wattenberg,

challenging the declinists in a 1990 collection of his syndicated columns, prophesied that the United States was a rising "omni-power,"
set to become the world's first "universal nation." Wattenberg ironically entitled one of his columns "The Rise and Fall of Paul
Kennedy."[21] Mortimer Zuckerman, in a 1998 piece in *Foreign Affairs*
entitled "A Second American Century," predicted that the United
States, having dominated the twentieth century, would also dominate the twenty-first.[22] On the economic front, the National Research
Council's *U.S. Industry in 2000* painted a fairly optimistic view of
American industrial performance, in stark contrast with many of the
dire predictions of the late 1980s and early 1990s.[23] In more academic articles, Ethan Kapstein and William Wohlforth provided empirical data and theoretical explanations for the proposition that
American unipolar hegemony could be a long-lasting state of affairs.[24] Zbigniew Brzezinski, in *The Grand Chessboard,* a book published in 1997, took a middle course. While optimistic about American power, he argued that the U.S. share of gross world product
will decline significantly as other economies grow, from 30 percent
to perhaps 20 percent in 2010 and 10–15 percent in 2020.[25]

In 2001 John Mearsheimer, a strong proponent of "realism" as a
theory of international relations, offered a fundamentally different
picture in his book *The Tragedy of Great Power Politics.*[26] The
United States, according to his analysis, is a regional hegemon, not
a global hegemon, because nuclear weapons prevent the establishment of global hegemony; but the United States has the potential to
block the emergence of any other regional hegemon. Whether it will
use its power in accordance with Mearsheimer's "offensive realism"
to keep its dominant position, he does not predict, but he believes
that it could.

Over the past four decades the expectations of America's decline
economically and militarily held sway until near the end of the Cold
War. Since that time, declinists still sound warnings, but more bull-
ish views on the durability of American hegemony have appeared
in the past fifteen years. Our book, of course, falls into this latter
category.

This brief survey by no means includes all the voices in this
debate, but it does track its main outlines, providing the context in
which our own book was written.

Notes

Introduction

1. Abraham Lincoln, "House divided" speech, delivered in Springfield, Illinois, to the Republican State Convention, 16 June 1858. Quoted in Roy P. Basler, ed., *The Collected Works of Abraham Lincoln,* 9 vols. (New Brunswick, N.J.: Rutgers University Press, 1953).

2. In order, the authors were Paul Kennedy, Francis Fukuyama, Robert Mueller, Michael Doyle (with several others as well), Zbigniew Brzezinski, and Samuel Huntington. Globalization has too many authors to list, although Thomas Friedman did a lot to popularize it.

3. They include the proponents of traditional power politics, or theories of "realism," and proponents of more subjective interpretations of world politics, or "constructivist" theories of international relations.

4. Nora Bensahel, "The Counterterrorism Coalitions," unpublished paper for the Project on Coalition Building and Maintenance, Institute for the Study of Diplomacy, Georgetown University, 6 May 2002, p. 1: "Terrorism cannot be 'defeated,' because it is a tactic, not an enemy." U.S. support for resistance forces in Afghanistan against Soviet occupation, for resistance to the communist regime in Nicaragua, and for many other such actions qualifies as "terrorist" operations by any legal definition of the term. That is why efforts to draft a law against international terrorism in the U.S. Senate in 1979 were eventually dropped: no variant could be devised that the United States had not violated.

5. Nye, *Bound to Lead.*

6. T. C. W. Blanning, *The Culture of Power and the Power of Culture: Old Regime Europe, 1660–1789* (New York: Oxford University Press, 2002), 121–26. Blanning quotes Frederick the Great to Voltaire, "I view my subjects like a herd of stags on some noble's estate; their only function is to reproduce and fill the space."

7. The authors are indebted to Kenneth Maxwell, reacting to an early version of the manuscript, for the term *subversive ideas.*

8. We will capitalize the words *Liberal* and *Liberalism* where they are used

in their original European definition of limited state power and the primacy of
individual rights. We lowercase *liberalism* when it is used in its contemporary
American definition, meaning left-of-center political views, including greater welfare distribution by means of the state budget and bureaucracy.

Chapter 1. The Sources of American Power

1. American "exceptionalism," of course, is an old issue that has inspired a
rich literature, which we draw on heavily. A recent example is Lipset's *American
Exceptionalism*. Hartz, *Liberal Tradition*, and Huntington, *American Politics*, are
important to our arguments here. The end of the Cold War has inspired a new
debate about it with the emphasis on limits and uses of U.S. power and the institutions that produce it. The debate began with Kennedy, *Rise and Fall*, and
continued with Fukuyama, *End of History*, Huntington, *Clash of Civilizations*, and
Brzezinski, *Grand Chessboard*. For a sampling of the contributions of several
other participants in this debate, see Lynn-Jones and Miller, *Cold War and After*.
A less well-known contribution is Geir Lundestad, *American "Empire"*; Lundestad describes the United States during the Cold War as an "empire by invitation,"
an idea we appropriate in this book.

2. See Hartz, *Liberal Tradition*, for the classic monograph on how Americans
lost touch with key words in the European vocabulary of political philosophy and
the impact of that loss on American political discourse.

3. Huntington, "The West," 30.

4. See Daphne I. Stroud, *Magna Carta* (Southampton, England: P. Cave,
1980), 5.

5. De Ruggiero, *History*, 1–2, 13, 20.

6. Revisionist history has raised serious questions about the traditional idea
of feudalism, but we do not believe they undercut de Ruggiero's assumption that
it marks a period of mutual obligations and liberties, albeit varying from country
to country and changing over time. See Susan Reynolds, *Fiefs and Vassals* (New
York: Oxford University Press, 1994).

7. Huntington, *Political Order*, chapter 2.

8. Huntington, *American Politics*, 87–91, 149–54.

9. Plattner, "Liberalism to Liberal Democracy," 121.

10. Zakaria, "Rise of Illiberal Democracy." See also Zakaria, *The Future of
Freedom*.

11. See, for example, Schedler, "What Is Democratic Consolidation?" 91,
which portrays the concept of democratic consolidation as chaotic and ill-defined;
Schedler would be less confused if he introduced the concept of Liberalism into
this analysis. See Diamond, "Is the Third Wave Over?" for considerable clarity on
this issue. Finally, see Huntington, "After Twenty Years," for similar clarity and
concern with "liberal" democracy as opposed to other kinds.

12. See Pipes, *Property and Freedom*, for a recent and extended explanation
of this ancient axiom from Western political thought.

13. See Lindblom, *Politics and Markets,* for an explanation of why all liberal democracies have private-property and market economies.

14. This point has been made repeatedly by neoclassical economists, and most pointedly by Friedrich von Hayek, in *Fatal Conceit* and in his monograph *Road to Serfdom,* and more recently by the Hungarian economist János Kornai, *Socialist System.* Still, it is far from universally accepted.

15. John Stuart Mill, *On Liberty* (New York: Appleton-Century-Crofts, 1947), especially 4.

16. Quoted in Kishlansky, *Monarchy Transformed,* 176.

17. Harold D. Lasswell, *Politics: Who Gets What, When, How* (Chicago: Peter Smith, 1936). Lasswell took this definition from the infamous Tammany Hall boss, William Marcy Tweed, whose succinct definition of politics has yet to be improved upon.

18. This is not, of course, universally true. Doyle, "Liberalism and World Politics," is highly explicit here and in all his other works. Fukuyama, *End of History,* is also clear on the distinction.

19. In American universities' political science departments, Liberalism has been so successfully conflated with democracy that students no longer learn, except through their own initiative, what it means, especially the historical evolution of its meaning. John Rawls, *A Theory of Justice* (Cambridge: Harvard University Press, 1971), has contributed heavily to the conflation of Liberalism and democracy by dressing up what are essentially socialist doctrines as "democratic."

20. Robert Dahl, perhaps the world's leading theorist on democracy, insists that "democratization and the development of opposition" are not identical. He prefers "to reserve the term 'democracy' for a political system one of the characteristics of which is the quality of being completely or almost completely responsive to all its citizens." Dahl, *Polyarchy,* 1–2. Thirty years later, however, in *On Democracy,* chapters 13 and 14, Dahl explains "why market capitalism favors democracy," but also "why market capitalism harms democracy."

21. Schumpeter, *Capitalism, Socialism, and Democracy,* 250–69, and Huntington, *Third Wave,* 6.

22. A huge amount of literature, of course, could be cited on this question, but most of it is highly technical, in that it depends on legal terms and concepts from the vocabulary of law professors and constitutional lawyers, or on the mathematical language of game theory devoted to coalition building, or on other such specialized approaches. For examples of less technical and more accessible essays, see Elster, *Constitutionalism and Democracy,* but even they do not boil the definition of a constitution down to its simplest terms. We want the most elementary definition here.

23. Rustow, "Transitions to Democracy." As an aside, this article is another example of erasing the distinction between Liberalism and democracy. Its great contribution is its focus on a fundamental Liberal principle—limiting the state's power through a "great compromise" among political elites.

24. See John A. Wickham, *Korea on the Brink: From the "12/12 Incident" to the Kwangju Uprising, 1979–1980* (Washington, D.C.: National Defense University Press, 1999), for a U.S. military commander's account of how close South Korea came to civil war at one point, notwithstanding the threat from North Korea.

25. Although the American record in the Philippines is mixed, Spanish, French, Dutch, and Portuguese colonial legacies have not included Liberal institutional legacies, either in Asia or elsewhere. Except for the British settlement colonies and two cities (Hong Kong and Singapore), the English record is no better.

26. Dahl, *On Democracy*, captures this change in his own views in chapters 13 and 14.

27. See, for examples, Joseph E. Stiglitz and Shahid Yusuf, eds., *Rethinking the East Asian Miracle* (Washington, D.C.: World Bank, 2001), for a collection of diagnostic essays, and Joseph E. Stiglitz, *Globalization and Its Discontents* (New York: Norton, 2002). Amusingly, Stiglitz belatedly awoke to the role of institutions several years after Douglass North won his Nobel Prize in 1993 for examining the role of institutions, but he entirely ignores North's work.

28. For example, see Lipset, *Political Man*, which also notes a high correlation between Protestantism and democracy.

29. Huntington, *Third Wave*, 59.

30. See North, *Structure and Change* and *Institutions*, as well as North and Weingast, "Constitutions and Commitment."

31. North, *Structure and Change*, 17.

32. Ibid., 18.

33. North, *Institutions*, 7.

34. North, *Structure and Change*, 147–57.

35. North and Weingast, "Constitutions and Commitment."

36. For the story of this development, see Brewer, *Sinews of Power*. Ferguson, *Cash Nexus*, adds critically important insights into the role of a central bank and a national debt in modern states that developed in eighteenth-century England.

37. Marx was flatly wrong in declaring the working class the enemy of capitalism. Workers need the jobs that effective markets create. Capitalism's real enemies are unconstitutional rulers and business entrepreneurs, as Adam Smith rightly recognized.

38. Brewer, *Sinews of Power*.

39. Ferguson, *Cash Nexus*.

40. North, *Institutions*, 57.

41. North writes, "Third-party enforcement means the development of the state as a coercive force able to monitor property rights and enforce contracts effectively, but no one at this stage in our knowledge knows how to create such an entity." He cites the inability of game theorists and others to account for the creation of this kind of cooperation, ibid., 59–60. North's use of the Glorious Revolution, of course, equates the resulting constitutional state to something close to "such an entity."

42. See W. Brian Arthur, "Competing Technologies, Increasing Returns, and

NOTES TO PAGES 29-34

Lock-in by Historical Events," *Economic Journal* 99, no. 1 (1989), 116–31. See also W. Brian Arthur, "Self-Reinforcing Mechanisms in Economics," in Philip W. Anderson, Kenneth J. Arrow, and David Pines, eds., *The Economy as an Evolving Complex Mechanism* (Reading, Mass.: Addison-Wesley, 1988). Paul David, "Clio and the Economics of QWERTY," *American Economic Review* 75, no. 3 (1985), 332–37, uses the history of the typewriter keyboard layout as an example of a less efficient solution that took hold as a quirk of initial engineering design constraints and would not yield to more efficient solutions later on when those constraints were overcome. Others have challenged the evidence David provides, but his principle can be seen in several other cases of technology for which the evidence seems beyond dispute.

43. North, *Institutions*, 59–60.

44. Pierson, "Increasing Returns."

45. As North states it in more technical language, "The increasing returns characteristic of an initial set of institutions that provide disincentives to productive activity will create organizations and interest groups with a stake in the existing constraints. They will shape the polity in their interests. Such institutions provide incentives that may encourage military domination of the polity and economy, religious fanaticism, or plain, simple redistributive organizations, but they provide few rewards from the increases in the stock and dissemination of economically useful knowledge. The subjective mental constructs of the participants will evolve an ideology that not only rationalizes the society's structure but accounts for its poor performance." North, *Institutions*, 99.

46. Huntington, "The West." Huntington not only makes an emphatic distinction between Westernization and modernization but makes the distinction a key assumption in his argument that non-Western countries can equal Western power in economic and technological terms while also being political hostile and threatening to the United States and its Western allies. His *Clash of Civilizations*, 68–72, defines Westernization in more detail: the classical legacy, Catholicism and Protestantism, European languages, and separation of spiritual and temporal authority, rule of law, social pluralism, representative bodies, and individualism. Except for the classical legacy, language, and religion, the other characteristics are highly likely under constitutionally limited government in other civilizations, not just in the West. This weakens his sharp distinction.

47. On this claim, see Migdal, *Strong Societies*, especially 279–86, and Lewis M. Snider, "The Political Performance of Third World Government and the Debt Crisis," *American Political Science Review* 84, no. 4 (1990), 1263–80.

48. See William E. Odom, *The Collapse of the Soviet Military* (New Haven: Yale University Press, 1998), chaps. 4 and 11.

49. Huntington's distinction between more and less institutionalized regimes, "civic versus praetorian," explains why few dictatorships are strong states and few are good at collecting taxes. See his *Political Order*, 78–98.

50. See Odom, *On Internal War*, 59. In the late 1960s, the government of South Vietnam was tapping only an estimated 10 percent of its potential tax base, depending for most of its revenues on U.S. aid. The Vietcong were able to provide

a large part of their resources by taxing the residual 90 percent of the base. Thus "It may not be an exaggeration to say that the crux of an internal war is taxation." Of three case studies treated in this book, El Salvador, Guatemala, and the Philippines, the country that received the least U.S. direct aid, Guatemala, did the best against communist insurgents. Forced to compete for tax revenue, it asserted stronger local governmental control, thereby denying resources to the insurgents.

51. Charles Tilly, *Capital, Coercion, and European States, AD 990–1990* (Oxford: Blackwell, 1992), 15. See pp. 14–28 for the logic of Tilly's rather complex arguments. Brewer, *Sinews of Power,* 138, sees the English case as not entirely explainable by the pressures of war: "The act of waging war did not inevitably lead to the development of new and more powerful state institutions. Indeed, in early modern Europe war often succeeded in diluting rather than concentrating state power." According to Brewer, two factors in addition to war were critical: first, William of Orange was the beneficiary of administrative reforms initiated earlier, and second, the parliament proved an effective watchdog against corruption.

52. Levi, *Of Rule and Revenue,* 122–44, 175–80. As she concludes from comparing England with other European states, "The crucial finding . . . is the paradoxical role of a strong parliament. Its emergence in England reflected the power of the nobility to delimit royal power, but in the long run it permitted English monarchs to reduce significantly the transaction costs of tax collection." Brewer, *Sinews of Power,* 127–30, makes the same case in more detail, offering illuminating comparisons with France's less efficient tax system. Ferguson, *Cash Nexus,* 13–15, adds the central bank and the national debt as key to England's superior capacity to handle large military budgets for war.

53. Here we follow the definition of the totalitarian regime-type in Friedrich and Brzezinski, *Totalitarian Dictatorship.*

54. Both regimes were also destroying those more efficient systems by their domestic policies. Had either lasted for several decades, it would have experienced a steady decline in economic performance and taxation capacity due to the rising transaction costs its policies were imposing.

55. Olson, *Power and Prosperity.* His arguments can be summed up as showing that the Soviet economy was like that of a single firm. It did not have an income tax but rather reallocated resources within the single state firm.

56. Olson, *Rise and Decline.* David R. Cameron, "Distributional Coalitions and Other Sources of Economic Stagnation: On Olson's Rise and Decline of Nations," *International Organization* 42, no. 4 (1988), 561–603, offers a penetrating criticism of Olson's thesis. Even if one accepts Cameron's critique of Olson's "logic," one can observe, nevertheless, the success that many small interest groups have had in using laws and government policy to obstruct the role of market forces in providing corrective feedback information on declining factor productivity. For example, the lobby in support of import tariffs on sugar in the United States has probably kept the price of sugar double what it would otherwise be if Central American producers could compete in U.S. markets. The rice farmers' lobby and the domestic steel industry's lobby in the United States are two other examples.

Chapter 2. An Empire of a New Type

1. We are proving the type as sui generis in the same way Carl J. Friedrich and Zbigniew K. Brzezinski did in describing the "totalitarian" regime-type as distinct from all other authoritarian systems. See Friedrich and Brzezinski, *Totalitarian Dictatorship*.

2. See www.unctad.org.

3. *Economic Report of the President* (Washington, D.C.: U.S. Government Printing Office, February 2002).

4. Lundestad, *American "Empire,"* 54.

5. Kennedy, *Rise and Fall,* especially pp. xv–xxv and 514–40.

6. Wattenberg, *First Universal Nation*. Wattenberg's idea of an American empire of a new type is very much along the lines we advance here.

7. It might be argued that the British Empire was Liberal in that it spread some Liberal institutions to its colonies. Where large numbers of British citizens migrated to its colonies to become the majority or a very large minority—in North America, Australia, and New Zealand—they implanted Liberal institutions which led eventually to rebellion in the American colonies and forced compromises in Canada, Australia, and New Zealand. In other colonies, where the indigenous population remained the large majority, manipulated and dominated by a small British elite, the resulting institutions were hardly Liberal. See Migdal, *Strong Societies,* chapter 3, for a description of the illiberal legacies the British left in Sierra Leone. India, which might be cited as an exception because it has democratic elections, has only a thin veneer of Liberalism that does not penetrate to local government.

8. Ikenberry, "The Myth of Post–Cold War Chaos," Also see his "Institutions, Strategic Restraint, and the Persistence of American Postwar Order."

9. For these points see Ikenberry, *After Victory*. Our concept of the American empire's constitutionalism is different from Ikenberry's in an important respect. In the Congress of Vienna system and the Versailles system, there was neither strong consensus on the kind of domestic political regimes that members ought to have nor pressure for members to create them. In the American system, the Liberal, or constitutional, regime-type is strongly approved by the core states—the large majority—and the United States and the European Union member states encourage and proselytize for the creation of constitutional systems.

10. See North, *Institutions,* for an explanation of the Northwest Ordinance framework as establishing an "increasing returns" process, locking in "path dependence" that made transaction costs for the economies of the new territories low, allowing a continuing expansion of the number of states in the union, each with the same or slightly adapted structure of property rights, inheritance laws, and political decision rules.

11. U.S. hegemonic power is the answer to "realist" theorists, who insist that no enforcement basis for supranational governance exists in the world. Those who acknowledge this answer consider it only temporary, not a stable arrangement. See, for example, Waltz, "Structural Realism."

12. Ikenberry, "Myth of Post–Cold War Chaos," does not capitalize "liberal" as we have.

13. J. L. Brierly, *The Law of Nations* (New York: Oxford University Press, 1963), 351–52.

14. For the more widely accepted versions of realism in the postwar American academic world, see Morgenthau, *Politics Among Nations;* Waltz, *Man, the State, and War* and *Theory of International Politics* (Reading, Mass.: Addison-Wesley, 1979); and Gilpin, *War and Change.*

15. For a few examples, see Mearsheimer, *Tragedy of Great Power Politics,* chapter 10; Kupchan, *End of the American Era;* and Gilpin, *Political Economy.* Gilpin sees this not as a consequence of the end of the Cold War but as the dynamics of international economics.

16. Waltz, "Structural Realism," 30.

17. Although France, Britain, and later Germany each attempted to dominate Europe, none proved capable of establishing unquestioned hegemony. Lacking a country that could become such a hegemon, Europe experienced repeated wars and shifting alliances aimed at preventing any country from becoming dominant. The historical record became one of periodic breakdowns in the equilibrium of balanced power followed by wars and diplomacy that reestablished the equilibrium. In East Asia, China's capacity to establish and maintain hegemony for long periods created a different pattern—periods of stability interrupted by invasions or breakdowns within China, followed by fighting that eventually reestablished hegemony. Realism is a compelling theory of the European experience, but less so of the Asian experience and probably for empires of the Middle East and other regions composed of mostly weak states, unable to play the balance of power game of European origin.

18. See Wohlforth, "Stability," especially 5–7.

19. Ibid., 13.

20. Ibid., 29.

21. Ethan B. Kapstein, "Does Unipolarity Have a Future?" in Kapstein and Mastanduno, *Unipolar Politics,* 481.

22. See Overholt, "Japan's Economy," for an important explanation of Japan's economic problems, an explanation that can be applied to a number of other Asian countries as well.

23. Kapstein, "Does Unipolarity Have a Future?" 475–84.

24. Ibid., 468.

25. Joffe, "How America Does It," 16.

26. Ibid., p. 24.

27. Waltz, "Structural Realism."

28. See Brendan Simms, *Unfinest Hour: Britain and the Destruction of Bosnia* (London: Penguin, 2001), for both the pernicious behavior of Britain and the reticence of the Clinton administration to override British and French resistance to effective intervention to stop the killing.

29. Régis Debray, *L'Edit de Caracalla, ou plaidoyer pour des Etats-Unis d'Occident par Xavier de C**** (Paris: Fayard, 2002).

30. Ibid., 21–22.

31. Ibid., 25.

32. Ibid., 91.

33. Ibid., 101.

34. Debray in the preface claims that he disagrees with his fictitious friend, but his arguments seem to lack conviction.

35. For a few recent and varied treatments of the concept, see Manfred B. Steger, *Globalization: The New Market Ideology* (Lanham, Md.: Rowman and Littlefield, 2001); Steven Weber, ed., *Globalization and the European Political Economy* (New York: Columbia University Press, 2001); John J. Kirton and George M. von Furstenberg, eds., *New Directions in Global Economic Governance: Managing Globalization in the Twenty-First Century* (Aldershot, England: Ashgate, 2001); and Heikki Patomaki, *Democratizing Globalization: The Leverage of the Tobin Tax* (London: Zed, 2001).

36. Russett, *Grasping the Democratic Peace,* offers one version of it, emphasizing "democracy" alone without requiring that a democracy must also be Liberal. For the analysis that kicked off the democratic peace thesis, see Michael W. Doyle, "Kant, Liberal Legacies, and Foreign Affairs," part 1, *Philosophy and Public Affairs* 12, no. 3 (1983), 205–35, and part 2, *Philosophy and Public Affairs* 12, no. 4 (1983), 323–53. Doyle's attention to property rights is entirely compatible with our Liberal empire thesis. For challenges to the democratic peace thesis, see Christopher Layne, "Kant or Cant: The Myth of the Democratic Peace," *International Security* 19, no. 2 (1994); David E. Spiro, "The Insignificance of the Liberal Peace," *International Security* 19, no. 2 (1994); and Gowa, *Ballots and Bullets.*

37. For a version emphasizing Liberalism's causal role, see John M. Owen, "How Liberalism Produces Democratic Peace," *International Security* 19, no. 2 (1994).

38. Russett, *Grasping the Democratic Peace.*

39. Immanuel Kant, *Perpetual Peace and Other Essays,* trans. Ted Humphrey (Indianapolis: Hackett, 1983), 107–43. Doyle, "Kant," rediscovered Kant's perpetual peace thesis and introduced it into contemporary discussions of peace and war in world politics. Also see Doyle, "Liberalism and World Politics," in which the author identifies three liberalisms in world politics: Schumpeter's liberal pacifism, Machiavelli's liberal imperialism, and Kant's liberal internationalism.

40. Kant, *Perpetual Peace,* 115.

41. Readers who are skeptical of this point should see Sandars, *America's Overseas Garrisons,* which traces the history of U.S. military deployments in both regions and efforts to reduce them on occasions during and since the Cold War. Sandar concludes that withdrawing U.S. garrisons from abroad will remain unwise and dangerous for long into the future.

42. Robert J. Art, "Why Western Europe Needs the United States and NATO," *Political Science Quarterly* 111, no. 1 (1996), 5–6.

43. For a French view of possible scenarios if U.S. military forces left Europe, see Crémieux, *Quand les "Ricains" repartiront.*

44. See David Yost, "Transatlantic Relations and Peace in Europe," *Interna-*

tional Affairs 78, no. 2 (2002), 277–300, for an insightful treatment of Crémieux's novel as a basis for understanding European security challenges today.

45. Olson, *Logic of Collective Action.*

46. Stuart Croft, Joylon Howorth, Terry Terriff, and Mark Webber, "NATO's Triple Challenge," *International Affairs* 76, no. 3 (2000), 503–10, offers a clarifying analysis of contemporary tensions between NATO and the EU over the European Security and Defense Initiative and the Common European Security and Defense Policy.

47. Ikenberry, "Myth of Post–Cold War Chaos," is an example; in *After Victory* Ikenberry shows more awareness of Waltz's challenge but does not really emphasize it for his "institutional" model of international system. Keohane and Nye, *Power and Interdependence,* and Keohane, *After Hegemony,* are more neglectful of Waltz's stance.

48. Quoted in North, *Institutions,* 60.

Chapter 3. The Military Power Gap

1. Rosen, *Winning the Next War,* and *Societies and Military Power: India and Its Armies* (Ithaca, N.Y.: Cornell University Press, 1996), are two useful books on this problem. It is, of course, a very old issue, which cannot be summed up easily because too much historiography has been devoted to finding "lessons."

2. For a textured examination of problems and ambiguities faced in military "net assessments," see Eliot A. Cohen, "Toward Better Net Assessment," *International Security* 13, no. 2 (1988), 50–89. More recently, it has been argued by a number of scholars that "democracies" have a significant military advantage in war. Dan Reiter and Alan C. Stam III, *Democracies at War* (Princeton: Princeton University Press, 2002), urges this view. Desch, "Democracy and Victory," raises rather compelling challenges to the thesis. This debate is beside the point for our arguments for two reasons. First, Liberal regimes are distinguished from illiberal democracies; second, the correlation is spurious in the same way that we showed in Chapter 2 that the "democratic peace" thesis is spurious.

3. Robert H. Scales, Jr., *Yellow Smoke: The Future of Land Warfare for America's Military* (Lanham, Md.: Rowman and Littlefield, 2003), 99–120.

4. Knowledgeable sources told one of the authors in 1993 that the French chief of defense told President François Mitterrand that French forces had difficulties because they had not been allowed to train within the NATO military structure. Once they overcame their shortfalls in tanks and supplies, however, French commanders performed with impressive competence. See Houlahan, *Gulf War,* chapter 14.

5. For some of the Soviet and Russian professional military reactions, see Mary C. FitzGerald, "Russia's New Military Doctrine," *Defence and International Security* (October 1992), 40–48.

6. As an alliance, however, NATO owns several Airborne Warning and Control System (AWACS) aircraft, giving it such capabilities.

7. The same thing happened in Kosovo: John Barry and Evan Thomas, "The Kosovo Cover-Up," *Newsweek,* 15 May 2000; Steven Lee Myers, "Damage to Serb Military Less Than Expected," *New York Times,* 28 June 1999. For a critical analysis of the bombing effects, see Barry R. Posen, "The War for Kosovo: Serbia's Political-Military Strategy," *International Security* 24, no. 4 (2000). In more than seventy days of NATO bombing, less than a score of tanks were destroyed. The number of other armored vehicles was even smaller.

8. Gordon and Trainor, *Generals' War,* 220. A Chinese-made radar, it was later determined, identified the F-117s as they approached Baghdad.

9. Ibid., 75–101, 206–66, for a description of the planning and execution of the air war.

10. Discussions with Eliot Cohen and Thomas A. Keaney. See their *Gulf War Air Power Survey Summary Report* (Washington, D.C.: Government Printing Office, 1993), for a detailed description and analysis of the air war.

11. Gordon and Trainor, *Generals' War,* 313, provides these aggregate figures.

12. Ibid., 335.

13. The defense damage estimates depended heavily on pilots' visual assessments, which historically have proven highly exaggerated.

14. Cohen and Keaney, *Gulf War Air Power Survey.*

15. Daryl G. Press, "The Myth of Air Power in the Persian Gulf War and the Future of Warfare," *International Security* 26, no. 2 (2001), 39–40. Press bases this claim on evidence and analysis undercutting all five of the following claims for the air campaign: that it (1) prevented the Iraqi forces from maneuvering, (2) severed Iraqi command and control, (3) cut Iraqi supply lines, (4) degraded Iraqi forces, and (5) broke Iraqi morale.

16. Cohen and Keaney, *Gulf War Air Power Survey,* 186.

17. Stephen Biddle, "Afghanistan and the Future of Warfare," *Foreign Affairs* 82, no. 2 (March–April 2003), 45.

18. See Kenneth W. Allen, "PLA Air Force Operations and Modernization," in *People's Liberation Army After Next,* ed. Susan M. Puska (Carlisle, Pa.: Strategic Studies Institute, 2000), 189–254.

19. The marines are not included here because they are neither structured nor equipped for land combat operations more than twenty miles or so inland. Their tanks were no match for Iraqi tanks; they could not maintain a fast pace of advance against retreating Iraqi forces; and they depended heavily on army logistics. Thus they are not a significant measure of U.S. land forces.

20. Brigadier General Volney J. Warner, Jr., provided these data from his experience with Tiger Brigade of the 2d Armored Division, which went ahead of and north of the marine units, sweeping to the north of Kuwait City before the marines reached the city itself. Warner was a major at the time.

21. See Houlahan, *Gulf War,* for detailed accounts of the army's performance.

22. For example, then-Major Volney Warner's unit advanced about 60 miles in one day of sustained combat, meeting resistance in Iraqi defensive positions about every 3 miles. The leading elements of General Barry McCaffrey's 24th

Mechanized Infantry Division moved farther and faster than any of General Patton's Third Army units during World War II. And McCaffrey's units outpaced the German offensive through the Ardennes to the English Channel in 1940.

23. Gordon and Trainor, *Generals' War*, are extremely critical. While they have valid points, these authors show little appreciation for the changes in lethality and size of division and corps combat formations, changes due to the new weapons, equipment, and logistics, as well as to the speeds of operations. Like many other critics, they show a poor grasp of the demands of command and control at the division and corps levels, especially the danger of large "friendly fire" casualties.

24. Cohen and Keaney, *Gulf War Air Power Survey*.

25. George Friedman and Meredith Friedman, *The Future of War* (New York: St. Martin's, 1996). The authors elaborate this concept and illustrate it with a number of weapons, including aircraft carriers. It is worth noting that they apply it to the tank, failing to grasp the astounding increase in killing power that characterizes modern tanks like the M-I, the British Challenger, the German Leopard, and the Russian T-80 and T-90.

26. See Gordon and Trainor, *Generals' War*. This is a continuing theme throughout the book that has not has been successfully refuted.

27. William G. Pagonis, *Moving Mountains: Lessons in Leadership and Logistics from the Gulf War* (Cambridge: Harvard Business School Press, 1992), 7. General Pagonis managed the Central Command's logistics during the first Persian Gulf War.

28. See Cohen and Keaney, *Gulf War Air Power Survey*, 188–89. In the repositioning of the 18th Airborne Corps, C-130s flew scheduled landings every seven minutes, twenty-four hours a day, for nearly fourteen days.

29. The British defeat of Argentine forces in the Falkland Islands is not an exception because U.S. assistance in intelligence and other areas was essential. Nor are the British and French interventions in Sierra Leone and the Ivory Coast, respectively, because they are not "forced entry" operations that require forces to fight their way into a country.

30. The Defense Department had nine such ships for movement to the Gulf in 1990, but only seven were sufficiently well maintained to move on schedule. Still, this capability is real—not the most advanced sealift technology, but easily available.

31. Information papers provided by the Department of the Army, May 2001.

32. The Hohenfels training area is near Grafenwoehr, allowing the two to be used together in limited ways, but it is much smaller and does not essentially change the comparison with the NTC made here.

33. Soviet military officers were particularly articulate about the implications of the first Gulf War. See, for some examples, Mary C. FitzGerald, "The Soviet Image of Future War: Through the Prism of the Persian Gulf," *Comparative Strategy* 10, no. 4 (1991), 393–435; Mary C. FitzGerald, "The Soviet Military and the New Air War in the Persian Gulf," *Airpower Journal* 5, no. 4 (1991).

34. Guay and Callum, "Transformation and Future Prospects."

35. See, for example, "Schroeder Refuses to Provide More Funds for Armed Forces," *Frankfurter Allgemeine Zeitung,* 7 March 2001 (English ed.). See *The Military Balance, 2001–2002* (London: IISS, 2001), 291, for a table on declining military budgets, 1998–2001.

36. Richard A. Bitzinger, "Towards a Brave New Arms Industry?" *Adelphi Paper* 356 (London: IISS, 2003), 6–9.

37. Ibid., 84.

38. See Odom, *On Internal War,* for a fuller analysis of this issue and the concept of "colonialism by ventriloquy."

39. For more on this point, see W. E. Odom, "Making NATO Interventions Work," *Strategic Review* 28, no. 2 (2000), 13–18; and National Science Foundation, "Interventions for the Long Run."

40. See Philip Zelikow and Condoleezza Rice, *Germany Unified and Europe Transformed* (Cambridge: Harvard University Press, 1995). This account offers excellent documentation of the first President Bush's use of U.S. power in Europe to prevent the efforts of British Prime Minister Margaret Thatcher and French President François Mitterrand to derail German reunification.

41. For debate leading up to enlargement in 1999, see William E. Odom, "NATO Expansion: Why the Critics Are Wrong," *National Interest,* no. 39 (1995), 38–49. For 2002 see hearings on NATO enlargement before the House Committee on International Relations, 17 April 2002, and before the Senate Foreign Relations Committee, 1 May 2002. This rationale was sharply disputed in 1996–98 but became the Clinton administration's line. It was little disputed as the Bush administration repeated it in 2001–2.

42. See William E. Odom, *Trial After Triumph: East Asia After the Cold War* (Indianapolis: Hudson Institute, 1992), especially the introduction and chapter 5.

43. This figure is undoubtedly much too high for both countries because it is based on "purchasing power parity" instead of international market exchange rates for their currencies.

44. Three field-grade army officers who served in Bosnia and Kosovo each explained this effect to one of the authors in slightly different ways, but the core message was common: telling professional soldiers that what they are doing is not worth risking lives demoralizes them.

45. Gelpi and Feaver, "Speak Softly and Carry a Big Stick?"

46. See Howard R. Winton and David R. Metz, eds., *The Challenge to Change: Military Institutions and New Realities, 1918–1941* (Lincoln: University of Nebraska Press, 2000); Rosen, *Winning the Next War.*

Chapter 4. The Demography Gap

1. Keynes, "Economic Consequences," 17.

2. European Union, Commission of the European Communities, "EU Economy," 12.

3. See Hudson and Den Boer, "Surplus of Men."

4. Eberstadt, "Population Implosion," 51.

5. Eberstadt, "Russia: Too Sick," 7.

6. INED (French demographic institute); www.ined.fr 1 December 2002.

7. U.S. Census Bureau, *International Data Base*, www.census.gov 6 July 2003.

8. For a detailed explanation of these issues see John Bongaarts, "Global Population Growth: Demographic Consequences of Declining Fertility," *Science*, 282, no. 5388 (16 October 1998), and Martha Farnsworth Riche, *America's Diversity and Growth: Signposts for the 21st Century* (Washington, D.C.: Population Reference Bureau, 2000, *Population Bulletin*, 55, no. 2, [2000]), box 1, p. 6.

9. U.S. Census Bureau projections and historical statistics (for 1950, both East and West Germany).

10. Historical statistics and U.S. Census Bureau estimates.

11. United Nations Population Division, *Replacement Migration*, 93.

12. Nicolas Baverez, *Les Orphelins de la liberté* (Paris: Plon, 1999), 123.

13. Haines, "Ethnic Differences," table 3.

14. Livi-Bacci, *Concise History*, 106–7.

15. See, for example, Mendras and Meyet, "L'Italie suicidaire?"

16. Todd, *Après l'empire*, 71.

17. Center for Immigration Studies, "Current Numbers," http://www.cis .org/topics/currentnumbers.html 16 March 2002 and "Illegal Immigration," http://www.cis.org/topics/illegalimmigration.html 24 February 2002. Higher estimates from Philip Martin and Jonas Widgren, "International Migration: Facing the Challenge," *Population Bulletin* 57, no. 1 (2002) (Washington, D.C.: Population Reference Bureau), table 2, p. 12.

18. William H. Frey, "Migration Swings," *American Demographics*, February 2002, 20 (25.9 percent).

19. Nine-million figure from "The Longest Journey: A Survey of Immigration," *The Economist*, 2 November 2002, 7.

20. D'Vera Cohn, "Immigrants Account for Half of New Workers," *Washington Post*, 2 December 2002.

21. Huntington, "The U.S.," 89. Huntington is now critical of Mexican immigration: "The Special Case of Mexican Immigration: Why Mexico Is a Problem," *American Enterprise Online*, December 2000.

22. Professor Philip Kasinitz of Hunter College, quoted in Bruce Lambert, "40 Percent in New York City Are Foreign-Born, Study Says," *New York Times*, 24 July 2000.

23. Data from Census Bureau, "Profile of the Foreign-Born Population in the United States," *Current Population Reports*, P23-195 (Washington, D.C.: U.S. Government Printing Office, 1999), 3.

24. Roberto Suro, "Movement at Warp Speed," *American Demographics*, August 2000, 63.

25. Wayne Kondro, "Canadian Universities: Massive Hiring Plan Aimed at 'Brain Gain,' " *Science*, 286, no. 5440 (22 October 1999), 651–53.

26. Center for Research on Innovation and Society, *Deutsche Nachwuchswissenschaftler in den U.S.A.*, exec. summary, 1; National Science Foundation,

www.nsf.gov/sbe/srs/issuebrf/sib99327.pdf 19 June 2003, 1995 data; National Science Foundation, *Report of the Senior Assessment Panel*, 25; "Survey: The United States," *The Economist*, 11 March 2000, 12 (U.S. ed.).

27. Devan and Tewari, "Brains Abroad."

28. Saxenian, *Silicon Valley's New Immigrant Entrepreneurs*, viii.

29. "Microsoft Clicks on India," *Financial Times*, 15 November 1997.

30. Sharon G. Levin and Paula E. Stephan, "Are the Foreign Born a Source of Strength for U.S. Science?" *Science*, 285, no. 5431 (20 August 1999), 1213–14.

31. Center for Research on Innovation and Society, *Deutsche Nachwuchswissenschaftler in den U.S.A.*, exec. summary, 1.

32. INRA (Institut national de recherche en informatique et en automatique), cited by Michel Alberganti in "Informatique: La Recherche française en quête de débouchés nationaux," *Le Monde*, 10 September 1999 (web edition at www.LeMonde.fr). See also Jean François-Poncet, "La Fuite des cervaux: Mythe ou réalité," Rapport d'information 388 (1999–2000), Commission des affaires économiques, French senate, http://www.senat.fr/rap/r99–388/r99–388_mono.html#haut 17 June 2000.

33. Robert Koenig, "Humboldt Hits the Comeback Trail," *Science* 291, no. 5505 (2 February 2001), 819.

34. Center for Research on Innovation and Society, *Deutsche Nachwuchswissenschaftler in den U.S.A.*, exec. summary, p. 2.

35. Horst Rademacher, "It's Not Nearly as Bad as You Might Think," *Frankfurter Allgemeine Zeitung*, English ed., 21 January 2001 (www.faz.com).

36. See, for example, Dennis Normile, "Japan: Blue Laser Pioneer Seeks Greener Pastures," *Science* 287, no. 5454 (4 February 2000), 782 (from www.sciencemag.org 10 July 2000), and Glenn Zorpette, "Blue Chip," *Scientific American*, August 2000, 31, for a famous example of "brain drain" from Japan.

37. MIT, http://web.mit.edu/iso/www/stats/1998/index.html/general_stats.html International Students Statistics 1998–99, MIT International Student Office, Accessed 19 June 2003.

38. Johnson and Regets, "International Mobility," 2, and Michael G. Finn, "The Stay Rate of Foreign Doctoral Students in Science and Engineering," 98/99 Open Doors on the Web, http://www.opendoorsweb.org/Lib%20Pages/For%20Studs/stay_rate.htm 19 April 2000); Douglas Fox, "U.S. Research Feels No Crisis," *Scientific American*, October 1999, says that in 1996 "68% of foreign citizens who received scientific or engineering doctorates planned to stay in the U.S" (89).

39. Richard R. Nelson, "U.S. Technological Leadership: Where Did It Come from and Where Did It Go?" in Jasanoff, *Comparative Science*, 225. Nikola Telsa, for example, came from Austria (Croatia), Michael I. Pupin from Hungary (Serbia), and Charles Steinmetz from Germany (Prussia).

40. Saxenian, *Silicon Valley's New Immigrant Entrepreneurs*, viii. Most of the Chinese in the study are from Taiwan.

41. *Forbes* magazine, 2002 list of the richest four hundred Americans.

42. "Survey: The United States," *The Economist*, 11 March 2000, 12 (U.S. ed.).

43. Jacoby, "How to Think About U.S. Immigration Policy," 5.

44. Saxenian, *Silicon Valley's New Immigrant Entrepreneurs.*

45. Sadanand Dhume, "Expatriates: Bringing It Home," *Far Eastern Economic Review,* 17 February 2000, 44–46.

46. See NSF, http://www.nsf.gov/sbe/srs/seind98/c2/c2s4.htm, National Science Foundation, 1998 Indicators, chapter 2, "Higher Education in Science and Engineering," section "Reverse flow of scientists and engineers to Asia."

47. Johnson and Regets, "International Mobility," 4, citing H. Choi, *An International Scientific Community: Asian Scholars in the United States* (New York: Praeger, 1995).

48. AnnaLee Saxenian, "Brain Circulation: How High-Skill Immigration Makes Everyone Better Off," *Brookings Review* 20, no. 1 (2002), 30.

49. Elliot Abrams, review of Peter Salin's *Assimilation American Style: The Public Interest,* 127 (1997), 125.

50. Glazer and Moynihan, *Beyond the Melting Pot.*

51. A point already made in the early 1980s by Sowell, *Ethnic America,* 286.

52. Alba, "Assimilation's Quiet Tide," 4.

53. Ibid., 14–15.

54. Suro, "Mixed Doubles." Kennedy, "Interracial Intimacy," 104, puts the number at around 40 percent (1990 census). Elliot Abrams, review of Peter Salin's *Assimilation American Style, The Public Interest,* 127 (1997), 126, on Japanese Americans.

55. Gregory Rodriguez, "Private Lives That Belie Public Words," *Los Angeles Times,* 10 February 2002.

56. "Speaking Graphically," *Population Today* 27, no. 2 (February 1999), 6. Many are black-white marriages that do not involve immigrants, but these partnerships also indicate a breakdown of ethnic barriers.

57. Glazer, "Immigration and the American Future," 55. See also Jacoby, "In Asian America."

58. Rodriguez, *From Newcomers to New Americans,* 17, from 1990 census.

59. Jacoby, "How to Think About U.S. Immigration Policy," 8.

60. "America's Best Colleges 2003," *U.S. News and World Report* (www .usnews.com 4 January 2003).

61. Cheryl Russell, *Racial and Ethnic Diversity* (Ithaca, N.Y.: Strategist, 1998), 8, 14, (1996 and 1997 data). Given patterns of Asian immigration, most of these students and M.D.s are either Asian-born or the children of immigrants.

62. Lipset and Marks, *It Didn't Happen Here,* 134, 155.

63. Patrick J. Buchanan, *The Death of the West: How Dying Populations and Immigrant Invasions Imperil Our Country and Civilization* (New York: St. Martin's/Thomas Dunne, 2002).

64. Sowell, *Ethnic America,* 172.

65. Alan Cooperman, "Robertson Calls Islam a Religion of Violence, Mayhem," *Washington Post,* 22 February 2002. For Robertson's claims of conspiracies, see *The New World Order* (Dallas: Word Publishing, 1991).

66. http://www.falwell.com/historical_data.html 15 June 2002, "Historical

Data About Muhammad." Susan Sachs, "Baptist Pastor Attacks Islam, Inciting Cries of Intolerance," *New York Times,* 15 June 2002.

67. Adam Clymer, "U.S. Attitudes Altered Little by Sept. 11, Pollsters Say," *New York Times,* 20 May 2002.

68. Shain, "The Mexican-American Diaspora's Impact," 690.

69. Shain, "Marketing the Democratic Creed Abroad," 102.

70. Wattenberg, *First Universal Nation,* 48–49.

71. Brzezinski, *Grand Chessboard,* 210.

72. Clark, Hatton, and Williamson, "Where Do U.S. Immigrants Come From and Why?" 36, table.

73. OECD, *Trends in International Migration,* Annual Report 2001, 198, 1999 data; Japan Ministry of Justice, www.moj.go.jp 26 June 2003.

74. United Nations Population Division, *Replacement Migration,* 51, 88, 75.

75. Papademetrious and Hamilton, *Reinventing Japan,* 1–4.

76. See Myron Weiner, "Opposing Visions: Migration and Citizenship Policies in Japan and the United States," in Weiner and Hanami, *Temporary Workers or Future Citizens?* 7.

77. Yad Vashem, www.yadvashem.org/about_holocaust/faqs/answers/faq _11.html 7 June 2001 (Jews from Germany and Austria, 1933–39).

78. Salim Ibrahimm, *Die "Ausländerfrage" in Deutschland: Fakten, Defizite und Handlungimperative* (Frankfurt am Main: VAS (Verlag für Akademische Schriften, 1997), table 1, p. 169; table 2, p. 172; and table 6, p. 174. Martin and Widgren, "International Migration," table 3, p. 16, for 1998 German data. OECD, *Trends in Annual Migration,* Annual Report 2001, for total percentage of foreign population. Andreas Goldberg, "Islam in Germany" in Hunter, *Islam, Europe's Second Religion,* 32, for estimate of number of Turks.

79. Martin and Widgren, "International Migration"; OECD, *Trends in International Migration Annual Report 2001,* 177. 1998 data.

00. Riphahn, "Dissimilation?" 21, figure (b)2.

81. INSEE, Tableaux du bilan démographique, tables 6 and 7, http://www .insee.fr/fr/ffc/pop_age3.htm#Tableau%207%20 -%20Naissances%20par%20nationalité%20des%20parents 16 March 2002

82. Remy Leveau and Shireen T. Hunter, "Islam in France," p. 6, and Andreas Goldberg, "Islam in Germany," p. 29, in Hunter, *Islam, Europe's Second Religion.* Estimates are based on country of origin, so "Muslim background" is more accurate because some immigrants from Muslim nations may themselves have abandoned the practice of Islam. (See Kaltenbach and Tribalat, *La République et l'islam,* chap. 2.)

83. "Speech That Has Raised a Storm," *Birmingham Post,* 22 April 1968; *Encyclopedia Britannica* compact disc 2000 deluxe ed., Enoch Powell entry.

84. Eberstadt, "Population Implosion," 49.

85. Albert Schäfer, "Year Saw Continued Big Increase in Number of Naturalizations in Germany," *Frankfurter Allgemeine Zeitung* 29 December 2000 (English ed., www.faz.com); "More Than Half a Million Naturalisations," *DE-NEWS,* 13 June 2003.

86. United Nations Population Division, *Replacement Migration*, 51, 88, 75.

87. OECD, *Employment Outlook* June 2001, chart 5.1, p. 179. See also Wihtol de Wenden, *L'Immigration en Europe*, 144. Statistics are not perfectly comparable; Old World nations distinguish between citizens and foreigners, whereas New World countries look at comparisons between native-borns and foreign-borns. See also "Special Report: Muslims in Western Europe," *The Economist*, 10 August 2002, 23; for the Netherlands see "The Longest Journey: A Survey of Immigration," *The Economist*, 2 November 2002, 9.

88. Far more immigrants to the United States than to Europe are college-educated. Devan and Tewari, "Brains Abroad," 1.

89. For France, see Xavier Ternisien, "44 aumôniers musulmans en France contre 460 intervenants catholiques," *Le Monde*, 30 October 2001. See also "A Survey of the Netherlands," *The Economist*, 4 May 2002, 15 (U.S. ed.).

90. Geoffrey Wawro, "Letter from Europe," unpublished, 2003.

91. Barone, *New Americans*, 169.

92. Peters, *Fighting for the Future*, 153.

93. World Bank, *World Development Indicators*, 1999, table 1.3, Gender Differences; for explanation of data see table 2.11, Illiteracy.

94. See U.N. statistics, *The World's Women 2000* at http://unstats.un.org/unsd/demographic/ww2000/tables.htm and www.un.org/Depts/unsd/ww2000/table6a.htm 8 August 2001.

95. OECD, *Education at a Glance: OECD Indicators*, 169, chart C4.6, 1998 data.

96. Japan Ministry of Health, Labor, and Welfare, http://www.mhlw.go.jp/wp/hakusyo/josei/00/gaiyo2.html 1 August 2001; Japan Ministry of Education, www.mext.go.jp/b_menu/toukei003/hyo14-2.htm 26 June 2003.

97. OECD, *Education Statistics* (Paris: OECD, 2001), 173, table C4.5.

98. Morley, *Mountain Is Moving*, 3.

99. Takahashi Hiroyuki, "Working Women in Japan: A Look at Historical Trends and Legal Reform." Washington, D.C.: Japan Economic Institute, 1998 (JEI Report no. 42A, 6 November 1998), 4.

100. Morley, *Mountain Is Moving*, 72.

101. On this issue, see Sylvester J. Schieber and Paul S. Hewitt, "Demographic Risk in Industrial Societies: Independent Population Forecasts for the G-7 Countries," *World Economics*, 1, no. 4 (October–December 2000), 16.

102. U.S. Dept. of Justice, http://www.ojp.usdoj.gov/bjs/correct.htm 19 June 2003 and other sources.

103. Source: OECD Health Data, http://www.oecd.org/els/health/software/fad.htm, 10 August 2001.

104. Mauer, *Crisis of the Young African American Male*, 3.

105. "Speaking Graphically: Obesity Among Adults in OECD Countries," *Population Today* 30, no. 6 (2002), 11.

Chapter 5. The Economic Performance Gap

1. IMF 2003 estimates, http://www.imf.org/external/pubs/ft/weo/2002/02/data/ngdp_r_a.csv 7 December 2002.
2. "America Rides the Wireless Wave," *The Economist*, 29 April 2000, 65 (U.S. ed.).
3. Coffee, "Convergence and Its Critics," 1 (abstract).
4. Steven Casper, "The Legal Framework for Corporate Governance: The Influence of Contract Law on Company Strategies in Germany and the United States," in Hall and Soskice, *Varieties of Capitalism*, 329.
5. La Porta et al., "Law and Finance."
6. Lipset and Marks, *It Didn't Happen Here*, 97.
7. "Survey, European Business: New Economy, Old Problems," *The Economist*, 29 April 2000, 17–19.
8. OECD, *Fostering Entrepreneurship*, 54.
9. Djankov et al., "Regulation of Entry," 4.
10. David C. Mowery and Nathan Rosenberg, "The U.S. National Innovation System," in Nelson, *National Innovation Systems*, 49.
11. Overholt, "Japan's Economy."
12. See Milhaupt and West, "Dark Side of Private Ordering."
13. See Alan Brender, "Japan Tries to Reform How It Trains Lawyers," *Chronicle of Higher Education*, 15 February 2002.
14. Brill and Carlson, "U.S. and Japanese Antimonopoly Policy."
15. Waller, "Internationalization of Antitrust Enforcement."
16. OECD, *Fostering Entrepreneurship*, 58–59.
17. "Survey, European Business."
18. Emily Thornton, "Going Belly-Up," *Business Week*, 5 May 1997, 22 (international ed.).
19. Katz, *Japan, the System That Soured*, 88–89.
20. See chapter 2 of Kornai, *Vision and Reality*, for the "soft budget" concept.
21. See, for example, Craig, Karolyi, and Stulz, "Why Are Foreign Firms Listed in the U.S. Worth More?"
22. Hideaki Miyajima, "The Impact of Deregulation on Corporate Governance and Finance," in Carlile and Tilton, *Is Japan Really Changing Its Ways?* 34–35. See also Kanaya and Woo, *Japanese Banking Crisis*, and Dore, *Stock Market Capitalism*.
23. Sigurt Vitols, "Varieties of Corporate Governance: Comparing Germany and the UK," in Hall and Soskice, *Varieties of Capitalism*.
24. See details in Davis Global Advisors, *Leading Corporate Governance Indicators ® 2001*, 79, table, and *Leading Corporate Governance Indicators ® 2002*, exec. summary, 5. Rankings are from the 2002 edition. We thank Stephen Davis for sending us the 2001 edition.
25. John T. Addison et al., "The Long Awaited Reform of the German Works Constitution Act," discussion paper no. 422, Bonn: Institute for the Study of Labor, February 2002.

26. Quoted in Charkham, *Keeping Good Company,* 10.

27. La Porta et al., "Law and Finance."

28. Peter A. Hall and David Soskice, "An Introduction to Varieties of Capitalism," in Hall and Soskice, eds., *Varieties of Capitalism,* 8.

29. See Almar Latour and Devin J. Delaney, "Toothless Watchdogs: Outside the U.S. Executives Face Little Legal Peril," *Wall Street Journal,* 16 August 2002.

30. See North and Thomas, *Rise of the Western World,* on the importance of providing private motives for undertaking socially desirable activities. Bhattacharya and Daouk, in "World Price of Insider Trading," note that the cost of equity decreases significantly after the first insider trading prosecution.

31. OECD, *Fostering Entrepreneurship,* 252–60.

32. National Science Board, *Science and Engineering Indicators, 2000,* appendix, table 7-14; "Survey: European Business."

33. For Japan, see Debra Lau, "American VCs Land in Japan: New Laws and Cultural Changes Fuel Western Interest," *Venture Capital Journal* 5 (1 May 2000), 46–49.

34. On venture capital and the professionalization of start-ups, see Hellmann and Puri, "Venture Capital."

35. David C. Mowery and Nathan Rosenberg, "The U.S. National Innovation System," in Nelson, *National Innovation Systems,* 48–49.

36. Goldie Blumenstyk, "American Universities' Patents Royalties Grow 10 Percent, Survey Finds," *Chronicle of Higher Education,* 14 November 2000; Goldie Blumenstyk, "Value of University Licenses on Patents Exceeded $1 Billion in 2000, Survey Finds," *Chronicle of Higher Education,* 9 March 2002; Goldie Blumenstyk, "Colleges Report $827 Million in 2001 Royalties," *Chronicle of Higher Education,* 6 June 2003.

37. "The Land of Disappointments," *The Economist,* 19 February 2000, 104 (U.S. ed.)

38. See Fujisue, "Promotion of Academia-Industry Cooperation"; National Science Foundation, Tokyo Regional Office, "Japanese Policies to Support High-Risk Innovation Research at Small and Medium Enterprises: A Comparison with the United States," report memorandum #00-09, 9 June 2000, 3, 8; Michael Chan, "2 Japanese Institutions Create Incubators for University-Based Start-Ups," *Chronicle of Higher Education,* 9 August 2001; Fumio Kodama and Lewis M. Branscomb, "University Research as an Engine for Growth: How Realistic Is the Vision?" in Branscomb, Kodama, and Florida, *Industrializing Knowledge,* 15.

39. OECD, *Employment Outlook* (July 2002), 323, table G.

40. In the late 1990s employment protection indexes, which measure the extent to which legislation makes it difficult to lay off employees, were 0.7 in the United States compared with 2.6 in Germany, 2.8 in France, and 3.4 in Italy. Card and Freeman, "What Have Two Decades of British Economic Reform Delivered?" 50, table 6 (from OECD, *Employment Outlook* 1999, table 2.5).

41. The U.S. minimum wage is much lower relative to average wage than in Europe. Heckman, "Flexibility and Job Creation: Lessons from Germany," 15.

42. Hans-Werner Sinn and Frank Westermann, "Two Mezzogiornos," working

paper no. 378 (Munich: CESinfo, December 2000), 22. See also Ochel, "Welfare to Work," 5.

43. Marc Gurgand and David N. Margolis, "Welfare and Labor Earnings: An Evaluation of the Financial Gains to Work," discussion paper no. 461, Bonn: IZA, March 2002, see a gain from work for most French welfare recipients, though not all, and in some cases the gains are very small. For comparison of U.S. and European jobless benefits, see Stephen Nickell et al., "Why Do Jobless Rates Differ?" *CESinfo Forum* 3, no. 1 (2002), 53, tables 2, 3. Also, OECD, *Benefit Systems and Work Incentives,* 43, table 3.10, for a comparison of gross replacement rates.

44. Heckman, "Flexibility and Job Creation," 21.

45. Konstanze Frischen, "The Situation Is Not That Bad in the East," *Frankfurter Allgemeine Zeitung* 26 February 2001 (English ed., www.faz.com).

46. http://www.stat.go.jp/data/idou/sokuhou/nen/index.htm, 5 July 2001; http://www.census.gov/prod/2001pubs/p20–538.pdf 5 July 2001.

47. Ralph Atkins, "Berlin Tackles Joblessness with Rent Reform," *Financial Times,* 20 July 2000, 2 (U.S. ed).

48. OECD, *Employment Outlook,* several editions.

49. Heckman. "Flexibility and Job Creation," 10. For a discussion of France's structural unemployment, see Heyer and Timbeau, "Le chômage structurel," 122 and 124, esp. tables 1 and 2.

50. For disability compensation in the Netherlands, see "A Survey of the Netherlands," *The Economist,* 4 May 2002, 7 (U.S. ed).

51. Friedrich Schneider, "The Size and Development of the Shadow Economies of 22 Transition and 21 OECD Countries," discussion paper no. 513 (Bonn: Institute for the Study of Labor [IZA], June 2002), 13, table 3.

52. OECD, *Employment Outlook,* July 2002, 305, table B.

53. OECD, *Employment Outlook,* July 2002, 307–9, table C.

54. Anchordoguy, "Japan's Software Industry."

55. See, for example, Johnson, *Japan, Who Governs?*

56. See Duesterberg, "The Japanese Economy in the 21st Century," 33 (of English-language original draft).

57. McKinsey Global Institute, *Why the Japanese Economy Is Not Growing,* 2 (exec. summary).

58. Card and Freeman, "What Have Two Decades of British Economic Reform Delivered?" 52, table 8, Source U.S. Bureau of Labor Statistics.

59. Heilmann, "China," 76.

60. Béja, "Crise sociale endémique," 128.

61. See Rosefielde, "Culture Versus Competition," 51.

62. Barry Naughton, *Growing Out of the Plan: Chinese Economic Reform, 1978–1993* (Cambridge: Cambridge University Press, 1996), 35–36.

63. OECD, *Synthesis Report: China in the World Economy* (Paris: OECD, 2002), 54, 26. 1999 data.

64. Heilmann, "China."

65. Xiabo Lu, "Booty Socialism." See also Chen, "Capitalist Development," 408.

66. See Chen, "Rebuilding the Party's Normative Authority"; Pei, "China's Governance Crisis."

67. For an analysis of these issues see Huntington, *Political Order in Changing Societies.*

68. For the concept of degeneration in communist polities, see Zbigniew Brzezinski, "The Soviet Political System: Transformation or Degeneration?" in Brzezinski, ed., *Dilemmas of Change in Soviet Politics* (New York: Columbia University Press, 1969), 30.

69. Finer, *History of Government,* 2: 656–57. See also Jones, *Great Qing Code,* 4–7.

70. See Friedrich and Brzezinski, *Totalitarian Dictatorship,* 146, on totalitarian states' attitudes toward civil law.

71. Finer, *History of Government,* 3: 1090–91.

72. Korea formally became a Japanese colony in 1910 but de facto lost its independence to Japan during the Russo-Japanese War of 1904–5.

73. On the colonial period and its role in economic development see, for example, Carter J. Eckert, *Offspring of Empire: The Koch'ang Kims and the Colonial Origins of Korean Capitalism, 1876–1945* (Seattle: University of Washington Press, 1997); and Gregory Henderson, *Korea: The Politics of the Vortex* (Cambridge: Harvard University Press, 1968), 78 on the legal system and 86–101 on Japan's role in modernization.

74. See Huntington, "Political Development," on the concept of decaying colonial institutions.

75. Ezra Vogel, *Japan as Number One: Lessons for America* (Cambridge: Harvard University Press, 1979); Kennedy, *Rise and Fall of the Great Powers;* Thurow, *Head to Head.*

76. Gabriel Schoenfeld, "Holocaust Reparations: A Growing Scandal," *Commentary* 110, no. 2 (September 2000).

77. Huntington, "Why International Primacy Matters," 72.

78. Richard Rosecrance, Introduction to Rosecrance, *America as an Ordinary Country,* 12.

79. From table B-107, Council of Economic Advisers, *Economic Report of the President,* February 2002 (http://w3.access.gpo.gov/usbudget/fy2003/sheets/b107 .xls 7 December 2002).

80. OECD Main Economic Indicators (www.oecd.org/std/indic.pdf, 35, 2 July 2001).

81. IISS, *The Military Balance, 2002–2003* (London: Oxford University Press, 2002), 332–37, table 26.

82. Huntington, *American Politics,* 257.

Chapter 6. The University Gap

1. Joe Plomin, "European Boost as U.S. Loosens Grip on Research," *The Guardian,* 21 June 2001.

2. Altbach, "International Academic Crisis?" 316.

3. Ibid., 318.

4. "University Challenge," editorial, *Financial Times*, 26–27 October 2002.

5. Adams et al., *Benchmarking of the International Standing of Research.*

6. "U.S. Share of World Papers Slides as Europe, Asia Rise," *Science Watch* 8, no. 3 (1997), 1.

7. "Research at the Top of the Table," *The Guardian*, 12 June 2001, computed by Evidence Ltd from data from the Institute for Scientific Information in Philadelphia.

8. National Science Board, *Science and Engineering Indicators, 2002*, vol. 2.

9. Source: www.nobel.se 26 June 2001.

10. These are some of the top prizes mentioned by Robert M. May, "The Scientific Wealth of Nations," *Science*, 7 February 1997, 796.

11. Paul R. Krugman, *Pop Internationalism* (Cambridge: MIT Press, 1996); the first of many editions of Paul A. Samuelson's enduring textbook is *Economics* (New York: McGraw-Hill, 1948). Our sources for the numbers of translations of Krugman and Samuelson are, respectively, e-mail from Maria Santos of MIT Press to Takuro Takeuchi, 25 June 2001; and www.mskousen.com/Books/Articles/perserverance.html 4 July 2001.

12. Paul Krugman, "The Myth of Asia's Miracle," *Foreign Affairs* 73, no. 6 (1994). Krugman argued that Asia's growth was due to increasing inputs, not to higher productivity. Quotation from Darren McDermott, "Singapore Swing: Krugman Was Right; Stung by a Professor, the Island Starts an Efficiency Drive," *Wall Street Journal*, 23 October 1996.

13. Daniel J. Goldhagen, *Hitler's Willing Executioners: Ordinary Germans and the Holocaust* (New York: Knopf, 1996).

14. Jan Tomasz Gross, *Neighbors: The Destruction of the Jewish Community in Jedwabne, Poland* (Princeton: Princeton University Press, 2001). Gross is Polish-born but left Poland in the 1960s. See Abraham Brumberg, "Poles and Jews," *Foreign Affairs* 81, no. 5 (2002).

15. Paxton's works include *Vichy France* (New York: Knopf, 1972), and, with Michael Marrus, *Vichy and the Jews* (New York: Basic, 1981).

16. Cumings's books include *The Origins of the Korean War* (Princeton: Princeton University Press, 1981–90); *The Two Koreas* (New York: Foreign Policy Association, 1984); and *Korea's Place in the Sun: A Modern History* (New York: Norton, 1997).

17. Dower, *Embracing Defeat;* Howard W. French, "An Outsider Teaches Japan About Itself," *New York Times*, 2 February 2002.

18. Alan Riding, "Belgium Confronts Its Heart of Darkness," *New York Times*, 21 September 2002.

19. Védrine, *Les Cartes de la France*, 8–9.

20. More than 20 percent for 1998–99, 31 percent for 2000, 18 percent for 2001.

21. Verzeichnis der besprochen Werke, *Philosophie Rundschau: Eine Zeitschrift für philosophische Kritik* 47 (2000); 26 out of 121 published in the United States.

22. Antonio Gramsci, *Selections from Cultural Writings,* ed. David Forgacs and Geoffrey Nowell-Smith, trans. William Boelhower (Cambridge: Harvard University Press, 1991), 405.

23. Institute of International Education, http://opendoors.iienetwork.org/?g =3390&ct=v2pages&pg_v=pg&pg_pid=8043&pg_fid=19750 26 November 2002.

24. Institute of International Education, IIE Network, 2001–2 data, http:// opendoors.iienetwork.org/?p=25182; http://opendoors.iienetwork.org/?p=25199 19 June 2003.

25. Institute of International Education, http://opendoors.iienetwork.org/file _depot/0–10000000/0–10000/3390/folder/19766/All+countries+of+origin1.xls 26 November 2002.

26. Institute of International Education, Open Doors on the Web, 2001–2 data. EU data includes only Germany, the United Kingdom, France, Italy, Spain, and the Netherlands (16,407); total EU representation is higher. http://opendoors .iienetwork.org/?pg_v=pg&pg_pid=8403&pg_fid=20488&g=3390&ct=v2pa 9 January 2003.

27. http://www.wharton.upenn.edu/mba/admissions/intl_students.html 20 June 2003 (Wharton class of 2005); http://www.hbs.edu/mba/experience/meet/ students/classprofile.html 20 June 2003 (Harvard MBA class of 2002).

28. *Financial Times* MBA 2003, Business Education Section, 20 January 2003.

29. "Ranking Business Schools: The Numbers Game," *The Economist,* 12 October 2002, 65 (U.S. ed.).

30. Beth Mcmurtrie, "Foreign Enrollments Grow in the U.S., but So Does Competition from Other Nations," *Chronicle of Higher Education,* 16 November 2001. Other sources say a third of the world total: Philip G. Altbach, "The American Academic Model in Comparative Perspective," in Altbach, Gumport, and Johnstone, *In Defense of American Higher Education,* 15.

31. E-mail from Sagano Akiko, Japan Information and Culture Center, to Robert Dujarric, 4 March 2002.

32. Center for Research on Innovation and Society, *Deutsche Nachwuchswissenschaftler in den U.S.A,* 4 (exec. summary).

33. See tables in *UNESCO Statistical Yearbook 1999* and Eurostat data for 2000. Europeans are aware of this problem: see Dufourg, *La Compétitivité éducative internationale.* See also Dieter Eissel and Alexander Grasse, "German Higher Education on the Way to the Anglo-Saxon System," *Debatte* 9, no. 1 (2001), 11–12.

34. Eurostat data for 2000.

35. Alan Brender, "Japan Sees 23% Increase in Foreign College Students," *Chronicle of Higher Education,* 6 November 2001; *Japan Times,* 16 November 2002.

36. See, for example, "College Relies on Chinese Students, but Tokyo's Neon Beckons," *Asahi Shimbun*, 20 March 2002 (English ed., www.asahi.com).

37. E-mail from Peking University graduate, 27 February 2002.

38. Kang Hong-Jun, "Ph. D. Holders from Foreign Universities Put at 22,064," *Jong-Ang Ilbo*, 10 July 2001 (English ed., http://english.joins.com).

39. Britta Baron, "Can Germany Remain Competitive in Attracting Internationals?" IIE Network, http://www.opendoorsweb.org/Lib%20Pages/Global/can_Germany.htm (19 April 2000); Dufourg, *La Compétitivité éducative internationale*, 12.

40. Burton Bollag, "European Governments Are Urged to Speed Alignment of Higher-Education Systems," *Chronicle of Higher Education*, 4 April 2001.

41. Bernd Waechter, "European Universities Must Adapt in an Era of Global Competition," *Chronicle of Higher Education*, 7 December 2001.

42. Burton Bollag, "European Union Plans Scholarship Program for Masters-Level Students from Elsewhere," *Chronicle of Higher Education*, 23 July 2002.

43. Clark, *Places of Inquiry*, 19 (quoting Joseph Ben-David, *The Scientist's Role in Society*).

44. Lohmann, "American University."

45. Ernst Nolte, *La Guerre civile européenne, 1917–1945: National-socialisme et bolchevisme*, trans. Jean-Marie Argelès (Paris: Editions des Syrtes, 2000), 475.

46. E-mail from Renata Stein of the Leo Beck Institute to Robert Dujarric, 11 December 2000.

47. Clark, *Places of Inquiry*, 38.

48. Rosovsky, *University*, 33.

49. See Lohmann, "American University."

50. From Philip G. Altbach, "Patterns in Higher Education Development," in Altbach, Berdahl, and Gumport, *American Higher Education*, 29.

51. Jurgen Enders, "A Chair System in Transition: Appointments, Promotions, and Gate-keeping in German Higher Education," in Altbach, *Changing Academic Workplace*, 50.

52. Quotation from Cicilie Rohwedder and David Wessel, "Outclassed: Despite Proud Past, German Universities Fail by Many Measures," *Wall Street Journal*, 26 February 2001. On German education, see also Emma Tucker, "German Education: Seriously Underachieving. Must Try Harder," *Financial Times*, 13 February 2002.

53. Clark, *Places of Inquiry*, 98; discussion with a senior French university professor, 4 March 2002.

54. Altbach, "Patterns in Higher Education Development," 25.

55. Sakakibara Eisuke, "First Reform the Educational Bureaucracy," *Japan Echo* 28, no. 3 (2001), 25.

56. Coleman, *Japanese Science*, 160.

57. Bureau of the Census, U.S. Dept. of Commerce, *Historical Statistics of the U.S., Colonial Times to 1957* (Washington, D.C.: Government Printing Office,

1960), Series H316–26, p. 210, and Dept. of Education, Digest of Education Statistics 2001, http://www.nces.ed.gov/pubs2002/digest2001/ch3.asp 7 December 2002.

58. Barbara Sporn, "Current Issues and Future Priorities for European Higher Education Systems," in Altbach and Peterson, *Higher Education in the 21st Century*, 68.

59. Clark, *Higher Education System*, 60.

60. Enders, "Chair System in Transition," 17.

61. See remarks by German Minister of Education and Research Edelgard Bulman, Center for Research on Innovation and Society, *Deutsche Nachwuchswissenschaftler in den USA*, 3.

62. Enders, "Chair System in Transition," 3.

63. Robert Koenig, "Germany: Panel Urges New Slots for Young Researchers," *Science*, 21 April 2000, 413–14. See also Enders, "Chair System in Transition," 11–12.

64. Enders, "Chair System in Transition," 15. See also "Junior Professorships Approved," *Frankfurter Allgemeine Zeitung*, 21 December 2001 (English ed., www.faz.com).

65. Koenig, "Germany," and Michael Balter, "Germany: Germany Tries to Break Its Habilitation Habit," *Science*, 3 Sept 1999, 1525.

66. Arthur Kornberg, Introduction to Coleman, *Japanese Science*, x; Dennis Normile, "Women Faculty Battle Japan's Koza System," *Science*, 2 February 2001, 818.

67. Dennis Normile, "Japan: Japanese Jump on Postdoc Bandwagon," *Science*, 3 September 1999; Brendan Barket, "Internationalizing Japanese Science," in Hemmert and Oberländer, *Technology and Innovation*, 76.

68. www.waseda.ac.jp/koho/databook 9 August 2000.

69. Clark, *Higher Education System*, 67. See also Kornberg, Introduction to *Japanese Science*, x.

70. Marius B. Jansen, *The Making of Modern Japan* (Cambridge, Mass.: Belknap, 2000), makes this point about the Imperial University in Meiji Japan, 408.

71. Park Sung-woo, "SNU Faculty Sees a University Adrift," *JongAng Ilbo*, 9 April 2001 (English ed., http://english.joins.com).

72. A point made by German scientists in Center for Research on Innovation and Society, *Deutsche Nachwuchswissenschaftler in den U.S.A.*

73. Clark, *Places of Inquiry*, 42.

74. Third International Mathematics and Science Study (TIMSS), 1995, http://nces.ed.gov/TIMSS/ 16 June 2003.

75. Joachim R. Frick and Gert G. Wagner, "Economic and Social Perspectives of Immigrant Children in Germany," Bonn, IZA (Institute for the Study of Labor), discussion paper no. 301, June 2001, 27 (1995–96 data).

76. OECD, *Knowledge and Skills for Life*, 4–12.

77. Boyer, Altbach, and Whitelaw, *Academic Profession*, 74.

78. Altbach, "American Academic Model," in 14.

79. OECD, *Education at a Glance*, 1998 ed., 95, 181.

80. David Cohen, "The Worldwide Rise of Private Colleges," *Chronicle of Higher Education*, 9 March 2001 (1998 statistics).

81. See OECD, *Education at a Glance*, 181.

82. Kumiko Fujimura-Fanselow, "Japan," in Postiglione and Mak, *Asian Higher Education*, 39.

83. Clark, *Places of Inquiry*, 166.

84. OECD, *Education at a Glance*, 2002 ed., chart B1.1, 146; chart B2.1, 161.

85. From *Chronicle of Higher Education*, University Endowments as of 30 June 2002, chronicle.com/stats/endowments/endowment_results.php3 23 June 2003, student population per schools' websites, accessed 2 March 2002.

86. John L. Pulley, "Private Giving to Colleges Surpassed Expectations in 2000–1," *Chronicle of Higher Education*, 25 March 2002; Goldie Blumenstyk, "College Fund Raising Dips for the First Time Since 1988," *Chronicle of Higher Education*, 13 March 2003.

87. Ziya Serdar Tumgoren, "Stanford Receives $400-Million from Hewlett Fund," *Chronicle of Philanthropy*, 3 May 2001; John L. Pulley, "Caltech to Receive $600-Million in Gifts From Computer Pioneer," *Chronicle of Higher Education*, 29 October 2001; Audrey Y. Williams, "1922 Graduate's $150 Million Bequest Will Endow 150 Chairs at NYU," *Chronicle of Higher Education*, 6 February 2002.

88. "Campaign Updates," *Chronicle of Philanthropy*, several issues, through spring 2001.

89. Johns Hopkins University Comparative Nonprofit Sector Project, comparative data: tables, http://www.jhu.edu/cnp/research.html 11 April 2001. Data for 1995. Other countries are France, Germany, and Japan.

90. Foundation Center, http://fdncenter.org/research/trends_analysis/top100 assets.html and http://fdncenter.org/research/trends_analysis/top100giving.html 23 June 2003. (Year end 2000 but some fiscal years do not end on 31 December.)

91. Japan Foundation Center data, www.jtc.or.jp 23 June 2003.

92. Pulley, "Private Giving to Colleges."

93. Contributions to the Metropolitan Museum: *Chronicle of Philanthropy*, 10 February 2000.

94. Clark, *Places of Inquiry*, 162; Jansen, *Making of Modern Japan*, 541; Fujimura-Fanselow, "Japan," 39.

95. Source U.S. Census Bureau, 2000 data.

96. Carnegie Foundation for the Advancement of Teaching, *The Carnegie Classification of Institutions of Higher Education*, 2000 ed., http://www .carnegiefoundation.org/Classification/index.htm 12 April 2001.

97. OECD, *Education at a Glance*, 2000 ed., 1998 figures.

98. Altbach, "International Academic Crisis?" 319.

99. Lohmann, "American University."

100. U.S. Census Bureau, *International Data Base*, http://www.census.gov/ ipc/www/idbsum.html 20 June 2003.

101. Madelaine Drohan and Alan Freeman, "English Rules," in O'Meara, Mehlinger, and Krain, *Globalization*, 428.

Chapter 7. The Science Gap

1. See Richard R. Nelson and Nathan Rosenberg, "Technical Innovation and National Systems," in Nelson, *National Innovation Systems,* 9–10; see also Landes, *Wealth and Poverty of Nations.*
2. Rudy, *Universities of Europe,* 130.
3. Kyoto, Crafoord, Wolf, Volvo, Draper, Bower, and Fields Medal.
4. National Science Board, *Science and Engineering Indicators, 2002,* appendix tables 6–12, 6–13, 5–14.
5. National Science Board, *Science and Engineering Indicators, 2000,* appendix table 6–56.
6. Richard R. Nelson, "U.S. Technological Leadership: Where Did It Come from and Where Did It Go?" in Jasanoff, *Comparative Science,* 223.
7. Albert Abraham Michelson, physics, 1907; Alexis Carrel, physiology and medicine, 1912; Theodore William Richards, chemistry, 1914; source www .nobelprizes.com 1 August 2000.
8. National Science Board, *Science and Engineering Indicators, 2002,* appendix tables 5–50 and 5–51.
9. Michael Balter, "Europeans Who Do Postdocs Abroad Face Reentry Problems," *Science,* 3 September 1999.
10. National Science Board, *Science and Engineering Indicators, 2000,* appendix table 7–13.
11. Francis Williams, "Demand for World Patents up Almost 25%," *Financial Times,* 14 February 2001.
12. Otto Keck, "The National System for Technical Innovation in Germany," in Nelson, *National Innovation Systems,* 126; Iain Cockburn et al., "Pharmaceuticals and Biotechnology," in Mowery, *U.S. Industry in 2000,* 366, writes that German companies produced "approximately 80% of the world's pharmaceutical output" until World War II. See Jonathan Liebenau, *Medical Science and Medical Industry: The Formation of the American Pharmaceutical Industry* (Baltimore: Johns Hopkins University Press, 1987), 37.
13. See National Science Foundation, *Report of the Senior Assessment Panel.*
14. National Academy of Sciences, *Experiments in International Benchmarking,* 1–9.
15. See Vannevar Bush's 1945 report *Science, the Endless Frontier.*
16. National Science Board, *Science and Engineering Indicators, 2000,* and p. 2–42; and National Science Board, *Science and Engineering Indicators, 2002,* appendix table 4–40.
17. National Science Board, *Science and Engineering Indicators, 2002,* appendix table 4–40.
18. National Science Board, *Science and Engineering Indicators, 2002,* O-2.
19. Christian Simm, Plenary Presentation, Science Policy and Expatriate Scientists and Engineers: The Case of Switzerland, *Deutsche Nachwuchswissenschaftler in den U.S.A.*
20. Martin Hemmert and Christian Oberländer, "The Japanese System of Tech-

nology Innovation: Preparing for the Twenty-first Century," in Hemmert and Oberländer, *Technology and Innovation*, 8.

21. Japanese Science and Technology Agency, New Developments in Science
and Technology: Responding to National and Social Needs (Summary), *Annual
Report on the Promotion of Science and Technology*, 1999, fig. 4, http://202.244
.24.5/ekg1999 20 June 2003.

22. Dennis Normile, "University Funding: Japan Wants Results to Influence
Budgets," *Science*, 4 June 1999.

23. See Porter et al., *New Challenge to America's Prosperity*.

24. National Science Board, *Science and Engineering Indicators, 2002*, 4–5,
1998 data.

25. See National Science Board, *Science and Engineering Indicators, 2002*, O-
3–O-5.

Chapter 8. The Media and Mass Culture Gaps

1. *Frankfurter Allgemeine Zeitung* circulation was 122,254 in 2000 (per
k.paerssinen@faz.de 18 July 2001).

2. *Encyclopedia Britannica*, http://www.britannica.com/eb/article?eu=55318
&tocid=5040 30 April 2001.

3. "125 Top Grossing Films Worldwide 2001," *Variety*, www.variety.com 5
January 2003.

4. www.mjifc.com/musiczone/albumsalescharts.html 23 April 2001.

5. United States Department of Commerce, U.S. Travel Service, Research and
Analysis Division, "Annual Summary of International Travelers to the U.S. January–December 1975," April 1976, 95–97; ITA Tourism Industries, "International
Arrivals to the U.S.-Historical Visitation, 1994–2000," http://tinet.ita.gov/view/f
-2000-04-001/index.html?ti_cart_cookie+20030620.002659.1405.151932.04135
20 June 2003.

6. Susan Levine, "Summer Across the Pond," *Washington Post*, 6 July 2002.

7. See Michael Medved, "That's Entertainment? Hollywood's Contribution to
Anti-Americanism Abroad," *National Interest*, no. 68 (2002).

Conclusion

1. Wohlforth, "Stability of a Unipolar World," makes a realist case that the
empire is highly durable. Kenneth Waltz, the dean of the realist school, argues
that U.S. power will be counterbalanced by other countries, but in reaction to
Wohlforth's article, he waffled to the point of making realism a truism of little
practical use: "Realist theory predicts that balances once disrupted will one day
be restored. A limitation of the theory, a limitation common to social science
theories, is that it cannot say when"; "Structural Realism," 27.

2. James Q. Wilson and Edward C. Banfield, "Public Regardingness as a Value
Premise in Voting Behavior," *American Political Science Review* 58, no. 4 (1964),
876–87. See also Edward C. Banfield and James Q. Wilson, *City Politics* (Cam-

bridge: Harvard University Press, 1963), and James Q. Wilson and Edward C. Banfield, "Political Ethos Revisited," *American Political Science Review* 65, no. 4 (1971), 1848–62. Wilson and Banfield revised their thesis in the 1971 article, showing that recent immigrant attitudes change over time to become more like Anglo-Saxon voting attitudes on public values versus private ones.

3. Charles A. Kupchan, for example, is highly confident that Europe is practically at the point of being a single political entity and capable of challenging the United States. See his *End of the American Era*, especially chapter 4.

4. Australia and New Zealand, of course, occupy another region, but their economies are small, and they are in many ways extensions of Britain and strongly linked to the U.S. economy.

5. Olson, *Rise and Decline*.

6. David R. Cameron, "Distributional Coalitions and Other Sources of Economic Stagnation: On Olson's Rise and Decline of Nations," *International Organization* 42, no. 4 (1988), 561–603.

7. For an early critique, see Bauer, *Dissent on Development*. This is only one of his many works on the subject.

8. Carl von Clausewitz, *On War*, ed. and trans. Michael Howard and Peter Peret (Princeton: Princeton University Press, 1976), 178.

9. Huntington, *American Politics*, cogently captures this dynamic process in his concept of an "institutions versus ideals gap." When the gap has become large at times in American history, protest and other kinds of corrective political action have reduced it, bringing institutions back into line with ideals.

Appendix

1. Servan-Schreiber, *Le Défi américain* (The American challenge), 115.

2. Gilpin, *U.S. Power*, 7.

3. Rosecrance, introduction to *America as an Ordinary Country*, 11, 16.

4. Chace, *Solvency*.

5. Olson, *Rise and Decline*. His earlier book is *The Logic of Collective Action* (1965).

6. Kennedy, *Rise and Fall*.

7. Caleo, *Beyond American Hegemony*, 4, 10.

8. Nye, *Bound to Lead*, 5.

9. Keohane, *After Hegemony*, 15, 9–10.

10. Tucker and Hendrickson, *Imperial Temptation*, 5–6.

11. Thurow, *Head to Head*, 14, 17.

12. Michael L. Dertouzos et al., *Made in America: Regaining the Productive Edge* (New York: HarperPerennial, 1990 [originally pub. 1989]).

13. Kennedy, *Preparing for the Twenty-first Century*, 293

14. Huntington, "Why International Primacy Matters," 72.

15. Ronald Steel, *Temptations of a Superpower* (Cambridge: Harvard University Press, 1998 [originally pub. 1995]), 5.

16. Johnson, *Japan*, 8.

17. In the early 1990s Japan was seen as a rising superpower, but during its prolonged economic slump most eyes focused on China as the challenger to American primacy in Asia. In its January 2000 issue *Commentary* invited leading foreign and defense policy experts to answer the question "American Power: For What?" Many of the commentators mentioned China's growing power as a key issue for the United States.

18. Kupchan, "After Pax Americana," 41. More recently he has elaborated this view in a book, *The End of the American Era.*

19. Pfaff, "Question of Hegemony," 227, 230.

20. Huntington, "The U.S.," 91.

21. Wattenberg, *First Universal Nation,* 25, 188.

22. Zuckerman, "Second American Century," 31.

23. Mowery, *U.S. Industry in 2000.*

24. Ethan B. Kapstein, "Does Unipolarity Have a Future?" in Kapstein and Mastanduno, *Unipolar Politics;* Wohlforth, "Stability of a Unipolar World."

25. Brzezinski, *Grand Chessboard,* 210.

26. Mearsheimer, *Tragedy of Great Power Politics.*

Bibliography

Adams, Jonathan, et al. *Benchmarking of the International Standing of Research in England: Report of a Consultancy Study on Bibliometric Analysis.* Leeds: University of Leeds, Center for Policy Studies in Education and Institute for Scientific Information, 1997.

Alba, Richard D. "Assimilation's Quiet Tide." *Public Interest* 119 (1995), 3–18.

Altbach, Philip G. "An International Academic Crisis? The American Professorate in Comparative Perspective." In *Daedalus: The American Academic Profession.* Issued as *Proceedings of the American Academy of Arts and Sciences* 126, no. 4 (1997), 315–38.

———, ed. *The Changing Academic Workplace: Comparative Perspectives.* Chestnut Hill, Mass.: Center for International Higher Education, Lynch School of Education, Boston College, 2000.

———, ed. *The International Academic Profession: Portraits of Fourteen Countries.* Princeton: Carnegie Foundation for the Advancement of Teaching, 1997.

Altbach, Philip G., Robert O. Berdahl, and Patricia J. Gumport, eds. *American Higher Education in the Twenty-first Century: Social, Political, and Economic Challenges.* Baltimore: Johns Hopkins University Press, 1999.

Altbach, Philip G., Patricia J. Gumport, and D. Bruce Johnstone, eds. *In Defense of American Higher Education.* Baltimore: Johns Hopkins University Press, 2001.

Altbach, Philip G., and Patti McGill Peterson, eds. *Higher Education in the 21st Century: Global Challenge and National Response.* Annapolis Junction, Md.: IIE, 1999.

Anchordoguy, Marie. "Japan's Software Industry: A Failure of Institutions?" *Research Policy* 29, no. 3 (2000), 391–408.

Angell, Norman. *The Great Illusion: A Study of the Relation of Military Power to National Advantage.* 4th ed. New York: Putnam's, 1913.

Archambault, Edith. *The Nonprofit Sector in France.* Manchester: Manchester University Press, 1997.

Ash, Mitchell G., and Alfons Söllner, eds. *Forced Migration and Scientific Change: Emigré German-speaking Scientists and Scholars After 1933.* Washington, D.C.: German Historical Institute/Cambridge University Press, 1996.

Bacevich, Andrew J. *American Empire: The Realities and Consequences of U.S. Diplomacy.* Cambridge: Harvard University Press, 2002.

Barone, Michael. *The New Americans: How the Melting Pot Can Work Again.* Washington, D.C.: Regnery, 2001.

Bauer, P. T. *Dissent on Development.* Rev. ed. Cambridge: Harvard University Press, 1976.

Baumol, William J. *The Free-Market Innovation Machine.* Princeton: Princeton University Press, 2002.

Béja, Jean-Philippe. "Crise sociale endémique et renforcement de la dictature en Chine populaire." *Esprit* 280 (2001), 126–45.

Bhattacharya, Uptal, and Hazem Daouk. "The World Price of Insider Trading." *Journal of Finance* 57, no. 1 (2002), 75–108.

Boniface, Pascal. *La France est-elle encore une grande puissance?* Paris: Presses de Sciences Po, 1998.

Boyer, Ernest L., Philip G. Altbach, and Mary Jean Whitelaw. *The Academic Profession: An International Perspective.* Princeton: Carnegie Foundation for the Advancement of Teaching, 1994.

Branscomb, Lewis M., Fumio Kodama, and Richard Florida, eds. *Industrializing Knowledge: University Industry Linkages in Japan and the United States.* Cambridge: MIT Press, 1999.

Brewer, John. *The Sinews of Power: War, Money, and the English State, 1688–1783.* New York: Knopf, 1988.

Brill, Charles A., and Brian A. Carlson, "U.S. and Japanese Antimonopoly Policy and the Extraterritorial Enforcement of Competition Laws." *International Lawyer* 33, no. 1 (1999), 75–118.

Brinton, Mary C. *Women and the Economic Miracle: Gender and Work in Postwar Japan.* Berkeley: University of California Press, 1993.

Brooks, Stephen G., and William C. Wohlforth. "American Primacy in Perspective." *Foreign Affairs* 81, no. 4 (2002), 20–33.

Brown, Simon. *European Foundation Fundamentals: A Portrait of the Independent Funding Community in Europe.* Brussels: European Foundation Centre, 1999.

Brzezinski, Zbigniew K. *The Grand Chessboard: American Primacy and Its Geostrategic Imperatives.* New York: Basic, 1997.

Buchanan, James. *The Political Economy of the Welfare State.* Stockholm: Almqvist and Wiksell International, 1988.

Bush, Vannevar. *Science, the Endless Frontier: A Report to the President on a Program for Postwar Scientific Research.* Washington, D.C.: National Science Foundation, 1990.

Caleo, David P. *Beyond American Hegemony: The Future of the Western Alliance.* New York: Basic, 1987.

Card, David, and Richard B. Freeman. "What Have Two Decades of British Economic Reform Delivered?" Working Paper 8801. Cambridge, Mass.: National Bureau of Economic Research, 2002.

Carlile, Lonny E., and Mark C. Tilton, eds. *Is Japan Really Changing Its Ways? Regulatory Reform and the Japanese Economy.* Washington, D.C.: Brookings Institution, 1998.

Center for Research on Innovation and Society. *Deutsche Nachwuchswissenschaftler in den U.S.A: Perspektiven der Hochschul- und Wissenschaftspolitik.* Workshop, Palo Alto, 18–20 January 2001. Santa Barbara, Calif.: Center for Innovation and Society, 2001.

Chace, James. *Solvency, the Price of Survival: An Essay on American Foreign Policy.* New York: Random House, 1981.

Chace, James, and Nicholas X. Rizopoulos. "Toward a New Concert of Nations: An American Perspective." *World Policy Journal* 16, no. 3 (1999).

Chapin, Wesley D. *Germany for the Germans? The Political Effects of International Migration.* Westport, Conn.: Greenwood, 1997.

Charkham, Jonathan P. *Keeping Good Company: A Study of Corporate Governance in Five Countries.* Oxford: Clarendon, 1994.

Chen, An. "Capitalist Development, Entrepreneurial Class, and Democratization in China." *Political Science Quarterly* 17, no. 3 (2002), 401–22.

Chen, Feng. "Rebuilding the Party's Normative Authority: China's Socialist Spiritual Civilization Campaign." *Problems of Post-Communism* 45, no. 6 (1998), 33–41.

Clark, Burton R. *The Higher Education System: Academic Organization in Cross-National Perspective.* Berkeley: University of California Press, 1983.

———. *Places of Inquiry: Research and Advanced Education in Modern Universities.* Berkeley: University of California Press, 1995.

Clark, Ximena, Timothy J. Hatton, and Jeffrey Williamson. "Where Do U.S. Immigrants Come From and Why?" Working Paper 8998. Cambridge, Mass.: National Bureau of Economic Research, 2002.

Coase, Ronald H. "The Institutional Structure of Production." *American Economic Review* 82, no. 4 (1992), 713–19.

Coffee, John C., Jr. "Convergence and Its Critics: What Are the Preconditions of the Separation of Ownership and Control?" Working Paper 179. New York: Columbia Law School, Center for Law and Economic Studies, 2000.

Coleman, Samuel. *Japanese Science: From the Inside.* London: Routledge, 1999.

Craig, Doidge, G. Andrew Karolyi, and Rene M. Stulz, "Why Are Foreign Firms Listed in the U.S. Worth More?" Working Paper W8538. Cambridge, Mass.: National Bureau of Economic Research, 2001.

Crémieux, Alain. *Quand les "Ricains" repartiront: Le journal imaginaire du nouveau millenaire*. Boofzheim, France: ACM, 2000.

Dahl, Robert A. *Democracy and Its Critics*. New Haven: Yale University Press, 1989.

———. "A Democratic Paradox?" *Political Science Quarterly* 115, no. 1 (2000), 35–40.

———. *On Democracy*. New Haven: Yale University Press, 2000.

———. *Polyarchy: Participation and Opposition*. New Haven: Yale University Press, 1971.

Davis Global Advisors. *Leading Corporate Governance Indicators*. Newton, Mass.: Davis Global Advisors, 2001 and 2002 editions.

De Grauwe, Paul, and Filip Camerman. "How Big Are the Big Multinational Companies?" www.ecol.kuleuven.ac.be 17 June 2003.

De Ruggiero, Guido. *The History of European Liberalism*. Trans. R. G. Collingwood. Boston: Beacon, 1959.

Desch, Michael, "Democracy and Victory: Which Regime Type Hardly Matters." *International Security* 27, no. 2 (2002), 5–47.

De Soto, Hernando. *The Mystery of Capital: Why Capitalism Triumphs in the West and Fails Everywhere Else*. New York: Basic, 2000.

Devan, Janamitra, and Parth S. Tewari. "Brains Abroad." *McKinsey Quarterly*, no. 4 (2001). www.mckinseyquarterly.com 16 August 2001.

Diamond, Larry. "Is the Third Wave Over?" *Journal of Democracy* 7, no. 3 (1996), 20–23.

Djankov, Simeon, et al. "The Regulation of Entry." Working Paper 7892. Cambridge, Mass.: National Bureau of Economic Research, 2000.

Domenach, Jean-Luc. "La Transition post-totalitaire en Chine." *Commentaire* 24, no. 93 (2001), 35–46.

Dore, Ronald P. *Stock Market Capitalism: Welfare Capitalism: Japan and Germany Versus the Anglo Saxons*. New York: Oxford University Press, 2000.

Dower, John W. *Embracing Defeat: Japan in the Wake of World War II*. New York: Norton, 1999.

Downing, Brian M. *The Military Revolution and Political Change: Origins of Democracy and Autocracy in Early Modern Europe*. Princeton: Princeton University Press, 1991.

Doyle, Michael W. *Empires*. Ithaca, N.Y.: Cornell University Press, 1986.

———. "Liberalism and World Politics." *American Political Science Review* 80, no. 4 (1986), 1151–69.

Duesterberg, Thomas J. "The Japanese Economy in the 21st Century." In Hudson Institute, ed. (English language draft), *The Re-emerging Japanese Superstate in the 21st Century*. Tokyo: Tokuma Shoten, 2002.

Dufourg, Bernard. *La Compétitivité éducative internationale de la France*. Paris: Chambre de commerce d'industrie de Paris, 1999.

Eberstadt, Nicholas. "China's Population Prospects: Problems Ahead." *Problems of Post-Communism* 47, no. 1 (2000), 28–37.

———. "The Population Implosion," *Foreign Policy,* no. 123 (2001), 42–53.

———. "Russia: Too Sick to Matter?" *Policy Review,* no. 95 (1999), 3–24.

Elster, Jon, ed. *Constitutionalism and Democracy.* Cambridge: Cambridge University Press, 1988.

European Union, Commission of the European Communities. "The EU Economy: 2002 Review, Summary and Main Conclusion." Brussels, 2002.

Ferguson, Niall. *The Cash Nexus: Money and Power in the Modern World, 1700–2000.* New York: Basic, 2000.

Finer, S. E. *The History of Government from the Earliest Times.* 3 vols. Oxford: Oxford University Press, 1997.

Friedman, Thomas L. *The Lexus and the Olive Tree.* New York: Farrar, Straus, and Giroux, 1999.

Friedrich, Carl J., and Zbigniew K. Brzezinski. *Totalitarian Dictatorship and Autocracy.* Cambridge: Harvard University Press, 1956.

Fujisue, Kenzo, "Promotion of Academia-Industry Cooperation in Japan: Establishing the 'Law of Promoting Technology Transfer from University to Industry,' in Japan." *Technovation* 18, nos. 6–7 (1998), 371–81.

Fukuyama, Francis. *The End of History and the Last Man.* New York: Free Press, 1992.

Gallagher, Mary E. " 'Reform and Openness': Why China's Economic Reforms Have Delayed Democracy." *World Politics* 54, no. 3 (2002), 338–72.

Gamble, William. "The Middle Kingdom Runs Dry: Tax Evasion in China." *Foreign Affairs* 79, no. 6 (2000), 16–20.

Gelpi, Christopher, and Peter D. Feaver, "Speak Softly and Carry a Big Stick? Veterans in the Political Elite and the American Use of Force." *American Political Science Review* 96, no. 4 (2002), 779–93.

Germany, Federal Ministry of Education and Research, Public Relations Division. *Basic and Structural Data, 1999–2000.* Bonn: Federal Ministry of Education and Research, 2000.

Gilpin, Robert. *The Challenge of Global Capitalism: The World Economy in the 21st Century.* Princeton: Princeton University Press, 2000.

———. *The Political Economy of International Relations.* Princeton: Princeton University Press, 1987.

———. *U.S. Power and the Multinational Corporation: The Political Economy of Foreign Direct Investment.* New York: Basic, 1975.

———. *War and Change in World Politics.* New York: Cambridge University Press, 1981.

Glazer, Nathan. "American Diversity and the 2000 Census." *Public Interest* 144 (2001), 3–18.

———. "Immigration and the American Future." *Public Interest* 118 (1995), 45–60.

Glazer, Nathan, and Daniel Patrick Moynihan. *Beyond the Melting Pot: The Negroes, Puerto Ricans, Jews, Italians, and Irish of New York City.* 2d ed. Cambridge: MIT Press, 1995. (Originally pub. in 1963.)

Goldsborough, James. "Out-of-Control Immigration." *Foreign Affairs* 79, no. 5 (2000), 89–101.

Gompers, Paul A., Joy L. Ishii, and Andrew Metrick. "Corporate Governance and Equity Prices." Working Paper 8449. Cambridge, Mass.: National Bureau of Economic Research, 2001.

Gordon, Michael R., and Bernard E. Trainor. *The Generals' War.* Boston: Little, Brown, 1995.

Gowa, Joanne. *Ballots and Bullets: The Elusive Democratic Peace.* Princeton: Princeton University Press, 1999.

Guay, Terrence, and Robert Callum, "The Transformation and Future Prospects of Europe's Defence Industry." *International Affairs* 78, no. 4 (2002), 757–76.

Haftendorn, Helga, Robert O. Keohane, and Celeste A. Wallander, eds. *Imperfect Unions: Security Institutions over Time and Space.* Oxford: Oxford University Press, 1999.

Haines, Michael R. "Ethnic Differences in Demographic Behavior in the United States: Has There Been Convergence." Working Paper 9042. Cambridge, Mass.: National Bureau of Economic Research, 2002.

Hall, Peter A., and David Soskice, eds. *Varieties of Capitalism: The Institutional Foundations of Comparative Advantage.* Oxford: Oxford University Press, 2001.

Hardt, Michael, and Antonio Negri. *Empire.* Cambridge: Harvard University Press, 2000.

Hartz, Louis. *The Liberal Tradition in America: An Interpretation of American Political Thought Since the Revolution.* San Diego: Harcourt Brace, 1991.

Hass, Ernst B. *Beyond the Nation State: Functionalism and International Organization.* Stanford: Stanford University Press, 1964.

Hayek, Friedrich A. von. *The Fatal Conceit: The Errors of Socialism.* Ed. W. W. Bartley III. Chicago: University of Chicago Press, 1989.

———. *The Road to Serfdom.* Chicago: University of Chicago Press, 1994.

Heckman, James J. "Flexibility and Job Creation: Lessons from Germany." Working Paper 9194. Cambridge, Mass.: National Bureau of Economic Research, 2002.

Hedlund, Stefan. *Russia's "Market" Economy: A Bad Case of Predatory Capitalism.* London: University College London Press, 1999.

Heilmann, Sebastian. "China: Expert, But Still Red" *Internationale Politik* (transatlantic ed.) 3, no. 2 (2002), 73–77.

Heisbourg, François. "American Hegemony? Perceptions of the U.S. Abroad." *Survival* 41, no. 4 (1999–2000), 5–19.

Hellmann, Thomas, and Manju Puri. "Venture Capital and the Professionalization of Start-Up Firms: Empirical Evidence," *Journal of Finance* 57, no. 1 (2002), 169–97.

Helweg, M. Diana. "Japan: A Rising Sun?" *Foreign Affairs* 79, no. 4 (2000), 26–39.

Hemmert, Martin, and Christian Oberländer, eds. *Technology and Innovation in Japan: Policy and Management for the Twenty-first Century.* London: Routledge, 1998.

Heyer, Eric, and Xavier Timbeau. "Le Chômage structurel à 5% en France?" *Revue de l'OFCE,* no. 80 (2002), 115–51.

Houlahan, Thomas. *Gulf War: The Complete History.* New London, N.H.: Schrenker Military Publishing, 1999.

Howard, Michael. *War and the Liberal Conscience.* New Brunswick, N.J.: Rutgers University Press, 1978.

Hudson, Valerie M., and Andrea Den Boer. "A Surplus of Men, a Deficit of Peace: Security and Sex Ratios in Asia's Largest States." *International Security* 26, no. 4 (2002), 5–38.

Hull, Charles Henry, ed. *The Economic Writings of Sir William Petty Together with the Observations upon the Bills of Mortality More Probably by Captain John Graunt.* New York: Augustus M. Kelley, Bookseller, 1963.

Hunter, Shireen T., ed. *Islam, Europe's Second Religion: The New Social, Cultural, and Political Landscape.* Westport, Conn.: Praeger, 2002.

Huntington, Samuel P. "After Twenty Years: The Future of the Third Wave." *Journal of Democracy* 8, no. 4 (1997), 3–12.

———. *American Politics: The Promise of Disharmony.* Cambridge, Mass.: Belknap, 1981.

———. *The Clash of Civilizations and the Remaking of World Order.* New York: Simon and Schuster, 1996.

———. "The Lonely Superpower." *Foreign Affairs* 78, no. 2 (1999), 35–49.

———. "Political Development and Political Decay." *World Politics* 17, no. 3 (1965), 386–430.

———. *Political Order in Changing Societies.* New Haven: Yale University Press, 1968.

———. "Robust Nationalism." *National Interest* 58 (1999–2000), 31–40.

———. *The Third Wave.* Norman: University of Oklahoma Press, 1991.

———. "The U.S.: Decline or Renewal?" *Foreign Affairs* 67, no. 2 (1988–89), 76–96.

———. "The West: Unique, Not Universal." *Foreign Affairs* 75, no. 6 (1996), 28–46.

———. "Why International Primacy Matters." *International Security* 17, no. 4 (1993), 68–83.

Ikenberry, G. John. *After Victory: Institutions, Strategic Restraint, and the*

264

BIBLIOGRAPHY

Rebuilding of Order After Major Wars. Princeton: Princeton University Press, 2001.

———. "America's Imperial Ambition." _Foreign Affairs_ 81, no. 5 (2002), 44–60.

———. "Institutions, Strategic Restraint, and the Persistence of American Postwar Order." _International Security_ 23, no. 3 (1998–99), 43–78.

———. "The Myth of Post–Cold War Chaos." _Foreign Affairs_ 75, no. 3 (1996), 79–91.

Institute for Scientific Information. _Journal Citations Reports: A Bibliometric Analysis of Science Journals in the ISI Database_. Philadelphia: Institute for Scientific Information, 1990–98 (selected eds.).

Ivey, Jamie, "Japan Hastens Corporate Governance Reform." _Corporate Finance_ 208 (2002), 52–53.

Jackson, Barbara Ward, and P. T. Bauer, _Two Views on Aid to Developing Countries_. Bombay: Vora, 1966.

Jacoby, Tamar. "How to Think About U.S. Immigration Policy and Its Post–9/11 Implications." Paper Presented at the Foreign Policy Roundtable, New York, 1 May 2002.

———. "In Asian America." _Commentary_ 110, no. 1 (2000), 21–28.

James, Harold. _The End of Globalization: Lessons from the Great Depression_. Cambridge: Harvard University Press, 2001.

Japan Foundation Center. _An Outlook of Japanese Grant-Making Foundations_. Tokyo, 2000.

Jasanoff, Sheila, ed. _Comparative Science and Technology Policy_. Cheltenham, England: Edward Elgar, 1997.

Joffe, Joseph. "How America Does It." _Foreign Affairs_ 76, no. 5 (1997), 13–27.

Johnson, Chalmers A. _Japan, Who Governs? The Rise of the Developmental State_. New York: Norton, 1995.

Johnson, Jean. _Statistical Profiles of Foreign Doctoral Recipients in Science and Engineering: Plans to Stay in the United States_. NSF 99-304. Arlington, Va.: National Science Foundation, Division of Science Resources Studies, 1998.

Johnson, Jean, and Regets, Mark. Issue Brief, "International Mobility of Scientists and Engineers to the United States: Brain Drain or Brain Circulation?" NSF 98-316. Arlington, Va.: National Science Foundation, 1998.

Jones, William C., trans., with the assistance of Tianquan Cheng and Yongling Jiang. _The Great Qing Code_. Oxford: Clarendon, 1994.

Kabashima, Ikuo. "The LDP's 'Kingdom of the Regions' and the Revolt of the Cities." _Japan Echo_ 27, no. 5 (2000), 22–28.

Kaltenbach, Jeanne-Hélène, and Michèle Tribalat. _La République et l'islam, entre crainte et aveuglement_. Paris: Gallimard, 2002.

Kanaya, Akihiro, and David Woo. _The Japanese Banking Crisis of the_

1990s: Sources and Lessons. Princeton: International Economics Section, Department of Economics, Princeton University, 2001.

Kannankutty, Nirmala, and R. Keith Wilkinson. *SESTAT: A Tool for Studying Scientists and Engineers in the United States*. NSF 99-337. Arlington, Va.: National Science Foundation, Division of Science Resources Studies, 1999.

Kaplan, Ann E., ed. *Giving U.S.A., 1999: The Annual Report on Philanthropy for the Year 1998*. New York: AAFRC Trust for Philanthropy, 1999.

Kapstein, Ethan B., and Michael Mastanduno, eds. *Unipolar Politics: Realism and State Strategies After the Cold War*. New York: Columbia University Press, 1999.

Kariya, Tajehiko. "The Baby Bust and the Lowering of Academic Standards." *Japan Echo* 28, no. 3 (2001), 20–22.

Katz, Richard. "Japan's Phoenix Economy." *Foreign Affairs* 82, no. 1 (2003), 114–29.

———. *Japan, the System That Soured: The Rise and Fall of the Japanese Economic Miracle*. Armonk, N.Y.: M. E. Sharpe, 1998.

Keller, Morton, and Phyllis Keller. *Making Harvard Modern: The Rise of America's University*. New York: Oxford University Press, 2001.

Kennedy, Paul. *Preparing for the Twenty-first Century*. New York: Random House, 1993.

———. *The Rise and Fall of the Great Powers: Economic Change and Military Conflict from 1500 to 2000*. New York: Random House, 1987.

Kennedy, Randall. "Interracial Intimacy." *Atlantic Monthly*, 290, no. 5 (2002), 103–10.

Kenny, Charles, and David Williams. "What Do We Know About Economic Growth? Or Why Don't We Know Very Much." *World Development* 29, no. 1 (2001), 1–22.

Keohane, Robert O. *After Hegemony: Cooperation and Discord in the World Political Economy*. Princeton: Princeton University Press, 1984.

Keohane, Robert O., and Joseph S. Nye, Jr. "Globalization: What's New? What's Not? (And So What?)" *Foreign Policy*, no. 118 (Spring 2000): 104–19.

———. *Power and Interdependence: World Politics in Transition*. Boston: Little, Brown, 1977.

———. "Power and Interdependence in the Information Age." *Foreign Affairs* 77, no. 5 (1998), 81–94.

Keynes, J. M. "The Economic Consequences of a Declining Population." *Eugenics Review* 29, no. 1 (1937), 13–17.

Kindleberger, Charles P. *World Economic Primacy, 1500 to 1990*. New York: Oxford University Press, 1996.

Kishlansky, Mark. *A Monarchy Transformed: Britain, 1603–1714*. London: Penguin, 1997.

Kissinger, Henry. "America at the Apex: Empire or Leader?" *National Interest* 64 (2001), 9–17.

Kitfield, James. "The Folk Who Live on the Hill." *National Interest* 58 (1999–2000), 48–55.

Kornai, János. *The Socialist System: The Political Economy of Communism.* Oxford: Clarendon, 1992.

———. *Vision and Reality, Market and State: Contradictions and Dilemmas Revisited.* New York: Routledge, 1990.

Krueger, Alan B., and Jitka Maleckova. "Education, Poverty, Political Violence, and Terrorism: Is There a Causal Connection?" Working Paper 9074. Cambridge, Mass.: National Bureau of Economic Research, 2002.

Kull, Steven, and Clay Ramsay. "The Myth of the Reactive Public: American Public Attitudes on Military Fatalities in the Post-Cold War Period." In *Public Opinion and the International Use of Force,* ed. Philip Everts and Pierangelo Isernia. London: Routledge, 2001.

Kunz, Diane B. *Butter and Guns: America's Cold War Economic Diplomacy.* New York: Free Press, 1997.

Kupchan, Charles A. "After Pax Americana: Benign Power, Regional Integration, and the Sources of a Stable Multipolarity." *International Security* 23, no. 2 (1998), 40–79.

———. *The End of the American Era: U.S. Foreign Policy and the Geopolitics of the Twenty-first Century.* New York: Knopf, 2002.

Landes, David. *The Wealth and Poverty of Nations: Why Some Are So Rich and Some So Poor.* New York: Norton, 1999.

La Porta, Rafael, et al. "Law and Finance." *Journal of Political Economy* 106, no. 6 (1998), 1113–55.

Lardy, Nicholas R. *China's Unfinished Economic Revolution.* Washington, D.C.: Brookings Institution, 1998.

Lebow, Richard Ned. "The Long Peace, the End of the Cold War, and the Failure of Realism." *International Organization* 48, no. 2 (1994), 249–77.

Lee, Sharon M. "Asian Americans: Diverse and Growing." *Population Bulletin* 53, no. 2 (1998), 5–11.

Levi, Margaret. *Of Rule and Revenue.* Berkeley: University of California Press, 1988.

Lindblom, Charles E. *Politics and Markets: The World's Political Economic Systems.* New York: Basic, 1977.

Lipset, Seymour Martin. *American Exceptionalism: A Double-Edged Sword.* New York: Norton, 1996.

———. *Political Man: The Social Bases of Politics.* Garden City, N.Y.: Doubleday, 1960.

Lipset, Seymour Martin, and Gary Marks. *It Didn't Happen Here: Why Socialism Failed in the United States.* New York: Norton, 2000.

Livi-Bacci, Massimo. *A Concise History of World Population.* 3d ed. Trans. Carl Ipsen. Malden, Mass.: Blackwell, 2001.

Lohmann, Susanne, "The American University: Why It Works, Where It Fails, How to Change It." New America Foundation talk, Washington D.C., 17 April 2001.

Lu, Xiabo. "Booty Socialism, Bureau-preneurs, and the State in Transition: Organizational Corruption in China." *Comparative Politics* 32, no. 3 (2000), 273–94.

Lundestad, Geir. *The American "Empire" and Other Studies of U.S. Foreign Policy in a Comparative Perspective*. Oslo: Norwegian Nobel University Press; Oxford: Oxford University Press, 1990.

——. *Empire by Integration: The United States and European Integration, 1945–1997*. Oxford: Oxford University Press, 1998.

Lynn-Jones, Sean M., and Steven E. Miller, eds. *The Cold War and After: Prospects of Peace*. Cambridge: MIT Press, 1993.

Ma, Ngok, Ka-ho Mok, and Anthony B. L. Cheung. "Advance and Retreat: The New Two-Pronged Strategy of Enterprise Reform in China." *Problems of Post-Communism* 48, no. 5 (2001), 52–61.

Ma, Shu-Yun. "Comparing the Russian State and the Chinese State: A Literature Review." *Problems of Post-Communism* 47, no. 2 (2000), 3–12.

Maddison, Angus. *The World Economy: A Millennial Perspective*. Paris: Organization for Economic Cooperation and Development, 2001.

Marks, Susan. *The Riddle of All Constitutions: International Law, Democracy, and the Critique of Ideology*. Oxford: Oxford University Press, 2000.

Martin, Philip L. *Germany: Reluctant Land of Immigration*. Washington, D.C.: American Institute for Contemporary German Studies, Johns Hopkins University, 1998.

Mauer, Marc. *The Crisis of the Young African American Male and the Criminal Justice System*. Washington, D.C.: The Sentencing Project, 1999.

May, Ernest R. *Imperial Democracy: The Emergence of America as a Great Power*. New York: Harcourt, Brace, and World, 1961.

May, Robert M. "The Scientific Wealth of Nations." *Science* 275 (7 February 1997), 793–96.

McKinsey Global Institute. *Why the Japanese Economy Is Not Growing: Micro Barriers to Productivity Growth*. Washington, D.C.: McKinsey Global Institute, 2000.

Mead, Walter Russell. "The Jacksonian Tradition and American Foreign Policy." *National Interest* 58 (1999–2000), 5–29.

——. *Mortal Splendor: The American Empire in Transition*. Boston: Houghton Mifflin, 1987.

Mearsheimer, John J. "The Future of the American Pacifier." *Foreign Affairs* 80, no. 5 (2001), 46–61.

——. *The Tragedy of Great Power Politics*. New York: Norton, 2001.

Mendras, Henri, and Sylvain Meyet. "L'Italie suicidaire?" *Revue de l'OFCE,* no. 80 (2002), 157–68.

Migdal, Joel S. *Strong Societies and Weak States: State-Society Relations and State Capabilities in the Third World.* Princeton: Princeton University Press, 1988.

Milhaupt, Curtis, and Mark D. West. "The Dark Side of Private Ordering: An Institutional and Empirical Analysis of Organized Crime." *University of Chicago Law Review* 67, no. 1 (2000), 41–98.

Milward, Allan S. *War, Economy, and Society, 1939–1945.* Berkeley: University of California Press, 1977.

Morgenthau, Hans J. *Politics Among Nations: The Struggle for Power and Peace.* New York: Knopf, 1948.

Morley, Patricia. *The Mountain Is Moving: Japanese Women's Lives.* New York: New York University Press, 1999.

Moschella, David C. *Waves of Power: Dynamics of Global Technology Leadership, 1964–2010.* New York: Amacom, 1997.

Mowery, David C., ed. *U.S. Industry in 2000: Studies in Competitive Performance.* Washington, D.C.: National Academy Press, 1999.

Mulgan, Aurelia George. "Japan: A Setting Sun?" *Foreign Affairs* 17, no. 4 (2000), 40–52.

National Academy of Sciences, National Academy of Engineering, Institute of Medicine, Committee on Science, Engineering, and Public Policy. *Experiments in International Benchmarking of U.S. Research Fields.* Washington, D.C.: National Academy Press, 2000.

National Science Board. *Science and Engineering Indicators.* Arlington, Va.: National Science Foundation, 2000 and 2002 editions.

National Science Foundation, Tokyo Regional Office. "A Radical Restructuring of Japan's Postwar S&T Policy and Institutions: The Politics and Rationality of the New Century." Report Memorandum 00-08, 15 May 2000.

Naitonal Science Foundation, William E. Odom, chair. *Report of the Senior Assessment Panel of the International Assessment of the U.S. Mathematical Sciences.* Arlington, Va.: National Science Foundation, 1998.

Nau, Henry R. *At Home Abroad: Identity and Power in American Foreign Policy.* Ithaca, N.Y.: Cornell University Press, 2002.

———. *The Myth of America's Decline: Leading the World Economy into the 1990s.* New York: Oxford University Press, 1990.

Nelson, Richard R., ed. *National Innovation Systems: A Comparative Analysis.* New York: Oxford University Press, 1993.

Nickell, Steve, and Jan van Ours. "The Netherlands and the United Kingdom: A European Unemployment Miracle?" *Economic Policy* 30 (2000), 135–80.

North, Douglass C. "Economic Performance Through Time." *American Economic Review* 84, no. 3 (1994), 359–68.

———. *Institutions, Institutional Change, and Economic Performance.* New York: Cambridge University Press, 1990.

———. *Structure and Change in Economic History.* New York: Norton, 1981.

North, Douglass C., and Robert Paul Thomas. *The Rise of the Western World: A New Economic History.* Cambridge: Cambridge University Press, 1973.

North, Douglass C., and Barry R. Weingast. "Constitutions and Commitment: The Evolution of Institutions Governing Public Choice in Seventeenth-Century England." *Journal of Economic History* 49, no. 4 (1989), 803–32.

Nye, Joseph S., Jr. *Bound to Lead: The Changing Nature of American Power.* New York: Basic, 1990.

———. *The Paradox of American Power.* Oxford: Oxford University Press: 2002.

Ochel, Wolfgang. "Welfare to Work in the U.S.: A Model for Germany?" CESinfo Working Paper 537. Munich: Center for Economic Studies and Ifo Institute for Economic Research, 2001.

Odom, William E. *America's Military Revolution: Strategy and Structure after the Cold War.* Washington, D.C.: American University Press, 1993. Lanham, Md.: University Press of America, 1998.

———. "Interventions for the Long Run: Strategies for Intervention and Governance." *Harvard International Review* 22, no. 4 (2001), 48–53.

———. *On Internal War: American and Soviet Approaches to Third World Clients and Insurgents.* Durham, N.C.: Duke University Press, 1992.

Olson, Mancur. "Dictatorship, Democracy, and Development." *American Political Science Review* 87, no. 3 (1993), 567–76.

———. *The Logic of Collective Action: Public Goods and the Theory of Groups.* Cambridge: Harvard University Press, 1965.

———. *Power and Prosperity: Outgrowing Communist and Capitalist Dictatorships.* New York: Basic, 2000.

———. *The Rise and Decline of Nations: Economic Growth, Stagflation, and Social Rigidities.* New Haven: Yale University Press, 1982.

O'Meara, Patrick, Howard D. Mehlinger, and Matthew Krain, eds. *Globalization and the Challenges of a New Century.* Bloomington: Indiana University Press, 2000.

Organization for Economic Cooperation and Development (OECD). *Benefit Systems and Work Incentives* (1999 edition). Paris: OECD, 1999.

———. *Fostering Entrepreneurship.* Paris: OECD, 1998.

———. *Knowledge and Skills for Life: First Results from PISA 2000.* Executive Summary. Paris: OECD, n.d.

———. *The Management of Science Systems.* Paris: OECD, 1999.

———. *Employment Outlook.* Paris: OECD, various eds.

———. *Synthesis Report: China in the World Economy.* Paris: OECD, 2002.

———. *Trends in International Migration.* Paris: OECD, various eds.

Organization for Economic Cooperation and Development, Centre for Educational Research and Innovation. *Education at a Glance: OECD In-dicators.* Paris: OECD, various eds.

———. *Education Statistics.* Paris: OECD, 2001.

Overholt, William H. "Asia's Continuing Crisis," *Survival* 44, no. 1 (2002), 97–114.

———. "Japan's Economy, at War with Itself." *Foreign Affairs* 81, no. 1 (2002), 134–47.

Owen, John M., IV. *Liberal Peace, Liberal War: American Politics and International Security.* Ithaca, N.Y.: Cornell University Press, 1997.

———. "Transnational Liberalism and U.S. Primacy," *International Security* 26, no. 3 (2001–2), 117–52.

Papademetrious, Demetrios G., and Kimberly A. Hamilton. *Reinventing Japan: Immigration's Role in Shaping Japan's Future.* Washington, D.C.: Carnegie Endowment for International Peace, 2000.

Pei, Minxin. "China's Governance Crisis." *Foreign Affairs* 81, no. 5 (2002), 96–109.

Peters, Ralph. *Fighting for the Future: Will America Triumph?* Mechanicsburg, Pa.: Stackpole, 1999.

Pfaff, William. "The Praetorian Guard." *National Interest,* no. 62 (2000–1), 57–64.

———. "The Question of Hegemony." *Foreign Affairs* 80, no. 1 (2001), 221–32.

Pierson, Paul. "Increasing Returns, Path Dependence, and the Study of Politics." *American Political Science Review* 94, no. 2 (2000), 251–67.

Pipes, Richard. *Property and Freedom.* New York: Vintage, 1999.

Plattner, Marc F. "From Liberalism to Liberal Democracy." *Journal of Democracy* 10, no. 3 (1999), 121–33.

Pomeranz, Kenneth. *The Great Divergence: Europe, China, and the Making of the Modern World Economy.* Princeton: Princeton University Press, 2000.

Porter, Michael E., et al. *The New Challenge to America's Prosperity: Findings from the Innovation Index.* Washington, D.C.: Council on Competitiveness, 1999.

Porter, Michael E., Hirotaka Takeuchi, and Mariko Sakakibara. *Can Japan Compete?* London: Macmillan, 2000.

Posen, Barry R., and Andrew L. Ross. "Competing Visions for U.S. Grand Strategy." *International Security* 21, no. 3 (1996–97), 5–53.

Postiglione, Gerard A., and Grace C. L. Mak, eds. *Asian Higher Education: An International Handbook and Reference Guide.* Westport, Conn.: Greenwood, 1997.

Putnam, Robert D., with Robert Leonardi and Raffaella Y. Nanetti. *Making Democracy Work: Civic Traditions in Modern Italy.* Princeton: Princeton University Press, 1993.

Qian, Yingyi. "How Reform Worked in China." Discussion Paper 3447. London: Centre for Economic Policy Research, 2002.

Reilly, John E., ed. *American Public Opinion and U.S. Foreign Policy, 1999*. Chicago: Chicago Council on Foreign Relations, 1999.

Reiter, Dan, and Allan C. Stamm III. *Democracies at War*. Princeton: Princeton University Press, 2002.

Renshaw, Jean R. *Kimono in the Boardroom: The Invisible Evolution of Japanese Women Managers*. New York: Oxford University Press, 1999.

Renz, Loren, and Steven Lawrence. *Foundation Growth and Giving Estimates: 2000 Preview*. New York: Foundation Center, 2001.

Riphahn, Regina T. "Dissimilation? The Educational Attainment of Second-Generation Immigrants." Discussion Paper 2903. London: Centre for Economic Policy Research, 2001.

Rodman, Peter W. *Uneasy Giant: The Challenges to American Predominance*. Washington, D.C.: Nixon Center, 2000.

Rodriguez, Gregory. *From Newcomers to New Americans: The Successful Integration of Immigrants into American Society*. Washington, D.C.: National Immigration Forum, 1999.

Rosecrance, Richard, ed. *America as an Ordinary Country: U.S. Foreign Policy and the Future*. Ithaca, N.Y.: Cornell University Press, 1976.

Rosefielde, Steven. "Culture Versus Competition: Economic Liberalization in Russia, China, and Japan." *Problems of Post-Communism* 49, no. 5 (2002), 51.

Rosen, Stephen Peter. *Winning the Next War: Innovation and the Modern Military*. Ithaca, N.Y.: Cornell University Press, 1991.

Rosenbluth, Frances McCall. *Financial Politics in Contemporary Japan*. Ithaca, N.Y.: Cornell University Press, 1989.

Rosovsky, Henry. *The University: An Owner's Manual*. New York: Norton, 1990.

Rostow, W. W. "Modern Japan's Fourth Challenge: The Political Economy of a Stagnant Population." *Proceedings of the American Philosophical Society* 144, no. 4 (2000), 384–96.

Roy, Olivier. "America and the New Terrorism: An Exchange." *Survival* 42, no. 2 (2000), 156–62.

Rudy, Willis. *The Universities of Europe, 1100–1914: A History*. Cranbury, N.J.: Associated University Presses, 1984.

Russell, Cheryl. *Racial and Ethnic Diversity: Asians, Blacks, Hispanics, Native Americans, and Whites*. American Consumer Series. 2d ed. Ithaca, N.Y.: New Strategist, 1998.

Russett, Bruce M., et al. *Grasping the Democratic Peace: Principles for a Post–Cold War Peace*. Princeton: Princeton University Press, 1993.

Russett, Bruce, and John R. O'Neal. *Triangulating Peace: Democracy, Interdependence, and International Organization*. New York: Norton, 2002.

Rustow, Dankwart. "Transitions to Democracy: Toward a Dynamic Model." *Comparative Politics* 2, no. 3 (1970), 337–63.

Sakakibara, Eisuke. "First Reform the Educational Bureaucracy." *Japan Echo* 28, no. 3 (2001), 23–26.

Salamon, Lester M. *America's Nonprofit Sector: A Primer*. New York: Foundation Center, 1999.

Salamon, Lester M., and Helmut K. Anheier, eds. *Defining the Nonprofit Sector: A Cross-national Analysis*. Johns Hopkins Nonprofit Sector Series, no. 4. Manchester: Manchester University Press, 1997.

Salamon, Lester M., Helmut K. Anheier, and Associates. *The Emerging Sector Revisited: A Summary*. Baltimore: Center for Civil Society Studies, Institute for Policy Studies, Johns Hopkins University, 1999.

Sandars, Christopher T. *America's Overseas Garrisons: The Leasehold Empire*. Oxford: Oxford University Press, 2000.

Saxenian, AnnaLee. *Silicon Valley's New Immigrant Entrepreneurs*. San Francisco: Public Policy Institute of California, 1999.

Schedler, Andreas. "What Is Democratic Consolidation?" *Journal of Democracy* 9, no. 2 (1998), 91–107.

Schneider, Friedrich. "The Size and Development of the Shadow Economies of 22 Transition and 21 OECD Countries." Discussion Paper 513. Bonn: Institute for the Study of Labor (IZA), 2002.

Schumpeter, Joseph. *Capitalism, Socialism, and Democracy*. 3d ed. New York: Harper and Row, 1950.

Science and Technology Agency (Japan). *Annual Report on the Promotion of Science and Technology 1999: New Developments in Science and Technology, Responding to National and Social Needs*. Summary.

Servan-Schreiber, Jean-Jacques. *Le Défi américain*. Paris: Denoël, 1967. Available in English as *The American Challenge*, trans. Ronald Steel. New York: Atheneum, 1968.

Shain, Yossi. "Marketing the Democratic Creed Abroad: U.S. Diasporic Politics in the Era of Multiculturalism." *Diaspora* 3, no. 1 (1994), 85–111.

———. "The Mexican-American Diaspora's Impact on Mexico," *Political Science Quarterly* 114, no. 4 (1999–2000), 661–91.

Shaw, Martin. *Theory of the Global State: Globality as an Unfinished Revolution*. Cambridge: Cambridge University Press, 2000.

Shenefield, John H., and Irwin M. Stelzer. *The Antitrust Laws: A Primer*. 3d ed. Washington, D.C.: American Enterprise Institute, 1998.

Shirakawa, Hideki. "A Nobel Laureate Discusses Japanese Education." *Japan Echo* 28, no. 1 (2001), 59–62.

Simon, Julian. *The Economics of Population: Classic Writings*. New Brunswick, N.J.: Transaction, 1998.

Sin, Hans-Werner. "Germany's Economic Unification: An Assessment After Ten Years." Working Paper 7586. Cambridge, Mass.: National Bureau of Economic Research, 2000.

———. "The Threat to the German Welfare State." CESifo Working Paper

Series 320. Munich: Center for Economic Studies and Ifo Institute for Economic Research, 2000.

Skowronek, Stephen. *Building a New American State: The Expansion of National Administrative Capacities, 1877–1920*. Cambridge: Cambridge University Press, 1982.

Slaughter, Anne-Marie, and David Bosco. "Plaintiff's Diplomacy." *Foreign Affairs* 79, no. 5 (2000), 102–16.

Solow, Robert M. "Unemployment in the United States and in Europe: A Contrast and the Reasons." CESifo Working Paper Series 231. Munich: Center for Economic Studies and Ifo Institute for Economic Research, 2000. *Ifo Studien* 46 (2000), 1–12.

Sowell, Thomas. *Ethnic America: A History*. New York: Basic, 1981.

Steinfeld, Edward S. "Moving Beyond Transition in China: Financial Reform and the Political Economy of Declining Growth." *Comparative Politics* 34, no. 4 (2002), 379–98.

Stelzer, Irwin M. "Immigration in the New Economy." *Public Interest* 141 (2000), 5–16.

Stern, Fritz Richard. *Einstein's German World*. Princeton: Princeton University Press, 1999.

Stevenson, David. *Armaments and the Coming of War: Europe, 1904–1914*. Oxford: Clarendon, 1996.

Suro, Roberto. "Mixed Doubles." *American Demographics* 21, no. 11 (1999), 56–62.

Takahashi, Hiroyuki. "Working Women in Japan: A Look at Historical Trends and Legal Reform." *Japan Economic Institute Report* 42A (1998), 1–10.

Thurow, Lester C. *Head to Head: The Coming Economic Battle Among Japan, Europe, and America*. New York: William Morrow, 1992.

Tijssen, Robert J. W., and Erik van Wijk. "In Search of the European Paradox: An International Comparison of Europe's Scientific Performance and Knowledge Flows in Information and Communication Technologies Research." *Research Policy* 28, no. 5 (1999), 519–43.

Tocqueville, Alexis de. *Democracy in America*. Trans. George Lawrence, ed. J. P. Mayer. New York: Harper Perennial, 1988.

Todd, Emmanuel. *Après l'empire: Essai sur la décomposition du système américain*. Paris: Gallimard, 2002.

Tribalat, Michèle. *Faire France: Une Grande Enquête sur les immigrés et leurs enfants*. Paris: Editions La Découverte, 1995.

Tucker, Robert W., and David C. Hendrickson, *The Imperial Temptation: The New World Order and America's Purpose*. New York: Council on Foreign Relations Press, 1992.

Ueda, Masako. "Banks Versus Venture Capital." Discussion Paper 3411. London: Centre for Economic Policy Research, 2002.

United Nations Educational, Scientific and Cultural Organization. *UNESCO Statistical Yearbook*. Paris: UNESCO (various eds., 1970–99).

United Nations Population Division (U.N. Secretariat, Department of Economic and Social Affairs). *Replacement Migration: Is It a Solution to Declining and Ageing Populations?* New York: United Nations, 2000.

Védrine, Hubert. *Les Cartes de la France à l'heure de la mondialisation: Dialogue avec Dominique Moïsi.* Paris: Fayard, 2000.

Vogel, Steven K. *Freer Markets, More Rules: Regulatory Reform in Advanced Industrial Countries.* Ithaca, N.Y.: Cornell University Press, 1996.

Waller, Spencer Weber. "The Internationalization of Antitrust Enforcement." *Boston University Law Review* 77, no. 2 (1997), 343–404.

Walt, Stephen M. "Why Alliances Endure or Collapse." *Survival* 39, no. 1 (1997), 156–79.

Waltz, Kenneth N. "Globalization and American Power." *National Interest* 59 (2000), 46–56.

———. *Man, the State, and War: A Theoretical Analysis.* New York: Columbia University Press, 1959.

———. "Structural Realism After the Cold War." *International Security* 25, no. 1 (2000), 5–41.

Wattenberg, Ben J. *The First Universal Nation: Leading Indicators and Ideas About the Surge of America in the 1990s.* New York: Free Press, 1990.

Wattenberg, Ben J., in collaboration with Richard M. Scammon. *This U.S.A.: An Unexpected Family Portrait of 194,067,296 Americans Drawn from the Census.* Garden City, N.Y.: Doubleday, 1965.

Wee, Herman Van der. *Prosperity and Upheaval: The World Economy, 1945–1980.* Trans. Robin Hogg and Max R. Hall. Berkeley: University of California Press, 1986.

Weiner, Myron, and Tadashi Hanami, eds. *Temporary Workers or Future Citizens? Japanese and U.S. Migration Policies.* New York: New York University Press, 1998.

Weintraub, Russell J. "Globalization's Effect on Antitrust Law." *New England Law Review,* 34, no. 1 (1999), 27–38.

Wendt, Alexander. *Social Theory of International Politics.* Cambridge: Cambridge University Press, 1999.

Wihtol de Wenden, Catherine. *L'Immigration en Europe.* Paris: La Documentation française, 1999.

Wohlforth, William C. "The Stability of a Unipolar World." *International Security* 24, no. 1 (1999), 5–41.

Woodall, Brian. *Japan Under Construction: Corruption, Politics, and Public Works.* Berkeley: University of California Press, 1996.

World Bank. *1999 World Development Indicators.* Oxford: Oxford University Press, 1999.

———. *World Development Report, 1999–2000.* Oxford: Oxford University Press, 2000.

Wright, Quincy. *A Study of War*. 2d ed. Chicago: University of Chicago Press, 1965.

Yamamoto, Tadashi, ed. *The Nonprofit Sector in Japan*. Johns Hopkins Nonprofit Sector Series, no. 7. Manchester: Manchester University Press, 1998.

Yergin, Daniel, and Joseph Stanislaw. *The Commanding Heights: The Battle for the World Economy*. New York: Simon and Schuster, 1998.

Yost, David S. "The NATO Capabilities Gap and the European Union." *Survival* 42, no. 4 (2000–2001), 97–128.

Young, Oran R. *Governance in World Affairs*. Ithaca, N.Y.: Cornell University Press, 1999.

Zakaria, Fareed. *From Wealth to Power: The Unusual Origins of America's World Role*. Princeton: Princeton University Press, 1998.

———. *The Future of Freedom: Illiberal Democracy at Home and Abroad*. New York: Norton, 2003.

———. "The Rise of Illiberal Democracy." *Foreign Affairs* 76, no. 6 (1997), 22–42.

Zuckerman, Mortimer B. "A Second American Century." *Foreign Affairs* 77, no. 3 (1998), 18–31.

Index

Woods, Tiger, 114
World Bank, 24, 36, 45, 211
World Trade Organization (WTO),
    36, 46

Yamasaki, Minoru, 113
Yang, Jerry, 113

Yeltsin, Boris, 20
Yugoslavia, 51

Zakaria, Fareed, 15
Zerhouni, Elias, 170
Zinni, Anthony, 113
Zuckerman, Mortimer, 223